HOLLINS AND VIYELLA
A Study in Business History

HOLLINS
AND VIYELLA
A Study in Business History

F. A. WELLS
Professor of Industrial Economics
University of Nottingham
England

AUGUSTUS M. KELLEY PUBLISHERS
New York 1968

© F. A. WELLS 1968

Published in the United States of America
by Augustus M. Kelley Publishers New York

Printed in Great Britain by
Latimer Trend & Company Limited Plymouth

Contents

List of Illustrations

PLATES

IN TEXT

Preface

ONE of the most interesting of recent developments in Britain's industrial structure is the changing organisation of textile manufacturing. Until a few years ago textile firms could usually be classified as belonging to a particular group, such as cotton, wool, worsted or hosiery manufacture. Within each group there was further specialisation, by process. In the cotton industry especially the separation of spinning, weaving, finishing and merchanting was still characteristic. The present tendency, however, is towards vertical integration. This implies not merely the conbination of firms engaged in different processes within one industry, as traditionally defined; it also implies the linking of firms across traditional boundaries, and thus the possibility of a single textile industry with the multi-fibre, multi-product firm as its characteristic unit.

Many factors, technological and commercial, have contributed to this transformation. On the technological side the main influence has been the remarkable development of manmade fibres and the ever-widening range of fabrics which these, often in combination with natural fibres, can produce. Further, success with these new materials owes much to improvements in finishing processes, so that the manufacturer, striving for a particular quality, must work in close association with the finisher. In the making of fabric too, the traditional distinction between weaving and knitting has lost some of its significance through the rapid growth of warp knitting. Again, the increasing use of manmade fibres makes for inter-dependence between textile manufacturing and a section of the chemical industry, and supplies a motive for the interlocking of commercial interests. Thus Imperial Chemical Industries and Courtaulds, as the main suppliers of manmade fibres in Britain, have, in different ways, sought to ensure their markets through investment in textile firms. Commerical influences making for integration are also seen at work in the use of brand names and trade names for fabrics and garments, which identify not merely the maker of the finished product, but also the proprietary material it contains and perhaps the special finishing process used.

The working of these various factors is seen in the creation, within the textile trades, of a small number of large, complex groups, each combining, under one ultimate control, a wide range of manufacturing and commercial activities. They are, in varying degrees, vertically organised, though by no means self-contained. They are also integrated laterally, in that their activities overlap the traditional trade boundaries. One such group is Viyella International Ltd, formed by Mr Joe Hyman in 1961.

This book recounts the history of William Hollins & Co Ltd, a founder member of the Viyella federation and the originator of its name. Hollins is one of our oldest textile firms, having started in 1784, and it is particularly interesting as an early example of the vertical form of organisation which has become so marked a feature of modern development in textiles. In its introduction of wool and cotton mixture yarns and its subsequent expansion into weaving, finishing and garment making, Hollins was among the pioneers. The firm was an innovator in selling methods too, being among the first to brand its products, undertake its own advertising and sell direct to retailers on the basis of fixed re-sale prices. It became a big exporter and built up an international reputation for its branded lines.

In writing the history of a firm one is obviously very much dependent on surviving records; and the form which the history takes, the degree of attention given to its various aspects, depends on the kinds of records available. In Hollins's case, the main sources for the earlier years are the annual statements of account, starting in 1786, and the deeds of partnership, the first dated 1785. There are, however, gaps in the series of accounts, between 1813 and 1831, and again between 1847 and 1873. There are no minute books until the conversion of the partnership into a joint stock company in 1882. From this time board meetings are regularly reported, but often less fully than one would wish; in the period of the private company, decisions are recorded, but little is revealed of the decision-making process. However, in the 1920s the board minutes become much fuller, and they are supplemented to an increasing extent by the minutes of various committees. Similarly, the amount of accounting and statistical information increases rapidly and its organisation for the purpose of this history proved to be a formidable task.

The most serious deficiency in the firm's archives is the almost complete lack of correspondence, except for the most recent years. This is unfortunate, for, from letters, much can be learned about the conduct of business and the personalities of business men. One would also like more information about changes in technique and organisation, and about labour conditions.

Such deficiencies have been remedied to some extent by the work of Mr Stanley Pigott, whose book, *Hollins, a Study of Industry*, was published by the firm in 1949. Pigott made a thorough investigation of the archives and he discovered much information about the Hollins and Paget families. He was also able to draw on the recollections of old employees whose memories, or those of their relatives, went back into the nineteenth century. His account is most interesting and valuable, but the last thirty years, down to 1949, are treated only very briefly.

I saw something of Pigott's work while it was in progress, and it was through this association that I was asked by the management of Viyella International to bring the history of Hollins up to date. I decided, however, that the only satisfactory way of doing this was to start at the beginning. Thus, although I have used the same material as Pigott for the earlier history, my treatment differs from his, and I have also been able to supplement his material from other sources, such as the local press. The greater part of the present book is concerned with the last fifty years. In covering this period Pigott, as a member of the firm, was unable to write freely or go into much detail; and, of course, a great deal happened after 1949. Indeed, from 1923 until the merger of 1961, Hollins passed through a series of crises. These events are fairly well documented and the study of them throws some light on the internal workings of an old-established business in a changing environment: still efficient and enterprising in some ways, weak in others and, at times, conspicuously weak in its central direction.

The story of Hollins ends in what may be described as a take-over in reverse. For the first move in the transactions that ultimately produced Viyella International was Hollins's successful bid for Mr Hyman's business, Gainsborough Cornard. This brought Hyman on to Hollins's board and soon to its chairmanship. Hollins then became the medium for the creation of a holding company and a new William Hollins was formed to operate as a subsidiary. Within the Viyella federation William Hollins & Co Ltd lives on as a distinctive unit with its characteristic trade in yarns, cloth and garments; but its fortunes are now merged with those of the much larger entity which is Viyella International.

Acknowledgments

I WISH to express my thanks to Viyella International Ltd for giving me the opportunity to undertake this work, and to the many past and present members of William Hollins & Co Ltd who have co-operated in its production. Their information, advice and critical comments have been most helpful.

My indebtedness to Mr Stanley Pigott's work is acknowledged in the preface. I have, however, had the benefit of free access to all Hollins's surviving records, including the most recent. I am particularly grateful to Mr Edgar Eagle and Mr John Saxton for their assistance in organising this material, and to Miss Margaret Aspden who so skilfully converted pages of untidy manuscript into a readable text.

CHAPTER ONE

The Enterprise and its Setting

THE importance of the East Midlands in the location of British textile trades is now mainly due to the concentration of hosiery manufacture in the region. At the end of the eighteenth century, however, Derbyshire and Nottinghamshire rivalled Lancashire in the development of cotton spinning by power-driven machinery. Most of the mills depended on water power; but one at Papplewick, a few miles north of Nottingham, had a steam engine installed as early as 1786, and was the first cotton mill to be so driven.

In Lancashire it was the growing demand for cotton cloth that stimulated invention in the spinning process. Using the spinning wheel with its single spindle, four spinners were required to supply one weaver with yarn.[1] Moreover, handspun cotton yarn was uneven and not strong enough for warp threads. There was an urgent need to speed up production and to improve quality; and the inventors whose efforts eventually transformed the domestic occupation of spinning into a factory industry had both these aims in view.

The spinning of either cotton or wool is a comparatively simple process, though cotton, especially the short-staple type, is the more troublesome material. First the fibres are carded to form a broad strip of fleecy substance, which may be further refined by combing. The strip is loosely twisted into a roving and then by further twisting and drawing the roving is converted into thread. The strength, fineness and uniformity of the thread depend on the co-ordination of the twisting and drawing processes, and to achieve this, together with speedier production, by mechanical means was a challenge to inventive skill.

The first attempt at machine spinning of which we have definite

[1] Daniels, G. W. *The Early English Cotton Industry*, p 74. 1920.

knowledge is that of Lewis Paul, who patented his device for roller spinning in 1738. This was a distinct advance on the spinning wheel method, in which the yarn was drawn out by hand; moreover, a later form of the machine was designed to spin four threads at once. Paul's machine was used in one or two places, but it was not a commercial success; its product was inferior to the best handspun thread and cost more.[1]

In the meantime the demand for cotton yarn was increasing, not only in Lancashire but also in the framework knitting industry of the Nottingham area. Cotton stockings were becoming popular; they were lighter than wool and because of their extreme whiteness they were coming to be preferred even to silk. But the stocking frame was exacting in its requirements; the yarn had to be fine and uniform. Hand spinners in the West of England woollen district, who were used to short-staple wool, were able to produce a tolerable cotton yarn, but the best had to be imported from India. Thus the expansion of the Nottingham trade in cotton stockings and other knitted articles depended on the prospect of more and cheaper yarn of suitable quality.[2]

The existence of this market was apparently known to Paul, for according to Henson he was experimenting with one of his machines in Nottingham about 1740. Over the next twenty-five years various abortive attempts at machine spinning were made in Nottingham, resulting in some progress, though the yarn was still inferior to the West of England handspun. At the same time similar experiments were going on in Lancashire and it was there that the first real successes were obtained, almost simultaneously, by Hargreaves and Arkwright.

James Hargreaves, the Blackburn weaver, built his first spinning jenny about 1764. For a year or two Hargreaves kept his invention to himself, using it to spin yarn at home, and even when, in 1767, a

[1] Henson, G. *The Civil, Political and Mechanical History of the Framework Knitters*. 1831.
[2] Wells, F. A. *The British Hosiery Trade*. 1935.

few machines were made for sale, they were not patented. Restricted as his activities were, however, it was not long before the inventor suffered from the activities of the machine smashers, who broke into his house and destroyed his frames. Such persecution, and the difficulties of coming to terms with the Lancashire manufacturers, drove Hargreaves to seek refuge in Nottingham. Here again he had difficulty in getting support owing to the failures of previous inventors, but eventually capital was supplied by Thomas James, a member of a prominent Nottingham family. A small mill was built in Hockley and the firm began to supply the local hosiers with cotton yarn spun on jennies with sixteen or more spindles.[1] In 1770 the machine was patented and in the next few years many jennies were sold to other spinners and to hosiers. But Hargreaves's business was only moderately successful. Nottingham had many frame-smiths capable of building jennies and some started making them on their own account.[2] When eventually Hargreaves tried to enforce his patent rights, the court held that these were nullified by the fact that the jenny had been used in industry before it was patented.

The spinning jenny marked a great advance on the spinning wheel in its ability to produce many threads at once. Further, it incorporated a movable carriage giving more precise control over the drawing action, so that a more even yarn could be spun with less skill. But it still required manipulation and had to be worked by hand. This was not always a disadvantage, and for certain kinds of work, and when operations were on a small scale, jennies continued in use for many years. In Derbyshire and Nottinghamshire, however, the jenny was soon superseded by the roller spinning machine, as developed by Richard Arkwright.

The merits of Arkwright's claim to the invention of roller spinning, which aroused so much controversy in later years, do not concern us here. In any case the idea was not new, though whether Arkwright or Hayes, whose invention the former is said to have

---

[1] Baines, E. *History of the Cotton Manufacture*, p 158. 1835.
[2] Henson, G., op cit, p 364.

appropriated, was acquainted with Paul's specification is doubtful. Whatever Arkwright, the Preston barber, may have lacked in mechanical genius, he certainly possessed extraordinary ability for the profitable exploitation of ideas. The distinctive feature of the roller frame was that it made spinning a continuous process, the yarn being drawn out by passing through successive rollers turning at different speeds. Thus the machine was adaptable to rotary motion and the application of mechanical power. This was not possible with the jenny, nor with the early versions of Crompton's mule, which, in addition to rollers, had a movable carriage. The mule, introduced about 1780, was superior to any other machine for spinning a fine and strong thread; but it was not until 1825 that a satisfactory self-acting type became available.

Arkwright was thus first in the field with a spinning machine to which power could be applied, and, like Hargreaves, he decided in

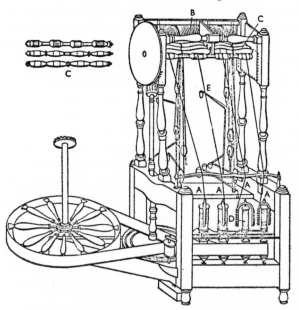

ARKWRIGHT'S ROLLER SPINNING MACHINE

1768 to try out his invention in Nottingham. There he secured the interest of the Wright brothers, the local bankers; but at the end of a year they became alarmed at the risk involved in continuing to finance such an enterprise and withdrew their support. However, they introduced Arkwright to Samuel Need, a prominent hosier, who became his partner and built him a small mill near that of Hargreaves. In the early stages the yarn spun was 'of wretched quality', much inferior to that made on the jenny, though this was by no means good, being lumpy and liable to break under the strain of knitting. Need, who is said to have expended £1,200 on the enterprise, grew impatient, but eventually a great improvement was effected by fluting the rollers.[1]

The next stage in Arkwright's progress is marked by his removal to the neighbouring county of Derby. Here Need was associated with Jedediah Strutt, who had patented the rib stocking frame in 1758 and was now in a considerable way of business. Strutt immediately recognised the possibilities of machine spinning and was able to bring inventive skill, capital and enterprise to the furtherance of Arkwright's schemes. The two men entered into partnership and proceeded to develop cotton spinning as a factory industry. Derbyshire was particularly suitable for starting such an industry because of the availability of water power. In Nottingham Arkwright had used horses to drive his machinery, but beside the swift-flowing Derwent there were many sites suitable for water mills and, moreover, labour was fairly plentiful in the area. The partnership lasted until 1781, and by this time mills had been built at Cromford, Masson and Belper. Roller spinning was much improved and good yarn was being produced. The partners demonstrated that machine-spun yarn could be used for fine-gauge stockings, and supplying the hosiery trade became an important part of their business.

After breaking their partnership, Arkwright and Strutt continued to expand, but as competitors. Very soon other competitors appeared, for Arkwright failed to maintain a monopoly of the new

[1] Henson, G., op cit, p 368.

spinning methods. His patent rights were repeatedly challenged and in 1785, after much litigation, they were cancelled. Machines similar to his were already being made and used by others, and the trade was now open to all comers. Most of the new spinning mills that came into existence were in Lancashire, but the demand for cotton hosiery continued to provide a growing market in the East Midlands. 'Cotton stockings have become very general for summer wear,' says a contemporary observer, 'and have gained very much on silk stockings, which are too thin for our climate and too expensive for common wear for people of middling circumstances.'[1] It is not known what quantity of cotton was used in hosiery manufacture before 1770, but it must have been very small. In 1787, however, it was estimated that 1,500,000 lb were consumed, and by 1836 the annual amount was over three times as great.[2] Silk hosiery had always been expensive and the price of wool was increasing with the growing shortage of supply;[3] on the other hand, cotton yarn was greatly cheapened by the new processes.[4] Wide markets were opened up for cotton hosiery both at home and abroad, and by 1815 the plain cotton hose branch employed the greatest number of frames in the trade.[5]

This boom in cotton hosiery gave a powerful stimulus to the local spinning industry. Some firms set up with machines licensed from Arkwright, but others were less scrupulous and built or bought machines on the expectation that Arkwright would be unable to enforce his patent rights. This was a reasonable assumption in 1784, when Arkwright made his last effort in the face of strongly organised opposition, and it was in that year that a partnership was formed to start a cotton mill at Pleasley, a small village in Derbyshire, but well removed from the scene of Arkwright's activities.

[1] Macpherson, D. *Annals of Commerce*, Vol IV, p.80. 1785.
[2] Baines, E., op cit, p 344.
[3] Cunningham, W. *The Growth of English Industry and Commerce in Modern Times*, p 644. 1925. The price of wool doubled between 1780 and 1791.
[4] Baines, E., op cit, p 357. Fine cotton yarn was 35s a pound in 1788, by 1793 it had fallen to 15s and by 1804 to 7s 10d.
[5] Blackner, J. *History of Nottingham*. 1815.

The five men who joined in this enterprise founded the business whose history we have now to relate.

The original partners were Henry Hollins, Thomas Oldknow, John Paulson, William Siddon and John Cowpe. All but Cowpe, who was employed by Oldknow, were already prosperous business men. Hollins was a brazier in Nottingham, and Oldknow, his brother-in-law, a Nottingham draper. Paulson and Siddon were also drapers, at Mansfield in Nottinghamshire, and a few miles south of Pleasley. Apart from general business experience and the possession of capital, the partners' qualifications for running a spinning mill are not obvious. But it must be remembered that manufacture by means of power-driven machinery was a new development. Inevitably, the pioneers of the new technology and organisation were men drawn from other walks of life. Arkwright himself had been a barber, Strutt a farmer, and these were characteristic figures in the industrial revolution now beginning.

Henry Hollins's family had been in the brass industry for generations. They came from Ashby-de-la-Zouch in Leicestershire. When Humphrey Hollins died there in 1695 he left to his son a 'shop of tools belonging to my trade', indicating that he was a worker in brass as well as a dealer. About 1724 the family moved to Nottingham and set up business in Long Row, facing the Market Place. In an advertisement inserted in *The Nottingham Journal* in 1789, Henry Hollins describes himself as a brazier and tinplate worker, and he wants to engage a 'journeyman brazier, likewise a tinplate worker'. It is fair to suppose that among his customers would be makers and repairers of stocking frames. Indeed, Henry Hollins may well have had dealings with Hargreaves and Arkwright during their sojourn in Nottingham; in any case he would know a good deal about their activities.

Thomas Oldknow was a draper, but an eighteenth-century draper often had wide interests covering wholesale as well as retail trade. It was a Nottingham draper who, a hundred years earlier, had established Smith's Bank, which became one of the best-known country banks in England. Moreover, a draper would have direct contacts with various branches of textile manufacture and would have some knowledge of their processes. A nephew and former apprentice of Oldknow's had, indeed, set up as a manufacturer, first of muslins and then of cotton yarn. Samuel Oldknow, a native of Anderton in Cheshire, became one of the leading men in the Lancashire cotton industry and was at times closely associated with the Arkwrights and the Strutts. He kept in touch with his uncle and visited the Pleasley mill on at least one occasion.[1]

Both Hollins and Oldknow were prominent citizens of Nottingham. They were members of a group of middle-class Whig dissenters,[2] mostly traders, who virtually ruled the town. Henry Hollins became sheriff in 1767, when still under thirty, his father having been mayor in 1762; Oldknow's father had twice been mayor and the son was made a senior councillor about the same time as Henry Hollins.[3]

Little is known of Paulson and Siddon, the Mansfield members of the partnership; but their local knowledge and influence were no doubt valuable, especially in the early stages of the enterprise. Hollins and Oldknow probably came to know them as fellow dissenters.[4] The fifth member, John Cowpe, was only twenty-five, but he must have had exceptional qualifications, as he assumed responsibility for equipping the mill. There is no evidence as to how he obtained his technical knowledge, or the capital for his investment. He had, however, been a fellow-apprentice with Samuel Oldknow in the Nottingham drapery business and perhaps the two discussed the prospects and problems of setting up in the textile industry. It is indeed possible that Cowpe had considered joining the young Old-

---

[1] See Unwin, G. *Samuel Oldknow and the Arkwrights.* 1924.
[2] The Hollins family were members of High Parliament Unitarian Chapel; the Oldknows supported the Particular Baptist Chapel in George Street Church: *Economic and Social Changes in a Midland Town,* p. 168. 1966.
[3] Pigott, op cit, p 24. Besides his Nottingham business, Hollins owned a considerable estate at Calverton, north of Nottingham, inherited through his mother.
[4] Paulson and Siddon signed a notice, by the Mansfield Dissenters' Committee, published in *The Nottingham Journal,* 5 June 1793.

know when the latter returned to Anderton to start his own business. But he remained in the employment of Thomas Oldknow and his opportunity came with the formation of the partnership. He may well have initiated it; for he undertook to contribute £1,400 to the total capital of £4,200, the other four members being committed for only £700 each. The capital was to be paid up by instalments, at such times and in such amounts as a majority of the partners, by value, should determine. Further evidence of Cowpe's leading part in the enterprise is shown in the decision that the firm should trade under the name of Cowpe, Oldknow, Siddon & Co; Hollins, for some reason, was not included. The style could, however, be changed at any time by majority decision.

The deed of partnership also provided that 'John Cowpe should undertake the care, management and superintendence of the joint trade and business'. As managing partner he was to be paid initially a salary of £52 10s a year. When the capital was fully subscribed and the business was operating, the salary was to increase by £10 10s, if profits were sufficient after paying the partners 5 per cent on their investment. If the business proved so profitable that the return on capital exceeded 15 per cent, Cowpe was to receive £5 for every £100 of the excess until his total salary reached £100. As a safeguard against possible mismanagement, Cowpe's fellow partners reserved the right to go to arbitration on any serious complaint against him and to replace him at six months' notice if the complaint should be upheld.

Although Cowpe was the chief executive, it is clear from the deed that all the original partners intended to take an active part in the direction of the enterprise. All outside agreements made by the partners were to be reduced to writing and handed to the bookkeeper. A partner's purchases were limited to £100 in any one month and none was to give credit to any person against whom the other partners had issued a warning. The partners were to meet on the first Tuesday on each month 'to make rules and orders'. All decisions were to be made by a majority, in value; they were to be

recorded in a minute book and were binding on all. On 1 June each
year an 'account, review and settlement' was to be drawn up and
and signed by all, and there was to be no going back on this, except
in the case of an obvious error. The profits were to be divided in
proportion to the shareholdings. None of the partners, other than
Cowpe, was to receive a salary; but a partner travelling on the
firm's business was to be paid expenses plus 'a reasonable allowance
made for the trouble of such journeys'.

The partners pledged themselves to work together for the ad-
vancement of their joint enterprise, and not to participate, as indivi-
duals, in any similar business. If one of them became bankrupt, he
was to be excluded, and the firm would be liable only to the extent
of his share. On the death of a partner his share might be adminis-
tered by his executors; but, if the share was divided the beneficiaries
could appoint only one representative to join the partnership, except in the case of Cowpe's successors, who could have two representatives, on account of his double share.

This provision was intended to keep the partnership compact and
intimate. But there were also safeguards against undue concentration of control. Shares might be transferred, but only on written
notice and at a price fixed by the partners; and, if a share was
offered to an outside purchaser, the other partners had the option of
buying it for 5 per cent less than the price obtainable outside. However, if a partner should acquire three shares, or half the capital, he
would exercise only equal power with the rest. Finally, there were
safeguards against admitting into the partnership persons who had
an interest in competing businesses. No partner was to sell or
assign a share to anybody 'in, or about to start in, the cotton yarn
or twist spinning trade' without the consent of all the other
partners.

The indenture embodying these provisions was made on 1 March
1785, but the lease on the property at Pleasley had been acquired
five months earlier. In this the partners were certainly fortunate, for
many enterprising business men were on the lookout for sites where

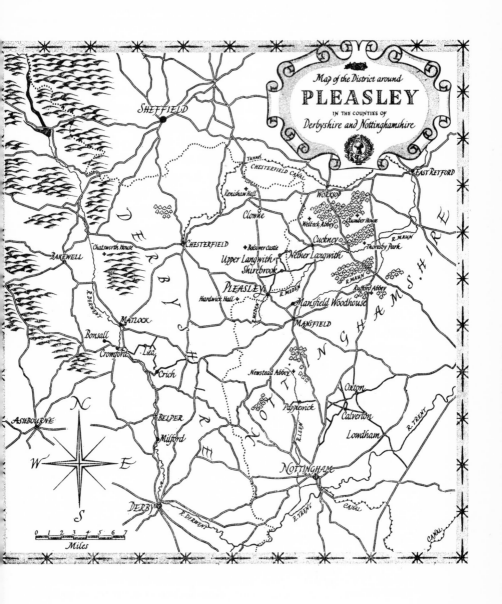

Map of the District around
PLEASLEY
IN THE COUNTIES OF
Derbyshire and Nottinghamshire

water power was available, and landowners were generally aware of their value. On the Pleasley site there was already a corn mill with its 'wheels machinery and works', and also a forge with various out-buildings and other items of equipment.[1] All this was secured, to-gether with 15 acres and a stretch of the River Meden, including the dam, on a 42-year lease for a premium of £105 and a yearly rent of £40. In taking over the existing buildings the partners were free to make what alterations they wished; but they were required to erect, 'with all convenient speed on some part of the premises in a good substantial and workmanlike manner a building (at least 60 ft long and 30 ft wide) of stone or other lasting material for the manu-facture of cotton.' The whole property, including this building, but not the machinery installed by the partners, was to revert to the lessor when the lease expired. But during the period of the lease Henry Thornton, the owner of the estate, undertook not to sell or lease any other site for a cotton mill, nor to divert the stream which fed the dam.

On these terms the partners made a good bargain and they were still more fortunate when, in 1827, they were able to buy the pro-perty outright. The firm they established has had its mills at Pleasley Vale ever since. It is a pleasant setting in wooded country with outcrops of limestone and with the former mill dam now forming an ornamental lake. The present multi-storey mills cover a wide area and include no trace of the original building. But there is a good example of a water-mill of about the same period at Nether Langwith, a few miles away, and which is the more interesting be-cause it was once worked by members of the Hollins family. This mill, long since disused, is a severely functional structure, with four rows of small square windows. The floors have disappeared but, from what can be seen of their place in the walls, it seems that the rooms were little more than 6 ft high.

---

[1] The site was known as Pleasley Forge long after iron working had ceased. Water power was used to drive the hammers and bellows in the making of cast and wrought iron.

Whether the Pleasley spinning mill was a new building or a reconstruction of the original corn mill is unknown, nor is there any description of the machinery that was installed. There had to be carding machines as well as spinning frames, and the latter would be of the Arkwright type, since this was the only form of spinning machine to which power had yet been successfully applied. The deed of partnership refers to the use of capital 'for the purchasing of such machines as shall be necessary'. But it is very likely that Cowpe built some of the machinery himself with the aid of local craftsmen, for in 1790 we find the firm advertising for a turner 'that understands iron and wood turning', and three years later for one or two turners, 'good hands who have been used to cotton mill work'.[1] It was quite common for manufacturers to build their own machines, copying or improving an existing design, or perhaps introducing a new type. The early spinning machines were about 4 ft long and about the same in height. Their frames were made largely of wood and there were plenty of carpenters capable of constructing them. As for the metal parts, there were many experienced and ingenious framesmiths in the hosiery districts, and workers in iron and brass, like those employed by Henry Hollins.

As an example of what could be done by clever and enterprising young men, there is the well-known case of Robert Owen. He was only nineteen when he formed a partnership in Manchester with a maker of wire bonnet frames and set out to produce spinning mules. They obtained the necessary wood, iron and brass on credit, and soon had forty men at work. After being bought out, Owen set up in a small way as a spinner and made £300 profit in his first year. He was then engaged, while still barely twenty, to manage a cotton factory employing 500 people. A few years later he joined David Dale, owner of much larger mills at New Lanark, and there built up, not only a highly successful business, but also a model indus-

---

[1] *The Nottingham Journal*, 31 July 1790 and 12 October 1793. The first advertisement asks also for a man to overlook a card room.
Advertisements for turners to work in cotton mills appear in *The Nottingham Journal* from 1785.

This Indenture of five Parts made the first day of March in the twenty fifth year of the Reign of our Sovereign Lord George the Third by the Grace of God of Great Britain France and Ireland King Defender of the Faith and so forth and in the year of our Lord One thousand seven hundred and eighty five *Between* John Paulson of Mansfield in the County of Nottingham Mercer of the first Part, Henry Hollins of the Town and County of the Town of Nottingham Brazier of the second Part Thomas Oldknow the Younger of the same place Mercer of the third Part, William Siddon of Mansfield aforesaid Mercer of the fourth Part and John Cowpe of the Town and County of the Town of Nottingham aforesaid Mercer of the fifth Part ——

Reciting part of the Lease from Mr Thornhill to the Copartners.

Whereas in and by a certain Indenture of Lease bearing Date on or about the 28th day of September last and made or mentioned to be made between Henry Thornhill of Mansfield Woodhouse in the said County of Nottingham Esquire of the One Part and the said John Paulson Henry Hollins Thomas Oldknow William Siddon and John Cowpe by their several Additions aforesaid of the other Part the said Henry Thornhill for the Considerations therein mentioned Did demise lease set and to farm let unto the said John Paulson Henry Hollins Thomas Oldknow William Siddon and John Cowpe their Executors Administrators and assigns *All* that Messuage Dwelling House or Tenement situate standing and being in the Parish of Pleasley in the County of Derby at or near a certain Place there called Pleasley Upper Forge then in Possession of Thomas Burrows or his assigns *And also all* that Water Corn Mill thereunto belonging with all and

THE FIRST PAGE OF THE INDENTURE OF CO-PARTNERSHIP, 1784

trial community.[1] John Cowpe's achievement at Pleasley was on a more modest scale, but it must have called for similar qualities: an understanding of machine construction and operations, the ability to organise work on factory lines, some knowledge of costing, and the capacity to train and manage labour.

[1] *Life of Robert Owen, Written by Himself.* 1857.

CHAPTER TWO

Growth and Consolidation at Pleasley

THE 'Indenture of Copartnership' was signed on 1 March 1785 and in July of the following year the first balance sheet was produced. Fortunately three books of these financial statements have survived, providing a continuous series down to 1813 and so illustrating the progress of the business in its early years. The first balance sheet is as on p 33.

As might be expected at this stage, nearly all the capital is represented by fixed assets. The fact that the water wheel and related items are valued at the round figure of £400 suggests that the existing installation was taken over in full working order. But it looks as though the valuation of premises and machinery includes the cost of work done by the firm in adapting the buildings and constructing machines. Much of the machinery must have been bought, however, to enable the mill to get into production in such a short time. It is, indeed, remarkable that the mill was turning out yarn in its first year, and that most of it could be described as 'good twist'.

Much of the first yarn spun was sent to Manchester. Although the intention was to supply the cotton hosiery trade, and this soon became the main outlet, there was a growing market for good twist in Lancashire and until the firm had built up its local connections it was probably convenient to deal with a Manchester merchant. There was also a stock of yarn at the mill which may have been for local distribution, and it will be noted that the firm used some of its own twist for manufacturing, that is for weaving. The cloth was calico, but two years later handkerchiefs are mentioned. Weaving was only a sideline, however; it would be done on handlooms, and it is perhaps surprising that the firm did not employ a few stocking

32

A PERSPECTIVE VIEW OF NOTTINGHAM MARKET PLACE.

Plate 1. Nottingham market place in the eighteenth century

Plate 2. A framework knitter

TABLE I

Statement of the Cotton Mill Account at Pleasley Works taken on the 8th day of July 1786

	£	s.	d.		£	s.	d.
Mill, Houses, Dam, Head and Cutt	2,472	5	9	Cash advanced by the Company	4,200	0	0
Water wheels, pit wheel and penstock	400	0	0	Debts oweing by the Company	309	5	9
Machinery as by Book	621	1	7½	Interest on £4,200 0s 0d at	210	0	0
Utensils as by Book	296	7	2	5 per cent			
Cotton wool on hand as by Book	146	2	6				
Good Twist at Manchester as by Book	186	12	6				
Good Twist at the Mill as by Book	133	15	3½				
Inferior Twist at the Mill as by Book	125	18	7½				
Callicoes and Twist to Manufacture	59	1	6				
Debts oweing to the Company	68	0	9½				
Loss sustained by the Company	210	0	0				
	£4,719	5	9		£4,719	5	9

c

frames too, but there is no record of this. Very soon the item 'manufactures' disappears from the accounts and it was many years before the firm went in for weaving again.

A loss of £210 was recorded in this first year; but it was entirely accounted for by the charge of 5 per cent on the partners' investment. In the following year a marked increase in productivity was achieved; little more was spent on machinery but, judging from the value of stocks, output was perhaps nearly three times as great. There was, however, a substantial increase in the company's balance of indebtedness, so no interest could be drawn. Year by year interest at 5 per cent was carried forward, but the partners had faith in the enterprise; for every year until 1792 they each contributed a further £133 6s 8d, a total of £800, to the capital. In this way the partners' stake in the firm increased to £9,835, well over twice the original investment; and by this time the accounts were showing a credit balance on the year's trade. This first appeared in 1790, when the amount was £1,283 16s 4d; in 1791 it was £1,886 19s 6d and it increased further to £2,193 8s 4½d in 1792. From 1790 Cowpe's salary went up to £100, as provided for in the deed of partnership.

Unfortunately the form of the accounts varies somewhat from year to year and in some statements only the combined stock of raw material and finished goods is shown; but it is clear that production was increasing and that it was now profitable. Moreover, there had been substantial additions to the plant, machinery being valued at £2,547 12s 9½d in 1792. An allowance for depreciation on the value of the buildings was made in 1790 and it was agreed to continue the charge at £70 a year, though in fact higher rates were sanctioned in subsequent years. There are entries for depreciation of machinery from 1800. The water wheel, in particular, was heavily written down, which was wise, for in 1803 it had to be replaced at a cost of £524.

The accounts show considerable expenditure on buildings, other than the mill, during the first ten years. A house on the estate was bought for Cowpe at a cost of £200, and £500 was spent on building ten houses for work-people in the Northfields, where a considerable area of land was bought for £1,010. A bridge and a new road were made. A smith's and joiner's shop and a cotton room were added to the mill. A particularly interesting item in the 1792 statement is 'new house and school house', which together with the brewhouse and cowhouse cost £180 12s 5d.

Dependence on water power meant that many of the early factories were isolated and their owners had the problem of attracting and retaining labour. Thus firms often had to provide workers' housing. For some jobs, especially 'piecing', or tying broken threads, children were employed and it was common for whole families to work in the mill. If, however, the local supply of child labour was insufficient, more children would be brought in from outside the locality and these had to be accommodated. Some were sent by their parents, but many were so-called parish apprentices placed in employment by the overseers, of the poor.

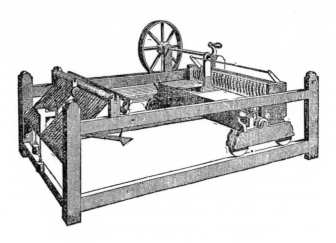

THE SLUBBING BILLY, 1783

Pleasley mill was a typical example of this. The population of the parish was only 473 in 1801 and the mill was some distance from the village; so Cowpe had to provide for apprentices living in. Four years after the firm started the following advertisement appeared in *The Nottingham Journal*. 'Wanted at the cotton mill, Pleasley, a middle-aged woman to have the care and management of from 12–15 boys and girls.' Soon afterwards, in 1791, a further batch of twenty-five apprentices were recruited. The indentures show that fifteen of these, all girls, aged between 9 and 16, were placed by the overseers; and John Cowpe, on behalf of the partnership, undertook to provide 'meet, competent and sufficient meat, drink and apparel, lodging, and other things necessary and fit for an apprentice', in return for their services. The others, including four boys, were apprenticed by their parents, and in these cases a small wage was paid, beginning as low as 2s 6d a week, out of which payment had to be made for board and lodging. Apprenticeship was normally for seven years and, where a wage was paid, it increased by small annual increments.

To accommodate these young workers an apprentice house and a school room were provided, which, together with the 'brewhouse next dyke' cost £171 6d 11½d. A further item recorded in the accounts for 1791–2 is the expenditure of £14 16s 10d 'in building Mrs Wood's kitchen'—Mrs Wood being evidently the 'middle-aged woman' referred to in the advertisement. The establishment of a school anticipated the provision of the Health and Morals of Apprentices Act of 1802. But the mill children, working perhaps 72 hours a week,[1] could attend only on Sunday.

The Act of 1802, just mentioned, provided that cotton mills employing apprentices should be visited by representatives of the local justices, and they reported on Pleasley this same year. There were then about 240 adult workers and 60 apprentices, all girls, and the visitors declared themselves 'on the whole satisfied from the remarkable healthful and clean appearance of the apprentices, and the very wholesome condition of this mill, and from the inspection of the domestic rules, and the writing and work in the school, that the great objects of the Act, the health, morals and instruction of the apprentices, have here been long and successfully attended to'.

This report was included in the minutes of evidence before the Select Committee on the State of Children Employed in Manufactories, 1816; and it was supplemented by Henry Hollins junior, who appeared on behalf of the cotton mill proprietors in the Mans-

---

[1] A contract with one William Wood, engaged as an overlooker in 1791, gives the hours of work as 'from six in the morning till seven in the evening, Sundays excepted'. This presumably includes meal times. Wood's wages were to be 8s a week in his first year, rising to 10s after seven years. The terms suggest that he was to learn the job. When the firm advertised for an overlooker in *The Nottingham Journal* in 1794 they stated that 'wages will be no object for an experienced man who has been employed in preparing for the hosiery trade'.

field area. He himself had now left the Pleasley firm and had mills at Langwith and Cuckney. It appeared that no further inspection of the mills had been made; but at the committee's request a sworn statement was delivered by William Pearsce, who had succeeded Cowpe as managing partner in the Pleasley firm. This gives more detailed employment information than the earlier report and may be summarised as follows:

TABLE 2

Employment at Pleasley 1816

Age Group	Males	Able to Read	Able to Write	Females	Able to Read	Able to Write
Over 18	50	47	41	98	85	52
10 to 18	28	28	9	64	56	20
Under 10	3	1	—	6	4	—
	81	72	50	168	145	72

It will be noted that total employment, at 249, was less than in 1802. There were now only forty apprentices. It seems likely that with more families now living nearby 'free' labour had become more plentiful and there was less need to bring in apprentices. According to Hollins' evidence before the Select Committee, few mills in the Mansfield area now employed apprentices, who were normally indentured until the age of twenty-one and for whom adult jobs were not always available. Many boys and girls left the mill at fifteen or sixteen, the boys to go into other trades or into farming and the girls mostly into domestic service until they married.

The conditions of children's employment were very similar to those of adults. They usually worked the same hours, for piecers were needed whenever the machines were spinning. The work, as the employers explained, may not have been laborious; but it was exacting and monotonous. There was often no break for meals, which meant that they had to be taken in the workroom with the machinery running. Yet most of the medical evidence submitted to the Select Committee was reassuring. 'The employment of the children is neither laborious nor sedentary,' says one report, 'constant motion being requisite for working the machinery.' Another doctor,[1] describing his visits to a group of mills, including Pleasley, found the children to be 'well fed, clothed, clean and healthy, more so than the generality of the poor of any other description, or in any other employ in the neighbourhood, and appearing cheerful and happy'. As a comparative statement this may well have been true, for there were worse employments for children than working in the mill. Framework knitting was the other main manufacture in the area and this was still organised on the domestic system. The work was done in cottages and small shops, usually overcrowded, and subject to no inspection at all. Winding and seaming were the common occupations of children, but some even worked frames. Hours were as long as in the factories, though more irregular, and earnings were low and less certain.

All the evidence taken by the Select Committee came from employers and other persons of the same class. Some, like Robert Owen, thought that working hours, especially for children, were too long and that no child should be employed in a factory under ten years of age. But most mill-owners faced the investigators complacently enough; many insisted on the marked improvement that had occurred since the early days of the industry. Against the general background, as revealed by the inquiry, Pleasley shows up rather well. Judged by the prevailing standards the partners could be regarded as good employers with a sense of responsibility for the welfare of their work-people.

They were certainly good men of business, prudent but not lacking in courage. Their prudence is shown in the policy of ploughing back most of the profits, which they could afford to do

---

[1] W. Paulson of Mansfield, probably a relative of John Paulson, one of the original partners.

Statement of Bolton Mills Account

Old Mill (Cam. Buildings & Out houses)		
with Workhouses, & Outhouses	2849	" "
Water wheel, Pitt wheel & Iron Work	300	" "
New Mill Quarr & butt	1190	" "
Machinery in the old Mill	2370	6 7
Sundries in Stock in Do	1224	" "
Machinery & Stock in new mill	2529	5 6
Cotton Work, weighing Waste Cotton	1925	3 10
Cotton Yarn	2549	5 5
Debts due to Company in La Ledge	12,665	8 —
Do in Smell Do	144	" "
Do in workmens Do	45	12 5
Land and Houses in the Northfield	1880	" "
Stable and alterations in Houses	50	" "
Balance of M. Maunes Book acc	61	10 10
Do of Henry Hollins Do	52	16 8

£ 29,752 9 3

(Deductions this year
Interest of money 750 17 1
Sundries 162 3 0
Repairs 102 13 10
Machinery 86 8 9
made into £ 399 15 11

Whereas 24 June 1800

Cash advanced	15,000	"	"
Ms M° of £25149. 5. 5 the amount of same	382	9	10
Poland Money	45	"	"
Debts owing by the Company in Ledge 1538	1538	"	2
Do to Smelt Do	366	13	3
Do in Workmens Do	4	5	11
Do to Mm Paulson	325	10	"
Do to Mr. A Liddelow	500	5	"
Do to Mm Liddelow M°	1240	10	9
Do to I Paulson	1970	4	6½
Do to M Hollins	5410	5	6½
Do Do	400	"	"
Do to Jno Oldknow	347	12	11½
Do to J Liddelow	2223	4	9½
Do to Mr Maunes	164	12	1½
Do to H Hollins Junr	369	13	2
Profits this year	240	1	3

£ 29,752 9 3

Statement of the Bolton Mill Accounts

The old Mill Dam and buildings }	2432	14	0
The Reservoir, House & Bridges }	3014	"	"
Machinery on Bush & Water wheels	5412	15	0
Stock belonging both Mills	1073	9	3
Stock of Cotton & yarn belonging both } Mills 1/2½ say less deduct }	639	10	"
New Mill Dam and buildings			
Machinery on Bush & Water wheels Compensation about 386 }	14786	7	"
Ballance of Debts in Large Ledger	349	"	"
Land and Houses on Portfield	403	"	"
Land and Houses on Shadywell	2	5	4
Ballance of Mr Matthews acct	76	5	2½
Ballance of Debts in Matthews Ledger	60	13	0
Ballance of Jos. Derrotts bank acct	2953	2	6¾
Ballance with Farries bank acct	42	13	4
allowed for carriage of Cotton woods on hand & in [...] }			
	£36066	11	3½

Taken up to this 1st January 1813

By Cash advanced	33,000	"	"
Ballance of Debts in small Ledger	560	3	9½
Ballance of Mr Derrotts acct	944	7	6
Profit the last year	2500	"	"

Deductions this year
from old Mill Dam and

Buildings	180.0.0
Machinery on Bush & } Water wheels }	304.8.0
New Mill Dam &c but	100.15.0
Machinery on Bush } Engine & Water wheels }	209.18.5¾
	615.1.5¾

	£36066	11	3½

since all but Cowpe had other businesses. But the money was not idle; it was used to finance expansion, and this needed courage. The firm had hardly started when it was threatened by the slump of 1786. 'Things go very slowly indeed,' wrote Sam Salte to Samuel Oldknow in December of that year; 'speculators have done infinite harm to every article made of cotton wool.' And later things were worse, 'When will the consequences of this hurricane be known?' the same writer wonders. 'Curse ambition and avarice, two principles that spread ruin and misery. My good friends this should be a warning to every man not to make too great haste to get rich.'[1]

The slump forced cotton spinners, led by Arkwright, to reduce their prices, and Cowpe, Siddon, Oldknow and Co must have suffered from severe competition. But the depression passed and after 1787 there was a marked improvement in the hosiery trade with a corresponding increase in the demand for stocking yarn. The improvement continued until 1793 when trade was hit by the outbreak of war with France. The firm made a loss of £1,618 in this year, and though the following year was better, with a profit of £2,471, the highest earned so far, no profit was shown in 1795 and only £1,439 in 1796. However in 1797, with capital now standing at £15,000 and the profit up to £2,643, confidence revived, and the partners decided to build a second mill in Pleasley Vale, lower down the stream.

The new mill must have been smaller than the first, for it cost, with the dam and cut, only £1,151, less than half the amount spent on the original mill. It apparently came into operation in 1799, when a further £136 had been spent on the building, and machinery installed to the value of £1,254. In the following years more machinery was added, making the total value £4,338 in 1804, after allowing for depreciation. Some of the machinery was built in the works, for the 1802 accounts include the item 'machinery in new mill, not finished, £133 19s 10d.'

---

[1] Unwin, G., op cit, pp 88 et seq. A letter of Richard Arkwright to Samuel Oldknow refers particularly to 'the drop my father has made in the stocking yarn'.

A major innovation in 1804 was the installation of a steam engine in the new mill. A start was made with an engine house only three years after the mill was completed, with its water wheel, dam and cut. Presumably the available water power had proved insufficient for the size of the plant now being put in. Unfortunately the cost of the steam engine is not revealed, but some indication is given by the sharp increase in the value of the equipment in 1804. In the 1803 statement 'machinery and water wheel' in the new mill stands at £2,800. In the following year the item is 'machinery, engine and water wheel' and the value is £4,338. It seems clear from this and subsequent financial statements that water power was still used along with steam in the new mill. No general changeover to steam was contemplated at this time. In 1803 and 1804 additional machinery to the value of £774 was put into the old mill and more power was needed there too. But this was provided by a new water wheel, costing £670, as an addition to the replacement wheel installed the year before. It was many years before water power was completely discarded; as late as 1841 water wheels are mentioned in the accounts, and according to Pigott water power was used even in 1900 for running a few machines on Saturday mornings.

These investments in buildings, power plant and additional machinery were all financed out of profits retained in the business. From 1797 to 1803 the nominal capital, built up in the way already described, remained at £15,000 and the profit for 1803, £6,900, gave a return of 46 per cent. It was now decided to fund most of the accumulated claims and so raise the capital to £36,000 in 1804. There are no turnover figures, but the accounts give some indication of the growth in the firm's production and trade. In the ten years 1794 to 1804 the value of stocks increased from £4,841 to £7,516 and debts due from £4,137 to £15,999. From 1804 until 1813, when the continuous series of early accounts ends, the recorded values of stocks and of debts due remain at about the same level. The business continued profitable over this period, but there is no evidence of further expansion. The labour force, was actually less in 1816 than in 1802, the increase in productive capacity being secured almost entirely by investments in capital equipment.

This lull in the firm's expansion after the burst of enterprise about the turn of the century may be attributed to several factors. The hosiery trade which provided its main market for yarn had had a fair run of prosperity in the latter years of the eighteenth century. Now it entered a long period of decline, which in some branches was accelerated by the closing of foreign markets following the resumption of war in 1804. The Nottingham trade, much of it in cotton hosiery, was especially dependent on exports, and it suffered severely. Peace, in 1815, brought no relief; for now there was a slump in the demand for warp plain and ribbed cotton pieces from which pantaloons had been made, and the manufacture of point net was ruined, as it was said, 'by constant striving after cheapness'.[1]

Under such conditions competition among spinners was intensified. Indeed this was true of the whole cotton industry. Firms were much more numerous than when the Pleasley company was formed. There were now at least eight other spinners in the immediate neighbourhood and very many in Lancashire and in southern Scotland. Spinning mills had also been set up abroad with, it was said, damaging effects on British exports. It must be remembered, too, that Cowpe, Oldknow and Siddons was a relatively small firm by current standards. Dale and Owen had over 2,000 workers at New Lanark. Arkwright employed 725 in one mill alone, at Cromford. There were two firms at Manchester with over 1,000 workers and the average employment in a sample of 43 mills in the Manchester area was 300 workers in 1816 when Pleasley had 249.[2]

The effects of adverse market conditions and intensified competition are reflected in the firm's profits. In 1810 they had again touched £6,000, but in 1812 they were down to £3,180 and they fell still further in 1813 to £2,400. There is now a gap in the records,

---

[1] Felkin, W. *History of Machine-wrought Hosiery and Lace Manufactures*, pp 138 and 440. 1867.
[2] Select Committee 1816, evidence.

but from what we know of general economic conditions in the period following the Napoleonic Wars, earnings were probably small. In 1831 they were only £265 and a mere £135 in 1832, and nothing had been added to the capital in the intervening years.

Many East Midlands spinners fared far worse. From 1813 onwards there are advertisements in *The Nottingham Review* of cotton mills offered for sale, and they were not easy to dispose of. A mill was usually advertised, in the first instance, for sale by private treaty, as a going concern. Then it would often appear again in the announcement of an auction. This was frequently followed by advertisements offering the contents for sale in lots.

Such was the fate of the Papplewick mill, which had been the first steam-driven cotton factory in the country. The whole plant was sold by auction in 1829, and the items listed are interesting as illustrating the range of processes and the extent to which these had now been mechanised. There were machines for opening up the raw cotton compressed in bales, spreading and carding machines, blowers and various kinds of spinning frames, including mules. There were also coppers, for use in scouring and bleaching, and dye vats. The most valuable item was the 'very superior Fire Engine, cost £200', presumably the successor to the original steam engine installed some fifty years earlier.

Some of the mills which closed down were evidently small and obsolete, and inconveniently located now that steam was replacing water power. But several had steam engines and were situated in towns, where there was no shortage of labour. This point was made, for instance, in advertising a mill at Sutton-in-Ashfield, not far from Pleasley: 'Sutton-in-Ashfield is a very populous place in the immediate neighbourhood of collieries, where a number of hands may be obtained at reasonable wages and coals procured at a moderate price.'

---

[1] After a few years of falling prices, trade improved in the early 1820s but depression returned, following the financial crisis at the end of 1825. The effects were still felt four years later. 'We think trade was never so bad as it is at the present time', writes the London agent of a Nottingham hosiery firm. Allen Solley Letter Book, 1829.

OLDKNOW, PEARSCE, & Co's.

PRICES OF COTTON YARN,

No.	Price per Bundle.				No.	Price per Bundle.		
	£.	s.	D.			£.	s.	D.
6½	1	15	4		33	2	14	0
6¾	1	15	5		34	2	15	0
7	1	15	6		35	2	16	0
7¼	1	15	7		36	2	17	0
7½	1	15	8		37	2	18	0
7¾	1	15	9		38	2	19	0
8	1	15	10		39	3	0	0
8¼	1	15	11		40	3	1	0
8½	1	16	0		41	3	2	0
8¾	1	16	1		42	3	3	0
9	1	16	2		43	3	4	0
9½	1	16	4		44	3	5	0
10	1	16	6		45	3	6	0
11	1	17	0		46	3	7	0
12	1	17	6		47	3	8	0
13	1	18	0		48	3	9	0
14	1	18	6		49	3	10	0
15	1	19	0		50	3	11	0
16	1	19	6		51	3	12	0
17	2	0	0		52	3	13	0
18	2	0	6		53	3	14	0
19	2	1	0		54	3	15	0
20	2	1	6		55	3	16	0
21	2	2	0		56	3	17	0
22	2	3	0		57	3	18	0
23	2	4	0		58	3	19	0
24	2	5	0		59	4	0	0
25	2	6	0		60	4	1	0
26	2	7	0		61	4	2	6
27	2	8	0		62	4	4	0
28	2	9	0		63	4	5	6
29	2	10	0		64	4	7	0
30	2	11	0		65	4	8	6
31	2	12	0		66	4	10	0
32	2	13	0		67	4	11	6

(J. DUNN, PRINTER, NOTTINGHAM.)

Two factors in particular helped the Pleasley firm to survive through these difficult years. One was the insistence on quality, which has been a feature of its products ever since. The yarn requirements of the hosiery trade were exacting, and with cotton, especially, it had always been difficult to spin an even yarn that would work smoothly in the knitting frame. Strutts, the biggest spinner of hosiery yarns and the most experienced firm in the industry, had many complaints about the poor quality of its yarn and Hollins was quoted as the standard of comparison. 'I am sorry to say,' writes Strutts' Nottingham agent in 1806, 'your cotton has not yet reached to that degree of improvement as to admit of my selling to those Houses who now buy of Hollins.'[1] Hollins had done well to establish such a reputation in its early years and it took care to maintain it.[2] The other factor was the conservative financial policy of the partnership, which was adhered to despite changes in its membership.

The first change came in 1796, when John Cowpe left. There is a local tradition, supported by a few notes in an 'observation book' kept by Cowpe's brother, the Mansfield farmer, that the break was due to a disagreement. This may well be true; for, as will be recalled, it was about this time that the idea of building a second mill came under discussion, though the business had only just become profitable and there had been a sharp fall in 1796. At all events, Cowpe was paid out and his two shares were bought by Samuel Siddon and Henry Hollins.[3]

Cowpe's place as manager was taken by William Pearsce, who had entered the partnership four years earlier, and in 1797 he was joined by Henry Hollins' son, who was also the nephew of Thomas Oldknow. Henry Hollins junior had just come of age and taken up his hereditary freedom of Nottingham as a 'burgess born'. He

---

[1] Fitton, R.S. and Wadsworth, A.P. *The Strutts and the Arkwrights*, p 307. 1958.
[2] Hollins was also notable for its wide range of yarns. See price list, opposite.
[3] According to his brother's record, Cowpe went into business at Normanton, Derbyshire, as a miller, maltster and farmer. Then, after a brief return to Pleasley Hill, he moved to Evesham where he joined a tanning firm. Pigott, S., op cit, p 44.

came into the partnership on the share which his father had bought from Cowpe and quickly assumed the responsibilities of management. The second mill was just being opened, and it seems likely that Pearsce and the young Hollins took charge of one mill each. Soon afterwards Hollins went to live in Cowpe's old house, and so began the long tradition of a Hollins living by the works in Pleasley Vale and directly involved in the management.

Henry Hollins the elder continued to live in Nottingham. Eventually, however, he gave up the old-established brazier's business and went into the hosiery trade. He appears in a Nottingham directory of 1814 as 'hosier, Angel Row', which was quite near to his former premises. This was a natural step to take for one who had a substantial stake in cotton spinning but had not been closely concerned with mill management. For the framework knitting industry was the main outlet for Pleasley's yarn. As a hosier, Hollins would own frames rented to outworkers; he would supply them with yarn and buy their finished goods, either directly or through middlemen or 'putters-out', as they were called. When Henry Hollins died in 1825, at the age of eighty-five, his hosiery business was continued by a son of his second marriage, Samuel Hollins, who later went into lace manufacture too.[1]

In the meantime further changes had occurred at Pleasley. After ten years as a partner and joint manager Henry Hollins junior decided to leave the firm and join his brother Charles in operating a cotton mill at Langwith, a few miles away. Just why this happened is not known. It is possible that relations between the joint managers had become strained. For instance, the accounts show that Pearsce's salary, as distinct from his share in profits, was only £63 in 1801, much less than Cowpe's, while Hollins, the younger and less experienced man, got £90. By 1807, when Hollins left, Pearsce's salary had gone up to £200, but Hollins' had been put up to the same figure. Each, like the other partners, had a one-sixth share in the firm's capital; but the partners' loan accounts show that Pearsce had

---

[1] Erickson, C. *British Industrialists. Steel & Hosiery*, p 182. 1959.

Plate 3. Cuckney Mill

Plate 4. Old Cotton Mill at Langwith 1948

Plate 5. Pleasley Lower Mill on fire

Plate 6. Via Gellia Mill

become by far the biggest creditor, with a balance of £1,040, as compared with Hollins' £329. Thus there may have been some resentment on Pearsce's side against having to share the management with Hollins, and some sense of frustration on Hollins' part, especially as the business was no longer expanding. On the other hand, it must be remembered that the production capacity of a water mill was dependent on the power available at any one site, and the power was liable to vary. In acquiring the Langwith mill the Hollins secured another unit which, though independently owned, could be operated in conjunction with Pleasley. This arrangement could still have seemed worthwhile even after the position at Pleasley had been relieved by the installation of a steam engine at one mill. For steam was, as yet, only an auxiliary source of power and not entirely reliable.

Whatever the reasons, Hollins departed with his share of the capital and his credit balance, and Pearsce moved into the manager's house. But the Langwith firm, which eventually acquired a second mill at Cuckney, maintained close relations with Pleasley. Pigott met people living in Pleasley Vale who could remember their grandparents describing how cotton wool and yarn used to pass to and fro between Langwith and Pleasley in ass carts. The two firms also set up a joint yarn agency in Nottingham, at the address of Henry Hollins the elder on Angel Row.

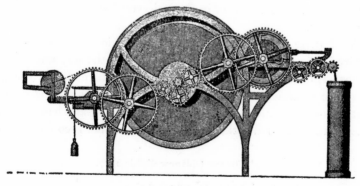

CARDING ENGINE *c.* 1830

D

When the first Henry Hollins died in 1825 his son decided to return to Pleasley. He had inherited, together with his brothers, his father's share in the business and soon afterwards he was able to buy the share of William Pearsce, who had died sometime previously. Hollins took over the management, and he brought in his eldest son, another Henry, who had gained experience at Langwith and Cuckney. Soon afterwards, in 1829, the Pleasley firm, whose name had been changed to Oldknow, Pearsce and Co in 1816, became known as Hollins, Siddon and Co.[1]

The Hollins family were now firmly established in the business, and it was the sons of grandsons of the second Henry Hollins who were mainly responsible for its subsequent development. But their achievement was shared by another family, the Pagets, whose connection with the firm lasted for more than a century. The first Pagets to enter the business were two brothers, William and Joseph, who bought the share of Henry Hollins the second when he withdrew in 1807. The Pagets were related by marriage to both Henry Hollins senior and to Thomas Oldknow and had similar religious affiliations.[2] But more important were their business connections. They were principals in the Loughborough hosiery firm of Paget and White, described as 'the most eminent manufacturers of hosiery and lace in the country', and which, later on, built some of the first circular frames to be driven by steam power.[3] One of the brothers was also a partner in the Leicester banking house of Paget and Kirby.

With these other interests the first generation of Pagets were not active in the management of Pleasley, so that the way was open for Henry Hollins to assume control when he returned. But their experience as hosiery and lace manufacturers and the direct contacts they provided with these industries introduced an element which the partnership had lacked hitherto. The banking connection was

[1] Thomas Oldknow died in 1817.
[2] Church R.A., op cit, p 130.
[3] Felkin, W., op cit, p 490.

MOST ELIGIBLE INVESTMENT.

Freehold
MANOR & ESTATE,
DERBYSHIRE.

To be Sold by Auction,

BY MR. BREAREY,

AT THE SWAN, IN MANSFIELD,

In the County of Nottingham,

On THURSDAY the 28th of AUGUST next,

AT THREE O'CLOCK:

THE

Manor of Pleasley,

WELL STOCKED WITH GAME,

IN THE COUNTY OF DERBY.

Also a very valuable Freehold Estate, &c.

WITHIN THE OLD MANOR,

Containing upwards of 1188 Acres,

COMPRISING SUNDRY GOOD

FARMS AND FARM-HOUSES,

With all necessary and commodious Outbuildings,

With a suitable proportion of capital Farming Land attached to each :

ALSO

A WATER CORN MILL OF GREAT POWER :

THE WHOLE TOWN OR VILL OF PLEASLEY,

(Except the Parsonage House,)

Together with Pleasley Park, containing 181A. 1R. 4P. of fine growing Oak and other Timber & Reserve-the whole (except the Park) being in the occupation of very responsible Tenants.

AT OLD RENTS AMOUNTING TO UPWARDS OF £1,200 PER ANNUM

Upon which a deduction of £20. per Cent. has lately been allowed

Several Plantations in different Parts of the Estate are in a most thriving condition.

The Estate offered for Sale has the advantage of the great Turnpike Roads from London to Chesterfield Sheffield and Rotherham through the same, with the Mail and other Coaches passing and repassing daily, and is situate 3 Miles from Mansfield and 9 from Chesterfield

Two thirds of the Purchase Money, at 4½ per Cent., may remain on Security of the Manor and Estate (if required) for a number of Years certain , and full printed Particulars may be had of Messrs. HOLME, FRAMPTON and LOFTUS, New Inn, London ; of Mr. DOWLAND, Cuckney, Nottinghamshire , of Mr. BREAREY, at Derby at the Swan, in Mansfield ; the King's Head, Derby ; the Black's Head, Nottingham , the Moseley Arm Manchester ; and of Messrs. BRITTLEBANK, Solicitors, Oddo, Derbyshire, at whose Office Plans of the Estate are deposited for inspection, and of whom further Particulars may be had.

ODDO, 28th July, 1823.

useful too. So far the partnership appears to have been entirely self-financing, and the resources were adequate so long as the individual partners were able and willing to hold substantial balances in their accounts with the firm. But it could happen that at times the firm had more capital than it could profitably use and at other times be short of working capital. Banks exist to relieve this situation, and the intimate relationship now established between Pleasley and the Leicester bank would be valuable to both businesses.

As previously remarked, there is a gap in the firm's accounts between 1813 and 1831,[1] so we have little direct evidence of its progress during this period. However, in 1828 an important property transaction was concluded. Until this time, the site of Pleasley mills and the water rights had been held on a lease. It was part of the Pleasley Manor estate, and the only land which the firm had been able to buy belonged to an adjoining property. The rent was still only £40 a year, but the lease was approaching its end and the partners must have viewed the prospect with some anxiety. In 1823 Pleasley Manor was sold for £38,000, but the leased land was reserved by the trustees of the estate in the expectation of a better price when the lease expired in three years' time. Eventually, after lengthy negotiations, the company managed to secure the freehold for £7,600. Thus the mills, with fifteen acres of land and the all-important water rights, became the firm's own property. It was decided to vest the property in an independent trustee. This was a wise precaution, since several of the partners were engaged in other businesses, and there was not the safeguard of limited liability; if any partner became bankrupt his creditors might then distrain on his assets in the partnership, with serious consequences for

---

[1] It appears that each partner had his own book containing a yearly balance sheet and a profit and loss account signed by all the partners. One of the three surviving books also records the personal account of each partner with the firm. In one book the entries finish in 1807; another continues till 1813. The ownership of these two books cannot be identified. But the third book belonged to the second Henry Hollins. The early entries begin in 1797, when he entered the partnership, and end in 1807, when he left. They are not resumed until 1831, which indicates that he did not become a full partner until some years after his return to Pleasley. The last entry was made in 1847, the year before his death.

the firm. The first trustee was George Walkden, a Mansfield solicitor, who happened to have married the sister of Mrs Henry Hollins.[1]

[1] The facts concerning the acquisition of the property are recorded in Pigott, op cit, pp 61–4.

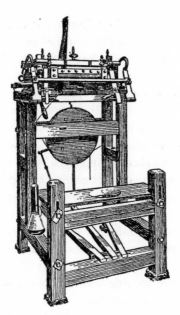

A STOCKING FRAME

CHAPTER THREE

Setback and Recovery

AT the time of the freehold purchase trade was still depressed. 'We are sorry to announce,' says *The Nottingham Review* for 15 September 1829, 'that trade is exceedingly flat at Mansfield, scarcely a factory or even a single frame being in full employ.' But although the company was making little profit, its financial position was sound and its members could draw on further resources to supplement the capital already invested. They could afford to take a long view of trade prospects. Fluctuations were inevitable; but by squeezing out the weaker competitors, with their desperate price cutting, a slump in trade could benefit a sound, well-equipped firm by enabling it to increase its share of the market when trade revived. The increase in market share was particularly important in the 1830s, for the hosiery industry was still depressed. Indeed the condition of the framework knitters became so bad that a government commission was appointed in 1845 to investigate the trade. This found that the trouble was due more to the chronic overcrowding of the occupation than to the decline of demand for hosiery goods. But there were certainly no signs of expansion; hosiery had become a stagnant industry and the abundance of cheap labour left manufacturers with little incentive to improve their methods of production.

Despite the unpromising conditions in its main market the Pleasley firm continued its policy of steady investment. The purchase of the property appears to have been financed by the partners making what is called in the accounts a 'further advance' of £8,005. The Pagets made substantial contributions in addition, especially William Paget, whose account never fell below £3,500 in the ten years 1831–41. During this period too, the firm borrowed fairly heavily from the Nottingham bankers, Messrs Maltby & Robinson, whose account reached nearly £9,000 in 1833. This additional capital was helpful during the period of low profits for it enabled the company to improve its equipment year by year, until in 1837 its valuation, after allowing depreciation at 7½ per cent, reached a total of £11,764 9s 4d. Then profits began to recover, reaching £4,260 in 1839, in addition to interest at 5 per cent on each partner's total investment. By 1837 the loan from Maltby & Robinson had been repaid, partly out of further investments made by the Pagets and partly from the return of funds borrowed from the firm by Henry Hollins and his son. These funds may well have been used for the Langwith business in which the two were still associated with Charles Hollins.

Unfortunately the recovery recorded in 1839 was not maintained. In the accounts for the following financial year stocks of cotton yarn are shown at £13,410, which is double the average figure for the preceding nine years. It had been the practice to write down the value of stocks by 15 per cent, but with stocks at this level it was wisely decided that 20 per cent should be written off. Trade was bad and profits slumped to £512. The setback was disappointing, but by no means critical. The partners still got their steady 5 per cent on invested capital and long experience had taught them to expect fluctuations in the net profits of the firm. If stocks were accumulating raw material buying would be reduced and the mills would go on short time until trade recovered.

But, at the end of the year 1840, Hollins, Siddon & Co encountered a setback of an altogether different order. On Christmas Day the upper mill was destroyed by fire. There are various accounts of the disaster. Pigott relates an interview with a Mr Sam Robinson, an engine-room attendant at the mills, who retired on pension in 1931. He recalled his grandmother telling how the sight of the mill in flames stirred the local people in the early hours of the morning and how she and the neighbours ran to the brow of Pleasley Hill to see the whole valley lit with reflections in the snow.

A week later the full story appeared in *The Nottingham Journal* and in *The Nottingham Review*. The latter made the most of it, and its account is worth quoting in full:

About three o'clock in the morning the inhabitants of Mansfield, instead of being aroused by the sweet voices of iterant singers, calling upon Christians to awake and salute the happy morn, had their slumbers broken by the hoarse cry of Fire! Fire! and the dismal rumbling of the engines as they rolled along the streets to the scene of destruction, while a lurid light shed its rays about the northern horizon and the darkly rolling clouds of the conflagration piling their giant towers upon the sky met the eyes of the astonished gazers.

The source of the alarm was soon ascertained and numbers proceeded to it; but before the engines could reach the place the fire had so far advanced as to prevent their being of any avail, save partly to protect the steam engine.

It appeared on enquiring that workmen were on the premises as late as 12 o'clock and also some singers were about at two, besides Mr Hollins's groom having only shortly previous gone to bed, when no trace of fire was then discernible; but in a little time after this a second set of singers were near the factory and discovered it to be on fire. A daughter of Mr Adams, the book-keeper, who lives close to the place, also observed the light and called her father up. The alarm was thus given, and Mr Adams, having obtained from Mr Hollins the key of the counting house, assisted by Mr Hollins, fortunately succeeded in rescuing most of the books. Nothing else could be saved, for after the fire was first seen, its progress was of such a sweeping character that the whole building was almost at once in flames.

A despatch was of course sent off for the engines from Mansfield, and a small one at the works was attempted to be played, but the trial was wholly useless and the giant destroyer seemed to laugh at the puny efforts which were made to stay his fierce progress. Indeed, considered apart from the calamitous consequences, the event was a glorious display of the element which, in its onward course, so speedily devoured the labour of many years, setting at nought strength of substance and skill in structure; the solid beam, the strong wall, the iron bar and the delicate machine were at once consumed or destroyed, as though they were of the fragile material which, but a short time before, was there in process of manufacture; while the hills, the dark woods, the humble cottages, the village church and the transparent lake, stood discovered before the consumer and added, by the beauty of their appearance, to the glory of his triumph.

We learn that the building and machines were only partially insured, in the Royal Exchange and Norwich Union Offices, and that 300 hands will, at this the worst season of the year, be deprived of employment. The loss has been variously estimated, but it is thought that it will amount to £12,000 or £15,000.

While this loss is to be deplored, we cannot but rejoice that no greater destruction took place, as it is probable, had the night been windy, that the dwelling house of Mr Hollins, which is very near the mill, and the houses of some of his dependents, which also adjoin, might have fallen a prey to the flames, and the loss of property would not only have been greater, but lives also might have been sacrificed.

The cause of the fire could not, of course, be ascertained. A few weeks later *The Review* reported that Henry Hollins had received an anonymous letter stating 'that if he did not take great care the other mill would be burnt and also that it would be useless to rebuild the one destroyed as the same fate would again befall it'. The incident is curious, especially in view of the fact that the other mill was burnt five years later. But this was probably no more than coincidence. Cotton mills, with their several floors supported by wooden beams, with their stocks of highly inflammable material, and now lighted by gas, were vulnerable to the risk of fire. The Pleasley mill was completely destroyed within two and a half hours, except for the engine house, on which the firemen had concentrated their efforts.

The first concern of the management was to maintain production and employment as far as possible. Fortunately the lower mill was half a mile away from the one destroyed and so suffered no damage. It was hoped that production might be restored by working this mill day and night; but it depended partly on water power and the head of water was insufficient for continuous working. Thus there was considerable loss of production capacity and more than a hundred workers remained unemployed. It is evident, however, that a great effort was made to keep things going, for in the four and a half months following the fire the firm made a profit of £727, more than in the whole of 1840.

The damage caused by the fire was estimated by the Norwich Insurance Office at 'somewhat over £10,000'. As *The Nottingham Journal* reported, 'the mill had, within the last few years, been filled with new machinery of the most approved description and was of great value'. Something of the building remained, for its value was entered in the firm's accounts at £1,400, but the loss on machinery is shown as £5,916. Another serious item was the amount of stock destroyed. As we have seen, yarn stocks had reached an abnormally high level at the time of the fire. In May 1841 they were valued at £9,658, a reduction of £3,752 on the previous year, which is an indication of the loss sustained.

So far as can be ascertained from the accounts, the total loss caused by the fire was about £11,500. Of this, £5,485 was covered by insurances, including a claim for £85 on the engine, which had been separately insured for £500. This left the company with a loss of assets amounting to some £6,000, and in a provisional balance sheet dated 1 January 1841 it was allowed for by writing down the value of premises and machinery. But the regular statement of accounts, produced in May, shows that more drastic action was taken, 'in pursuance of this day's resolutions for future guidance'. The effect was to reduce the value of premises and machinery from the 1840 figure of £23,667 to £9,754, a depreciation of £13,913. At the same time, and presumably in accordance with the same resolutions, the item 'further advance' of £8,005 was removed from the liabilities side of the account.

The meeting at which these decisions were taken had been preceded by Henry Hollins's retirement from the firm. He had managed the Pleasley mills for the past fifteen years. He was now sixty-five and one can imagine his reluctance to face the urgent task of reconstruction. For a short time he maintained his connection with his brother Charles at Langwith, but when he died, in 1848, this mill closed down. His son Henry, who was not included in the new partnership, died in the same year, and it was a younger son, William Hollins, who took his father's place.

Within a few years of the partnership being reconstituted, several further changes occurred. Joseph Paget died in 1842 and was succeeded by his son Charles, who already had a financial interest in the firm. William Paget, the younger, became a full partner when his father died four years later. In 1846 too, Sam Siddon died. His family had been members of the firm for some fifty years and the name was retained in the style adopted in 1841: William Hollins, Siddon & Company. Now it became simply William Hollins & Company, as it is today.

The change of name signifies the position assumed by William Hollins in the reconstituted partnership. He was only twenty-five when he took over the management from his father in 1841, and was not yet a full partner. But no other member of the two families was able to give his whole time to the firm's affairs. An older brother, Edward, acquired Henry Hollins's share of the capital but he was already in business on his own account. As early as 1832 he had an office in Manchester and ten years later was established as a cotton spinner at Park Mills, Stockport. Of the three Pagets with shares in the firm, Thomas was a surgeon at Leicester, William managed the hosiery manufacturing business in Loughborough, and Charles, although he later came to live at Stuffynwood Hall in Pleasley Vale, was increasingly absorbed in public affairs. In 1844 he became High Sheriff of Nottinghamshire; he was active in the Anti-Corn Law League, and from 1856 to 1865 he represented Nottingham in Parliament as a Whig Liberal. But it was not by mere accident that the choice as manager of Pleasley Mills fell on William Hollins, for he must, as a young man, have shown something of the qualities that enabled him to direct a constantly expanding business over a period of fifty years. He was made a partner in 1844 and the revised deed of co-partnership explicitly provided that William Hollins need bring in no part of his share initially but was to acquire it by leaving in two-thirds of his yearly profit until sufficient capital had been accumulated.

The first major task under William Hollins' management was the replacement of the burnt-out upper mill. This was not undertaken immediately. Trade was not good at the time of the fire,[1] and the older partners may well have felt it best to conserve their resources by concentrating production in the remaining mill and so reduce overheads. By this policy the firm managed to make a profit of £3,450 in 1842, though it fell to £2,106 the following year. However, a new generation was now taking over. They were not content

---

[1] The depression continued throughout 1841. *The Nottingham Review* of 5 November reported 'great distress and unemployment in Mansfield'. The poor rates had doubled. The latest blow was the discharge of forty mill-hands by Leavers and Greenhalgh, who could only employ their remaining workers half-time.

to see the firm merely jogging along at this level, and with signs of a trade revival appearing towards the end of 1843 they decided to build. 'We understand,' says *The Nottingham Review* of 16 February 1844, 'that in consequence of the increased demand for cotton yarn Messrs Hollins & Co, of Pleasley Works, have come to the determination of erecting another mill near to the site occupied by the former one which was destroyed by fire. Plans have been prepared and it is expected the building will be proceeded with in the spring.' Later, in August, the paper refers to the mill being under construction.

The statement of accounts dated 10 May 1845 shows that £8,085 was spent on the new mill. The total cost of the building, including expenditure in the previous year was £8,406, and the accounts for 1846 record that machinery to the value of £11,099 was installed. In preparation for this increased investment in fixed assets, the new co-partnership deed of 1844 provided for raising the nominal capital to £48,000; some of the partners advances were funded, but the increased capital was only partly paid up. In 1846 further payments were made, especially by Charles Paget, whose account increased to £16,458. A profit of £2,439 was shown for the year ended 10 May 1847.

It is remarkable that any profit was earned in the financial year 1846–7; for in October 1846[1] another disaster occurred, which, though less damaging financially than that of five years before, must have caused a sharp fall in production. *The Nottingham Journal* of 9 October 1846 reported as follows: 'Soon after 5 o'clock on Tuesday evening last a fire broke out in the old mill at Pleasley Works, belonging to Messrs Hollins and Co. The wind being very brisk, the fire raged so as to baffle all attempts to stay its progress. By half-past six the roof had fallen in, and although the Mansfield fire engines were soon on the spot and at work, the whole fabric, with the greater part of the goods and machines was, destroyed, and by midnight nothing but bare blackened walls remained. We understand that the property was insured.'

[1] Pigott, S., op cit, p 65, gives the date as 1844. This is clearly a mistake.

The mill now destroyed was the second mill, built in 1798; it had, however, been greatly extended over the years and the estimated damage, £12,000, was slightly higher than for the upper mill. But this time a bigger proportion was covered by insurance. A few weeks after the fire *The Journal* gave the amount of the claim as £9,000 and added that the mill was to be restored 'as speedily as possible'. The loss through the fire explains the low valuation of the firm's premises in the accounts for 1847. The recently completed

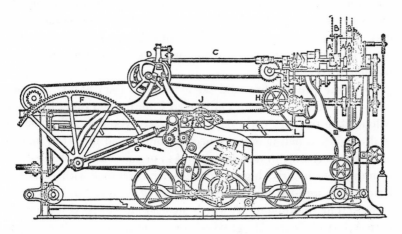

ROBERTS'S SELF-ACTING MULE

new upper mill had been heavily written down and the total attributed to premises was only £6,938. Machinery, for which the depreciation rate is given as 12½ per cent, stood at £14,252; evidently there had been further installations in the new mill and perhaps some machines had been saved from the fire.

In contrast with their reaction after the first fire, the partners, with William Hollins as the dominant member, showed no hesitation in their decision to rebuild. Indeed, they provided not merely for restoration but for growth. In 1847, by a special endorsement to the co-partnership deed of 1844, the nominal capital of the business was raised to £80,000. The money was to be obtained, 'as the erection of new buildings and other occasions of the said business shall require it', presumably, as before, by the funding of partners' accumulated claims by way of interest and profits and from any additional investments they chose to make. In the meantime some short term borrowing from outside the partnership was arranged.[1]

In acting as they did now the partners were doubtless inspired by the success of the new upper mill, which had fortunately come into full production before the second fire. They saw the destruction of the old lower mill as an opportunity for repeating this success. They may, indeed, have contemplated rebuilding and re-equipping the lower mill in any case. Now, if the business was to grow, they had no alternative.

So in the end the fires did far more good than harm. The old mills had been added to and improved from time to time. But they belonged to the very early days of the factory system. The industrial revolution had long since been accomplished in cotton manufacture, but change in technology and in organisation continued. In spinning particularly, bigger and heavier machines with cast-iron frames had speeded up the process and economised in the use of labour.[2] The spinning mule, which incorporated the best features of both Arkwright's and Hargreaves's inventions, had now been made self-acting, so that all the movements, including the travel of the carriage, could be power-driven. Another notable innovation about 1850 was the combing machine. Hand combing had been a man's job, but the machines could be worked by women.[3]

New equipment necessitated changes in work organisation and progressive firms were giving more attention to factory layout. It was

---

[1] The only surviving evidence of this for the period in question is a bill dated 29 September 1848. This shows that £3,000, repayable at three months' notice, was borrowed from relatives of William Hollins: Charles Hollins of Leicester, Gentleman, John Hollins of Melton Mowbray, Agent, and Samuel Hollins of Nottingham, Lacemaker.

[2] 'So much has been done in the increase of speed that a few years since was thought impossible,' said a cotton spinner in evidence before the Royal Commission on Factories, 1833.

[3] Singer. *History of Technology*. 1958.

coming to be realised, too, that the efficiency of labour could be raised by improving the working environment. Indeed, higher minimum standards of accommodation were now laid down in the Factories Act and inspectors had been appointed to ensure conformity.

Many firms failed to keep pace with such development, either from lack of resources or a flagging of enterprise, and their obsolete mills became derelict. But for the opportunity fortuitously created by the fires, and the way it was seized by William Hollins, a similar fate might have overtaken Pleasley.

The new mills, like the originals, were built of stone; a good deal came from the ruins and its salvage value was recorded in the accounts; the rest was quarried on the estate. Many extensions have since been made to both buildings, but it is still possible to recognise the structures as shown in the engravings on a billhead of the 1850s.[1] They are plain, functional buildings, well-proportioned, like most factories and warehouses of this period; and being of stone they blend happily with the pleasant landscape of Pleasley Vale. The lower mill was now the larger of the two, with four storeys, the upper mill having only three. Water power was used in both mills, but each had its chimney stack and engine house. With the opening of pits in the neighbourhood Pleasley could get plenty of cheap coal; but water power was cheaper still, when enough was available.

[1] p 64.

Stanley Works
Mansfield
NOTTINGHAMSHIRE.

CHAPTER FOUR

The Pleasley Industrial Community

THERE is unfortunately little direct information on conditions of employment at Pleasley during this period. The labour force had naturally grown with the expansion of the business, but far less than the capital employed and the capacity of the mills. At the time of the first fire one newspaper suggested that 300 people were likely to lose their jobs. But a later report put the figure at no more than 180, which suggests that the two mills might have had some 350 workers altogether. This accords with the estimate of between 300 and 400 given in a local directory for 1846. Thus employment seems to have grown by about one-third in the thirty years since 1816.

Labour supply was always something of a problem for factories whose location was determined by the availability of water power. Hollins, in Pleasley Vale, was less isolated than some; it could draw on three nearby villages, Pleasley, Mansfield Woodhouse and Shirebrook, all quite small, and there was also Mansfield town four miles away. But the journey to and from work, on foot and along rough roads, added to the burden of a working day that normally extended from six in the morning to six at night. There was a 1½ hr break for meals; but we can well believe the factory commissioners of 1833 who mentioned the strain of standing for long hours in humid conditions as one of the worst features of mill work.

Labour turnover must have been high. The earlier expedient of using pauper apprentices as a form of tied labour had been generally abandoned with the prohibition on the employment of children under nine in cotton mills. But the practice of hiring on long contracts was still common, and workers could be prosecuted and sent to jail for breach of contract. In 1838 Hollins of Langwith was in-

volved in such a case.[1] This concerned the Walker children, a girl
of 17 and four boys aged from 9 to 15 years. Their father had sent
them to work in the mill so long as they could earn enough to
maintain themselves. Their starting wages ranged from 1s 9d to
5s 6d a week and they were promised, after a year, 26s for the girl
and 13s for the older boys. However, for various reasons, including
the 'breaking of the great wheel', which stopped the mill for five
weeks and put everybody on half pay, the children's wages were
never sufficient. Their father then took them away. Hollins sued
for breach of contract, claiming that they had been hired for the
year, and the Mansfield justices upheld the claim, adding, signi-
ficantly, that their decision would provide 'a suitable example to
Messrs Hollins's other hands'. Although Hollins, having won his
case, would have taken the children back, the magistrates insisted
on sending four of them to prison. Eventually, after a public appeal
and a petition to the home secretary, a pardon was secured.

Another and more creditable means of attaching workers to the
mill was to build houses on the site. This was done on a considerable scale by the Strutts and the Arkwrights in the Derwent valley,
and Hollins, too, made such provision in Pleasley Vale. The settlement, which had begun in 1790 with John Cowpe's ten houses in
Northfields, grew in the course of time to a village with twenty-six
cottages in the vale and another eight at Pleasley Hill. Thus, by the
time William Hollins established himself in the Vale House, a large
proportion of his employees would be living in the vicinity; for the
tenants' children often followed their parents into the mills and it
was common for several members of a family to be working there at
the same time. In this way an industrial community was formed. Its
nucleus was in Pleasley Vale, but its activities brought in many
others living farther afield yet sharing a common interest as
Hollins' employees.

[1] The case is described by Pigott, quoting Home Office Papers and a handbill in
Nottingham Public Library. The Langwith firm was separate from Hollins of
Pleasley. The managing partner at the time was Henry Hollins III; his father,
Henry Hollins II had now rejoined the Pleasley partners.

Close by the upper mill was the house where William Hollins now lived.[1] He was the first Hollins really to belong to Pleasley Vale. His grandfather, who had helped to found the firm, had remained a Nottingham man, with business interests there, and had been influential in local affairs. William's father lived at Pleasley for many years, but his connection had been broken by the long absence during which the mills at Langwith and Cuckney had claimed most of his attention. In the fifteen years following his return, however, he had been the dominant influence in the firm; its workers and their families were his neighbours and he their respected head. This patriarchal role in the community was now assumed by William Hollins.

Glimpses of the social environment at Pleasley Vale about this time are provided by reports in the local press. There is, for instance, a lively account of the Sunday-school tea meeting in *The Nottingham Review* for 17 November 1843. It took place in the juvenile school room belonging to Messrs Hollins, the tea being given as a reward to the scholars for good behaviour during the past year.

> About 140 sat down to tea. The room was tastefully decorated with evergreens and rosettes, which did credit to the taste of Mr John Sanderson, the schoolmaster. At one end of the room was placed a large circular board, lined with cotton wool, bearing this inscription, formed with berries: 'Henry Hollins Esq, the friend of education.' In the centre was hung a splendid copper crown formed of piping, which was beautifully lighted up with gas.[2] At the other end of the room was a square board, lined as before, with the inscription: 'To Hollins, Siddon & Co, our kind benefactors.' The entrance was imposingly grand. The scholars were waited upon by Miss Hollins, Mr and Mrs Howard, Mr Sanderson and the teachers in general. After the children had partaken of the cheering beverage, the superintendent, teachers, parents, and friends of the children sat down to tea and were honoured with the company of W. Hollins, Esq, the Rev W. Linwood and Miss Hollins. A variety of sacred music was performed during the evening by Messrs Harp and Slaney, associated with three youths connected with the works. When tea was concluded, Mr Howard, the indefatiguable and respected manager of the works, gave out a hymn, after which the children sang and recited a

[1] The house, though much altered, still exists. After the death of Henry Ernest Hollins it was converted into offices.

[2] The firm's gas plant was installed in 1839 at a cost of £876 17s 9d.

variety of pieces in a style which would have done honour to scholars
of much higher pretensions. On the thanks of the meeting being given
to the proprietor of the works, W. Hollins Esq rose and assured the
meeting that it gave him and the gentlemen with whom he was connected great pleasure in having the opportunity to give their support
to an institution which had for its object the education of youth.
Henry Hollins Esq not being present from unavoidable circumstances,
Mrs Howard proposed a vote of thanks to him for his donation.

The provision of schooling for the Pleasley children was not entirely a private benefaction. It had been started in accordance with
legislation governing the employment of pauper apprentices. Later
on the Act of 1833 made the employment of children in textile mills
conditional upon attendance at school for two hours a day on six
days a week. But the Hollins, like the Strutts at Belper and Milford,
were always mindful of their obligations. They came out well in the
inquiry of 1816 and the subsequent development of both the day
school and the Sunday school owed much to the personal interest of
the second Henry Hollins. This was continued by his son, and in
the 1850s the mill children attended school half-time, one week in
the mornings and the next in the afternoons. Physical recreation
was also provided for, as is shown in the following report from *The
Nottingham Review* in 1843 : 'Messrs William Hollins, Siddon & Co,
with their usual kind attention to the health and comfort of their
workpeople, have opened a spaceous playground for the children
belonging to their infant and junior school, and a plentiful supply
of articles for athletic amusements have been provided for the workpeople generally, of both sexes and all ages.' Another amenity introduced about the same time was penny baths for the workpeople.
The Review expressed the hope that 'this praiseworthy example
will be followed by the proprietors of other establishments'. Bearing
in mind the long hours of work and the distance that many workers
had to travel, one imagines that a canteen would have been welcome. But not until forty years later was such provision made.

The conditions in which the Pleasley community developed
tended, inevitably, to emphasise the dependent relationship of
master and men. But in William Hollins there was nothing of the

hard taskmaster as portrayed in some accounts of the early factory system. He represented the third generation of his family as mill owners; and the Pagets, too, had inherited an established position in business and professional life. The partners could afford to take a wide view of business affairs, which included an awareness of social responsibilities and an appreciation of the fact that the welfare of one's employees is an important element in business efficiency. In William Hollins, who had assumed the leadership under particularly difficult conditions, the sense of responsibility for his people was manifest; it won him their respect and even their affection.

This was demonstrated on the occasion of his marriage in 1849, when *The Nottingham Journal* records that 'the workpeople employed by Messrs Hollins & Co have purchased, by subscription, a beautiful silver salver and four silver salts, which they have presented to William Hollins Esq, their master, as a testimony of their gratitude and attachment'. The paper goes on to quote the letter which accompanied the gift.

> Worthy Master, I am deputed by my fellow workpeople to present this small token of our esteem and respect for your kindness shewed to us during the time you have had the management of this concern, and more particularly upon the approaching union with a lady, though unknown to us, we are assured, well worthy of your choice; and may that event be long and happily blessed with health and prosperity for many years, and your posterity become successors in this concern for many generations, is the prayer of Your most obedient servant, William Adams.[1]

[1] It is interesting to compare this tribute with an address presented to William's elder brother Edward Hollins, who was briefly associated with the Pleasley business, but was now a cotton manufacturer at Stockport. The following extract is quoted from Pigott.

> While, sir, we would as much disdain to address you in the language of flattery as you would be disgusted at accepting it from our lips, we nevertheless feel, ourselves impelled . . . to refer to a few traits in your character which, were they more generally conspicuous in individuals of your station, would go far to dissipate those local differences, which have too frequently existed between the employer and ememployed. In you, sir, the MASTER is blended with the FRIEND. Convinced yourself that ignorance is incompatible with happiness, you have laboured with unwearied energy, in raising us in the scale of intelligence—in proving to us by personal argument, that the interests of master and servant are identical—that class interests are opposed to

In his reply, Hollins asked the writer to assure the contributors 'that, apart from the valuable nature of the gift itself, I attach the greatest estimation to their expression of good will and confidence. As regards the past,' he added, 'I feel very doubtful of deserving such a token of my fellow workpeople's esteem; but I trust that by a wife's aid and a future long connection, we may jointly be enabled more effectively to promote the welfare and happiness of all those engaged at Pleasley Works.'

It was given to William Hollins to see these hopes amply fulfilled. Under his leadership the business prospered and grew until its interests extended far beyond Pleasley Vale. But its heart was in Pleasley where Hollins continued to live in the Vale House, within sight and sound of the mills. Everybody knew 'Mr William', and memories of his time, stored in the minds of a later generation, could still be drawn upon when Pigott's *History* was written. 'It was Mr William himself who came round the mill almost daily and who lived in the big house. If you had an idea for an improvement, you could tell him so, and hear what he thought of it. There was no need for a suggestion box; you dealt with people, not committees. The personal note was dominant.'

Ideas for improvements would often relate to technical matters and the firm owed much to intelligent and enterprising men who had started as ordinary operatives in the mills. But such men had wider interests too. Some joined the growing trade union movement, though we hear nothing of trade unionism in the semi-rural environment of Pleasley in this period. Others found an outlet in associations for adult education, in friendly societies and in various

---

the welfare of the community—and that the prosperity of a nation must depend on a harmonious union and reciprocity of interests, between the sons of toil and the wealthy capitalists. But, sir, more than this, we have ever witnessed in you the tender sympathizer in affliction, the secret benefactor in seasons of distress, the anxious designer of our comforts, the encouraging enquirer into our wants, the ready promoter of our wishes; in short, sir, your conduct towards ourselves and others, has been of a character which has disarmed envy and established peace—emplanted hope in bosoms which once rankled with despair and wretchedness.

forms of co-operative enterprise. These interests all found expression in the Pleasley community. They indicate the growth of a spirit of independence and self-reliance which William Hollins and his partners were concerned to encourage.

Prominent among the many organisations for workers' education in the 1830s and 1840s were the Mechanics Institutes with their reading rooms and libraries, their programmes of lectures and meetings for 'mutual improvement'. In 1845 Charles Paget, recently appointed as High Sheriff of the County, spoke at the opening of the Nottingham Mechanics Institute, and he may well have referred to Pleasley's experience, for two years earlier this small community had set up its own Institute. At the same time a Mutual Aid Society was established, and within a few months the membership of the two bodies was sufficient for a joint celebration on an impressive scale. The event is recorded in *The Nottingham Review* of 1 July 1843.

> On Saturday last a handsome supper was provided by members of the Pleasley Works Mechanics Institution and Mutual Aid Society, for the purpose of celebrating their formation. The societies have been in existence about five months and the number of members amounts to nearly 70. The library contains about 200 volumes of excellent works, inclusive of private presentations, especially from the Rector of Pleasley. Wm Hollins, Esq, is the President of the Mutual Aid Society, and from the kind and gentlemanly manner in which the discussions are conducted there is a cheering prospect that the members will materially improve in moral and intellectual character. The societies also possess the advantage of an excellent reading room where the various periodicals of the day are regularly seen. A toast was proposed to Wm Hollins Esq, and we need scarcely advert to the manner in which this proposition was met; the feelings of all present being unanimous that he might long live to see the happy returns of numerous anniversaries of the formation of the two societies. The following were then given: Mr Adams, an old and faithful servant of the firm, Mr Armson and Mr Howard, the committee of management. At the close of this business dancing commenced among the wives and sweethearts and the numerous assembly and continued until the approach of midnight.

It is evident from this account that the two bodies worked closely together and had a common membership. They apparently merged later on, for we hear of the Mutual Aid Society running the library, with the aid of the schoolmaster, who was paid five shillings a quarter for his services. It also arranged public lectures and excur-

sions. Its main purpose, however, was to operate an insurance
scheme. Membership of this was in three classes, according to age,
full membership being attained at the age of eighteen. No information is available about contributions or benefits, but the funds were
invested in the firm and there may have been some provision for a
share in profits as well as the payment of interest. This is suggested
by a resolution of 1869, quoted by Pigott: 'that J. Chatsworthy
junior be deprived of his share of stock for neglect of duty and
spoiling the Company's work and other misconduct.'

The later history of the Mutual Aid Society is obscure. It was
still in existence in the 1870s, though its membership was not much
higher than at the beginning. Saving bank facilities continued,
however, and there was a suggestion in 1894 of offering shares in
the firm to senior employees on special terms. Nothing came of
this, but when the public company was formed in 1908 many of
Hollins's people bought shares in the ordinary way.

Because of its financial connection with the firm the Mutual Aid
Society could not be entirely independent but it did provide for
employee participation in its management. More spontaneous in its
origin was the Pleasley Works Co-operative Society, founded on the
principles of the Rochdale Pioneers, to supply its members with
groceries and other goods through their own store, and distributing
its surplus as a dividend on purchases. The firm's permission was
required at the outset, if only to secure the site, but the store was in
no sense a company shop. Indeed, one of the objects of retail
co-operative societies was to free workers from dependence on
goods sold by the employer. Hollins did supply milk, eggs and
vegetables from the Vale farm, which they continued to run, but
this was for the convenience of their tenants. There was no opposition to the co-operative store; on the contrary it appears to have
received every encouragement from the firm.

The records of the co-operative society go back to 1860, but it
was then well established and must have started some years before.
The shop on the Pleasley estate is still there, and from this small

beginning there eventually developed the Pleasley and Pleasley Hill Co-operative Society. This is in pleasant contrast with the fate of a similar enterprise started much earlier by the cotton mill operatives of Belper. Here the society came to be dominated by the overlookers, who so exploited the poorer members that it lost support and was eventually wound up.[1]

Information on these various activities is scanty, but from what there is one gets the impression of a quite lively community. The common interest in Pleasley Mills as a place of work and source of income spread out and found expression in many directions. There was not much leisure time, unless trade was slack or the water failed. But Pleasley Vale was a pleasant place in which to live and there was enough to occupy such free time as people had. There were the cottage gardens supplemented by a field which was ploughed each season for planting potatoes. With the provision of the recreation ground a cricket club was formed, which became a particularly important institution. There was the Mutual Aid Society with its library, its meetings, usually attended by members of the Hollins family, and its occasional lectures. There were the events connected with the day school and the Sunday school and church services, the anglicans having a small church of their own and the methodists using the schoolroom. Then, when the railway came to Mansfield, an occasional works outing would be arranged. The first of these, one Monday in June 1856, was reported in the press:[2] 'William Hollins Esq, of Pleasley, with his usual liberality, instead of giving the hands a treat at the works, engaged a special train to convey the whole of them, numbering upwards of 430, to the fete at Derby Arboretum. In addition, he paid their expenses as well as their wages for the day. The Pleasley brass band accompanied them. Everyone appeared highly delighted with the day's excursion.' Later on, such trips became annual events, with seaside places like Skegness and Cleethorpes as a popular venue.

---

[1] Fitton and Wadsworth. *The Strutts and the Arkwrights*, pp 250–2. 1958.
[2] *The Nottingham Journal*. 27 June 1856.

CHAPTER FIVE

The Achievement of William Hollins

WILLIAM Hollins took over as managing partner at a time of crisis. The upper mill had just been destroyed and then, with the rebuilding barely completed, the lower mill was lost. The partners' financial resources were enough to withstand the strain but difficult decisions, involving considerable risk, had to be taken. Trade was not good, and it remained depressed while more capital was being sunk in the enterprise. The year 1847 was particularly bad and on 28 May *The Nottingham Journal* reported: 'Trade continues in a most lamentable condition in Mansfield, Sutton-in-Ashfield and the villages around having a share in the hosiery trade. . . . The workhouse is full and some hundreds are receiving relief in food; it is to be feared that many more are all but starving.'

From its start the Pleasley firm had specialised in the spinning of cotton yarn for hosiery manufacture but the boom in cotton hosiery was long since passed and this branch of the trade was now the most depressed. The lace manufacture was expanding in Notting-ham, following the inventions of Heathcoat, Leavers and others, and it provided a growing, if unsteady, market for cotton yarns in which Hollins & Co interested themselves to some extent, though it never became very important with them. What Hollins needed to ensure their future prosperity was a new line and in the middle 1840s they found it; they introduced the mixture yarns which have ever since been a characteristic product of the firm.

It is a curious fact that while the cotton hosiery trade had created its own spinning industry in Derbyshire and Nottinghamshire, worsted spinning did not develop to anything like the same extent in Leicestershire where most of the woollen hosiery was made. There had been strong opposition to worsted spinning machinery, based on Arkwright's principle, when it was introduced in Leicester towards the end of the eighteenth century, and although efforts were made to re-establish worsted spinning after about 1830, hosiery manufacturers were now accustomed to getting their yarn from the main centre of production in Yorkshire.

MULE SPINNING

In contrast with the cotton section, the worsted branch of the hosiery trade did fairly well in the 1830s and 1840s. To quote a contemporary report: 'The worsted hosiery trade is not a speculative business, its annual demand is subject to little variation, its machinery has been stationary for the last twenty years, and is now even less in amount than at the conclusion of the war, while more stocks are required for the supply of numerous wholesale houses, new markets are opened and we have more customers at home and abroad.'[1] The main obstacle to the further growth of the trade was the high price of wool, but a new source of supply was now being opened up in Australia. The first small shipment came in 1821; in 1848 Australia exported 36 million lb of wool.

[1] Wells, F. A., op cit, p 132, quoting *Leicestershire Mercury*, 1 April 1837.

The Australian wool was called merino after the Spanish breed of sheep from which the first flocks were established. It was fine and soft, relatively short in fibre, and therefore more suitable for spinning on cotton machinery than other types then available. Indeed it proved so adaptable as to prompt experiments in mixing cotton and wool. Merino was found to blend extremely well with good quality cotton like the Caracoa, Surinam and Pernambuco varieties from the West Indies and South America which Hollins had always used. The resulting yarn had several advantages: it was cheaper than a pure wool yarn and was less liable to shrinkage; yet it was fine and strong, and fabric made from it had a unique quality, being smoother than wool but more comfortable in wear than pure cotton. A yarn with these qualities was admirably suited to the needs of the hosiery trade, in which a new spirit of enterprise and technical innovation was at last beginning to stir.

William Hollins & Co was among the first to see these possibilities. A small stock of merino, worth £1,641, appears in the accounts for May 1846, by which time the firm had evidently succeeded both with the mixing process and with the adaptation of its spinning machines; for the special endorsement to the 1844 co-partnership deed, signed in 1847, refers specifically to merino. As mentioned in the previous chapter, the endorsement provided for an increase in the capital to £80,000 'as the erection of new buildings and other occasions of the said business shall require it'. One of the 'occasions' was evidently the prospective development of merino; for the endorsement goes on to say that 'Charles Paget, William Hollins, William Paget and Edward Hollins will continue to carry on the business of preparing and spinning yarn or twist and vending the same when so prepared and spun, and shall and will also carry on the business of preparing and spinning Merino, and all matters incident thereto'.

The decision to specialise on mixture yarns was a turning point in the history of the firm. Moreover, it pursued a policy of giving its yarns a distinctive quality. The fact that the mills were having to be rebuilt and re-equipped at this time meant that Hollins got off to a good start; for they had the opportunity of installing the machinery best suited to their needs instead of having to adapt older equipment. New machinery of the latest design made it easier to maintain quality standards and it also reduced the waste of valuable material, which had always been a problem in worsted spinning. In time Hollins went in for still better qualities of wool, especially high grade lamb's wool, of which they became the biggest buyer in Australia. By emphasising quality and always striving for higher standards Hollins won an almost unique reputation in a highly competitive trade, and this was well maintained in later years, when they came to extend the range of their products still further.

Information from the firm's accounts (which have so far been the main source of information on its progress), is unfortunately lacking for the period 1847–73; nor have any minute books or correspondence survived. There are, however, various documents recording the acquisition of properties, and from these and a few external sources some of the main developments can be described.

Some of the most important developments were in the location of the firm's activities. Until about 1850, all manufacturing had been concentrated at Pleasley and the company continued to expand there. But Pleasley Vale was somewhat remote from the main centres of industry and of population, and problems of labour supply may well have arisen with the improvement of trade in Mansfield and Sutton which had now set in. It was in Mansfield that Hollins's first extension beyond Pleasley was made. Here the Sherwood Mills, just off the Nottingham Road, were rented for silk spinning. The arrangement did not last long, however, for Hollins soon turned their attention to possibilities in Nottingham.

The firm had, from its earliest days, maintained a sales office and yarn warehouse in Nottingham. When William Hollins took over the management the original premises in Angel Row were given up and for some twenty-five years the business was done through an agent in Mills Yard between Long Row and Parliament Street.

Then in 1870 the firm established its own office and warehouse at
Fletcher Gate in the heart of the Lace Market, in which many
hosiery firms were represented. Foreign merchants were also established in the Lace Market and buyers of lace, yarns and knitted
goods from overseas were regular visitors. A commercial establishment in Nottingham was essential for Hollins's trade and contacts
with foreign merchants were increasingly important. For instance,
the official catalogue of the Great Exhibition of 1851 refers to
William Hollins & Co as 'manufacturers of Merino, Cashmere and
cotton hosiery yarns, used in the Midland counties for the manufacture of hosiery, and on the Continent for knittings and hosiery
purposes'.[1] British yarn exports to the Continent, especially to
Germany, were growing, assisted by the generally low import
duties, in contrast with those imposed on piece goods, and Hollins
were well placed for participating in this trade.

With this commercial base in Nottingham it was natural for
Hollins, now bent on expansion, to consider setting up a manufacturing establishment in Nottingham, where textiles were the
predominant industry. In 1856 an opportunity came to lease a
former starch factory in Spring Close, Lenton, at that time just
outside the Nottingham boundary. Silk spinning was now transferred from Mansfield to Lenton and additional machinery was
installed; when the freehold of the premises was acquired in 1873
the total investment was valued at about £5,000.

In the meantime, another venture had been started in nearby
Radford, which was to become a major part of the firm's organisation. It began in the same way, with the acquisition of an existing
mill. This, which came to be known as the old silk mill, was already
equipped for silk spinning, and for many years Hollins carried on
this trade both at Lenton and Radford. The hosiery trade used a
fair amount of silk, especially for stockings, and now that Hollins
were extending their range of yarns, silk seemed an obvious line to

---

[1] In the yarn trade merino had, by this time, come to mean a wool-cotton
mixture yarn.

develop. But the silk department was never very successful. Soon after its expansion, the removal of the duty on silk imports from France, under the Cobden Treaty of 1860, intensified competition. Further, fluctuations in silk prices made the business very speculative, since raw material formed a big proportion of the yarn's selling value. Then there were difficulties in combining the management of the silk mills with other activities at Radford, as these became more and more important. In 1882 the Lenton Mill was sold and its machinery transferred to Radford, which relieved the position to some extent. But in the end, at the turn of the century, Hollins sold out their silk interests to a specialised firm, the Bent Ley Silk Spinning Co Ltd, in which it made a small investment.

It was not in silk, but in other lines, that Radford contributed to Hollins's growth. Along with the old silk mill the firm was able to buy a considerable area of adjoining land and here it built a new mill, with a number of houses for workpeople, in what was then a growing industrial suburb of Nottingham. The main business of this mill, and eventually of the old silk mill, was the manufacture of coloured yarns. Pleasley continued to spin cotton, merino mixtures and also worsted yarns. But these were sold in their natural shades, or, in the case of cotton, bleached. Such yarns were suitable for underwear, though if colours were required hosiers would have the dyeing done by specialist firms. This was satisfactory for cotton and worsted, but mixture yarns were difficult, since the two materials reacted differently to dyes. Hollins, who had become specialists in mixture yarns, therefore determined to undertake the dyeing too, and so ensure a high standard of quality in the finished product.

The 'coloured mill', as Radford came to be called, was designed as a specialised unit for spinning and dyeing all types of coloured yarn, the fibres for mixing being dyed before spinning. It also included a bleaching plant and dealt not only with material manufactured at Radford itself but also with a considerable amount of Pleasley yarn which was sent to the 'coloured mill' for dyeing and bleaching. It was many years before a dyehouse was provided at

Pleasley. In 1874, when the new mill had been in operation ten years, the value of the two Radford mills and their machinery was shown in the accounts as £28,900, of which nearly two-thirds was attributed to the new mill. In 1882 the mill was enlarged and eventually the capacity of the old silk mill was brought in.

Hollins' extension into dyeing is particularly significant, for it marks the first stage in the growth of the vertical organisation which was to become characteristic of the firm. It is to be seen as a further expression of its policy of emphasising the distinctive quality of its products, and of its belief that this could best be maintained by having all the processes of manufacture under its own control. But there was another factor too; the demand for coloured yarns was increasing, especially for hand knitting. Yarns for this purpose, known in the trade as 'knittings', were specially mentioned in the description of Hollins' products in the catalogue of the Great Exhibition of 1851. Twenty years later knittings and other coloured yarns represented perhaps a third of the firm's production.

An indication of the various lines and their relative importance in Hollins's trade about this time may be obtained from the stock figures recorded in the annual accounts. The following table shows the position in 1876.[1]

TABLE 3

	£
Raw material	64,577
White Merino and Cashmere	30,269
Brown cotton yarn	6,255
White knittings	4,240
Silk Imperial	2,210
Spun silk	5,963
Patent spun hosiery yarn	1,220
Lace yarn	1,570
Coloured Merino and cotton	14,036
Coloured knittings	10,524
Total	£140,864

[1] The amount of detail varies from year to year. The accounts for 1876 give the most detailed classification. Stock values can give only a rough indication of production in the various lines—unfortunately there are no production figures.

During this period of expansion, involving the introduction of new lines and the establishment of manufacture in Nottingham, Hollins increased its paid-up capital on three occasions: to £120,000 in 1859, to £162,000 in 1865, and to £180,000 eleven years later. This was done, as before, by funding part of the partners' loan balances, on which fixed interest was paid. Profits figures for the period between 1847 and 1873 are lacking, but in the latter year £42,000 was earned, giving a return of 26 per cent on the capital, apart from loan balances. In 1874 the dividend was 24 per cent; it fell to 18 per cent for the next year, but with profits recovering to £33,000 in 1876 the dividend was maintained at 18 per cent on the increased capital.

The prosperity of these years was due not merely to the enterprise of the partners and the technical skill which they commanded, but also to the buoyancy of the firm's markets. In the 1860s the hosiery trade began to share in the general expansion of British industry and the long-delayed transition to factory production was accelerating. With more efficient methods, making for cheaper production, and a rising standard of living among consumers, the hosiery trade was doing well and the demand for yarns was good. On the Continent too hosiery manufacture was expanding, especially in France and Saxony; and although this meant more competition with British hosiery, it benefited yarn exporters, among whom Hollins were well established. A further factor favourable to profits was the rise in the prices of raw materials. After the slow fall of prices between 1830 and 1852 a persistent rise had set in, reaching a peak in 1873. So long as wool and cotton prices were rising, stocks of wool, cotton and finished yarn automatically appreciated in value; for the yarn was readily sold at current prices to manufacturers buying in anticipation of still higher prices in the future.

In 1873, however, the favourable trend of prices, which had several times showed signs of breaking, was abruptly reversed, and the period known to economic historians as the great depression began. Like the still greater depression of the 1930s, it started in the

F

USA and it affected all the industrialised countries of the world. But for Britain the depression was more than a mere phase in the trade cycle, it marked the end of our world supremacy in industry and trade. The industrial revolution which Britain had started was now rapidly spreading to other countries, some better endowed with natural resources and with more efficient equipment than that relied upon by many of our older-established manufacturers. In the export trade, on which Britain had become so heavily dependent, competition intensified; and while most other countries protected their home markets by tariffs, Britain adhered to her free trade policy and imposed no restriction on foreign imports. The whole experience was a test of the capacity for adaptation in the British economy. In this we were ultimately successful and a new period of growth and prosperity set in; but Britain was no longer, as it had been in the middle years of the nineteenth century, 'the workshop of the world'.

The history of Hollins in the last quarter of the century illustrates the impact of these conditions on a particular firm. For the same three phases can be distinguished: setback, then adaptation through technical and commercial innovation, and finally recovered prosperity.

Until 1876 Hollins' profits held up quite well; at £33,000 they were better than in the previous year. But 1877 brought a sharp fall to £21,000 and they declined further to £16,000 in 1881. This, however, still gave a return of 9 per cent on capital, in addition to loan interest, and was, of course, much better than the record for the previous major depression in the 1840s. It was also better than what many other spinners could show. In the late 1870s the cotton trade was particularly bad and a fall in exports was affecting the woollen trade, though here the state of home demand provided some compensation. It was Hollins' policy to spin yarn to order rather than make for stock; they followed the practice described in a contemporary trade article as 'the only paying mode of doing business'.[1] But apparently orders could not always be relied upon,

[1] *Statist.* 18 March 1882.

for an order book of this period for the Radford mill records, in bold handwriting, an instruction by William Hollins himself: 'Always get *positive* orders as to quantity of each sort and nos. to be spun from Mr. Place. The present way is loose and may lead to your making useless stock at times.'[1]

Another problem was the extended credit, as much as nine months, which spinners were driven to concede to hosiery manufacturers when trade was slack.[2] Even substantial firms were slow payers. For instance, Allen Solly & Co of Nottingham, which bought about £25,000 worth of yarn a year from Hollins, had to be pressed for payment on more than one occasion. In 1872 Solly's letter book records a request for a cheque to be sent to Hollins whose account was overdue and the cashier was instructed to 'send all you can by Saturday'. Another letter some months later refers to a visit from Mr Hollins who had said 'they will be open to receive any cash as they are in need just now'. The writer adds, 'I shall be glad to reduce this as far as possible as we must order freely later end of month or shut up altogether for want of yarn.'

With the onset of trade depression the risks of cancelled orders and bad debts increased. Hollins were in a stronger position than many of their competitors, but as the depression lengthened the effects were serious enough in view of the firm's extended commitments. This was one reason for the change in its constitution which was now decided upon. For nearly a hundred years the firm had operated as a partnership. When the enterprise began, partnership was practically the only legal form in which a group of persons could be associated as owners of a business. It was highly complicated, involving the drawing up of a new deed of partnership whenever the membership changed. Moreover, in the event of failure the liability of the partners for the firm's debts was not limited to the capital they had invested in it. However, by a series of Company Acts, particularly that of 1862, the former onerous re-

[1] Pigott, op cit, p 87. Place was the firm's yarn agent in Nottingham.
[2] Wells, op cit, p 173.

strictions on the formation of joint stock companies had now been removed and the principle of incorporation with limited liability introduced. Apart from the limitation of liability, the great advantage of the joint stock company was in its recognition as a legal entity with ownership vested in the holders of transferable shares. In 1882 the owners of William Hollins & Co adopted this form, by dissolving their partnership and setting up a joint stock company to acquire its assets.

William Hollins & Company Ltd, as the firm now became, was at this stage a private company. Its original shareholders were members of the same two families, the Hollins and the Pagets, that had been associated for so long in the partnership. The draft scheme for conversion of the business proposed a capital of £300,000, but in the memorandum of association this was reduced to £250,000, with power to increase. All the capital was in ordinary shares of £1,000 each, and the three largest shareholders, William Hollins and William and Joseph Paget had equal allotments. William Hollins continued as head of the business with W. B. Paget as vice-chairman. Henry Ernest Hollins, William's nephew, was named as managing director with a salary of £350 a year and 10 per cent of all profits exceeding a 5 per cent return on capital. The other directors were Henry's brother, Richard Arthur, and William Hollins's elder son, Humphrey.

As in the partnership, precautions were taken against possible fragmentation of shareholdings or the intrusion of outsiders. Thus no share was to be sold to anyone but a member of the company without having first been offered to the directors at par; and if any member died the directors were empowered to buy his shares on payment of a price 10 per cent above par. The firm was still very much a family concern.

Most of the directors representing the two families were also active in the firm's management. In the early days of the partnership only one member appears to have taken part in day to day management and this was still the position when William Hollins came in. It was indeed provided on several occasions when the partnership was reconstituted that partners should not be required to assume managerial responsibilities. The practice changed in 1865 when, with mills established in Nottingham, two deputies were appointed to assist William Hollins. One was W. B. Paget, who looked after Radford and Lenton for a time; the other, R. A. Hollins, had similar responsibilities at Pleasley. Each was paid a salary of £250 a year, while William Hollins got £500 for exercising 'a general supervision and authority'.

It was about this time that Henry Ernest Hollins entered the firm, which he was ultimately to lead for so many years. His father, Edward, was an older brother of William Hollins and had cotton mills in Lancashire. He also had an interest in the Pleasley firm and it was to Pleasley that Henry was sent to learn the yarn business. The young man quickly made his mark and in 1870 he replaced W. B. Paget, who then retired from active management. By the time the company was formed, Henry Ernest had emerged as the leading member of the management team and had become managing director. Claude Hollins, his younger brother, combined the duties of company secretary with the management of Radford mill and William Hollins's son, Humphrey, was an assistant manager at Pleasley. The Vale House was, of course, still occupied by William Hollins, but Henry Ernest also established himself in the Vale, at the Uplands, where he continued to reside until his retirement.

Besides the Hollins and the Pagets there were many others who, though they never became partners or directors, rose to responsible positions in the expanding firm, and Hollins owed a great deal to them. Pigott mentions several such men. There was James Cutler, for instance, an ordinary employee who rose to become a mill manager at Pleasley at the time when William Hollins was preparing his plans for expansion. He died suddenly while visiting Nottingham in 1859, at the age of 51, and he is buried in Pleasley churchyard. William Hollins wrote this epitaph for him: 'This stone is

placed here by the workpeople, Sunday School children and Company of Pleasley Works in remembrance of his many virtues as
Manager, Neighbour and Friend. His warm family affection and
earnest piety, and his fidelity to daily duty, have left an abiding
record in the hearts of all who knew him.'

James Cutler had a younger half-brother, Thomas, who managed
Radford mill in its early days. 'Thomas was an enormous man,
weighing about twenty stone, and he came to the mill each day
carrying a long stick and wearing a grey top hat, for all the world
more like a showman than a work's manager.' Then there was
Thomas Hardwick, who started work in 1844 at the age of eight,
and who rose to manage the cotton bleaching and wool-scouring
department. His son, William Hardwick, who joined in 1877, followed his example; he eventually assumed a position of considerable responsibility and served the firm for more than fifty
years. Herbert Kenyon, who started in 1853 when he was nine
(his father having been employed by the company), was pro-
moted overlooker while still quite young and later became a
manager at Upper Mill. Herbert Healey, born in 1860, spent fifty-
seven years at Pleasley 'in and out of card rooms' before he retired
in 1926.

There were families whose members had served the firm through
successive generations. The Sissons were such a case: James,
Robert and William, whose father and grandfather had been employed by Hollins. 'James, who was born in 1847, and his brother
Robert, two years younger, started work at Pleasley when they were
nine. Both became men of exceptional ability; they also became
intense rivals, especially after Robert was transferred from Pleasley
to take charge at Radford, under Claude Hollins.'

Such men owed little to formal education. They learned on the
job and they went on learning, by observation and patient experiment. Textile machinery was being constantly improved; but the
high and, in some respects, unique quality of Hollins's products
could not be achieved and maintained merely by installing the

latest equipment, which was equally available to their competitors. Much depended on the technical skill and enterprise of men like the Sissons, who rose to responsible positions in middle management and who trained and inspired others to succeed them.

CHAPTER SIX

The Birth of Viyella

THE year 1890 is a significant landmark in the history of Hollins. William Hollins died in the February and there followed a major reconstitution of the firm, involving the creation of a new company and the beginnings of a new form of expansion through the absorption of other businesses. It was in this year too that experiments began in making the cloth that was to become famous as Viyella.

Although in his latter years William Hollins had shed some of his responsibilities and had divided his time between Pleasley Vale and his London residence in Queen's Gate Place, he remained, until his death, head of the firm, and there were very few of its members who could remember any other. He died in London but was brought home to Pleasley for burial in the churchyard, after a service in Mansfield Town Hall. As reported in the local press, the funeral was the occasion for a remarkable demonstration of respect and affection by the firm's workpeople and by representatives of the various institutions which he had supported—the Mansfield hospital, the Mansfield Mechanics Institute, the Unitarian Chapel, the Mansfield Improvement Commissioners and others.[1] Hollins died a wealthy man, leaving a personal estate of £321,294. His financial interests in the firm went to his son William.

The formation of the new company, a few months later, was connected with a capital reconstruction. Instead of having all the capital in ordinary shares, as in the first company of 1882, 10,000 6 per cent preference shares were now issued together with £90,000 of 4 per cent debentures, and there were 14,280 £10 ordi-

---

[1] Most of Hollins's interests, outside the firm, were in the Mansfield area but it is recorded that the building fund for Manchester College, Oxford, was 'begun with a donation of £5,000 from Mr Hollins of Pleasley'.

nary shares. Allowing for unissued ordinary shares, the total capital was £300,000 but, as before, the business was owned entirely by the directors. W. B. Paget, the former vice-chairman, succeeded William Hollins as chairman, and William's son, another William, joined the board as one of the three largest shareholders. He was twenty-eight at the time and unlike his elder brother, Humphrey, who had died in 1886, he had not been trained in the business. He did, however, continue as a director for many years. Equal in shareholding with William Hollins and W. B. Paget was Joseph Paget; he was now sixty-five and died a few years later.

On the board so constituted Henry Ernest Hollins, who continued as managing director, inevitably had great influence. The chairman had long since given up his executive responsibilities; he now lived at Loughborough, and, though he regularly presided at board meetings, he had only a part-time function in the firm. It was the managing director, closely involved in day-to-day management as well as in the affairs of the board, who was the true successor of William Hollins. Like his predecessor he lived at Pleasley. In recognition of his enhanced status his salary was raised to £1,000 a year with, as before, a share in profits. Henry Ernest was assisted in the management by his two brothers, Richard Arthur and Claude Hollins, both of whom continued as directors.

The value of the properties as assessed for transfer to the new company was approximately £134,000. Of this £76,500 was attributed to Pleasley where, in addition to the two mills, a new gas works had now been established and railway sidings laid out. The rest, £57,500, represented the investment at Radford. There was also £10,500 due from I. & R. Morley Ltd to whom Hollins had just sold their warehouse in the Nottingham Lace Market. They had now built new premises in Warser Gate, in the same area, and it was here that board meetings were usually held, although the office was transferred to Pleasley in 1891, leaving Warser Gate as the Nottingham warehouse.

The establishment of the Radford mills had been the most im-

portant new development in William Hollins' time. It represented a
continuation of the firm's traditional policy of expansion by adding
to its buildings and plant. But now expansion began to take a
different form, involving the acquisition of other businesses. The
first transaction of this kind was already being negotiated before the
new company was formed and at the second meeting of its board
the deal was completed for the purchase of the Via Gellia Mills,
near Matlock, as a going concern.

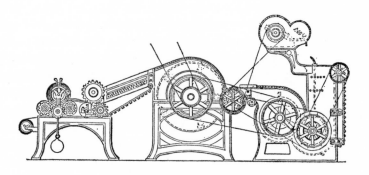

A WOOL-CLEANING MACHINE, *c.* 1880

The history of the Via Gellia business is in some ways similar to
that of Hollins at Pleasley. It began with the adaptation of an old
water mill, which had been used originally for corn, and recon-
structed in the eighteenth century for the processing of lead, at that
time an important industry in Derbyshire. In 1839 there were two
smelting houses, a rolling mill and a plant for grading slag, but the
exhaustion of the local lead mines eventually put an end to this
enterprise and a cotton mill was built on the site, though steam was
now substituted for water power. After two owners had failed to
make it pay, this business was bought cheaply by Thomas Hill, a
director of I. & R. Morley, the Nottingham hosiery manufacturers,
and it was Hill's son, Charles, who first made a success of it. By

1888 he had two other mills in the area, which he rented, one at Milford, near Belper, where he spun Shetlands, and the other, originally owned by Arkwright, at Cromford, where he did reeling and spooling. Via Gellia itself was used for merino yarns. The total turnover for the whole business was about £55,000 a year and the merino section was in direct competition with Hollins. Moreover, it had this close connection with I. & R. Morley, who were among the oldest and best of Hollins' customers.[1]

Another competitor in the same field was the firm of A. Cockroft & Sons Ltd of Huddersfield. Its works, the Fairfield Mills, were about twice the size of Via Gellia, or half the size of Pleasley and Radford taken together. In 1889 the brothers Fred and Charles Cockroft were in touch with Charles Hill with a view to buying Via Gellia, a purchase which would have given them a capacity rivalling that of Hollins.[2] The prospect of such an amalgamation was clearly unwelcome to Hollins, but fortunately the Cockrofts delayed in coming to terms. They wanted to have Hill's business valued, but Hill stood out for his own price. Moreover, he was aware of Hollins' interest, and between the two potential purchasers he was in a strong position. While the Cockrofts hesitated Henry Ernest Hollins moved in and got an offer from Hill, which the board accepted at its meeting in May 1890.

By this transaction Hollins acquired the three mills with some houses for £20,398, together with stocks valued at £19,633. At the same time Charles Hill joined the board, where he was to stay for many years to come. But it was only the merino business that Hollins really wanted and it soon decided to dispose of the Cromford and Milford Mills, even at a loss. At this time, however, it clearly intended to expand production at Via Gellia; more land was bought and new equipment installed, including a softening plant, carding engines and spinning mules.

A few years later negotiations were opened with the other and bigger competitor, Cockrofts, with a view to absorbing them too. The

---

[1] Pigott, op cit, p 95.   [2] Ibid, p 96.

intermediary was C. J. Lewis, who had formerly acted for Cockrofts in their dealings with Hill, but was now Hollins's yarn agent and an important figure in the firm. Lewis approached Cockrofts in 1895, but progress was slow. However in 1897 they entered into an agreement with Hollins to limit the credit terms extended to their customers in the hosiery trade. This encouraged the hope of a closer relationship, and on the proposal of H. E. Hollins Cockrofts was offered £35,000 in cash and £25,000 in debenture and share capital as a take-over bid. It was not enough, and there were further obstacles, with regard to the management of Fairfield and its degree of autonomy within the Hollins organisation. However, early in 1898 agreement was reached on an offer of £65,000. It had been hoped that the Cockrofts would agree to take up half the purchase price in Hollins's shares and debentures, but in the event the family took only 1,250 ordinary shares and £7,500 worth of debentures and Hollins had to issue more shares and debentures to provide the rest in cash.

As things turned out, the Cockrofts did quite well. They did not secure a seat on Hollins' board, as Hill had done, but they retained considerable independence in the management of Fairfield Mills. The advantage to Hollins was in securing virtual control of the merino yarn market. With the addition of Via Gellia and Fairfield it had almost doubled its capacity. Moreover its dominant position in the trade offered the prospect of planning production on more economical lines. For instance, the recent intensification of competition had forced spinners to offer what C. J. Lewis described as 'an appalling variety of yarns', two-thirds of which, he believed, could be thrown out after the merging of interests. It should also be possible to rationalise production; orders could be so distributed among the various plants that each could specialise and get the benefit of long runs. This, in turn, meant that re-equipment, experiment, and expansion could be undertaken with greater confidence.

The Fairfield purchase was, however, essentially a defensive move intended to safeguard the merino trade under conditions of gradually declining demand. Hollins' directors expressed some concern about this at their December meeting in 1897. Selling prices were falling while production costs tended to rise because plant was not working to full capacity. Some relief was given to Pleasley by restricting production at Via Gellia, which was 'not allowed to compete with the other mills in bad times'. The same policy was now applied to Fairfield; profits on this business fell in 1898 'owing to the large amount of cotton we have had to spin in place of Merino', and there was a proposal for compensating the Cockrofts if Hollins decided 'to remove qualities or interfere with their sale of Merino'.

But a merely defensive policy was not in keeping with Hollins's tradition nor with the character of its present managing director. If the trade in merino yarns was now less promising, other types of yarn must be developed or a new use found for merino itself. In 1894 it was thought that silk might be worth expanding and £1,000 was invested in silk spinning machinery at Pleasley. This venture was disappointing, however, and Hollins eventually abandoned this trade altogether. Then two years later, a worsted spinning plant, bought secondhand for £2,000, was installed at Pleasley. Worsted spinning had been started in a small way at Radford in 1889 and this plant was now transferred to Pleasley. The early results were not satisfactory but the management committee could 'see no reason why, when we have more experience and have got our qualities well on to the market, the loss should not be turned into a profit. Considering the poor prospect we have for a better trade in White and dyeing Merinos,' the report continues, 'we think it will be advisable to fill another room at the Upper Mill with this class of (worsted) machinery. If we do not make a profit we shall at least make something towards interest and at the same time reduce the cost of spinning Merinos.'

In the event, the firm's modest expectations for worsted spinning were more than fulfilled. There were considerable fluctuations, but

the trade continued to grow and when the Upper Mill at Pleasley
was enlarged in 1905–6 it had already become known as the Worsted
Mill. Hollins, however, was not a specialist in worsted yarns as it
was in merino mixtures, and there was still the problem of finding
an adequate outlet for the product in which it had made its reputation. For this, as with worsted and cotton yarns, it was still dependent on the hosiery industry, which provided a none too stable
market. German and French manufacturers, like the British, were
now equipped with power-driven frames and were keen competitors, especially in cotton hosiery. Foreign goods entered our home
market duty-free, while our exports encountered rising tariffs abroad.
The American 'McKinley' tariff of 1890 was particularly damaging
to British hosiery exports. Moreover, technical and commerical conditions in the hosiery trade favoured the proliferation of small
businesses in any brief burst of prosperity that might occur, and this
intensified competition and price-cutting in the succeeding slump.

Such was the situation that Hollins faced in the early 1890s. In
merino yarns it had a distinctive, but rather expensive, product.
They had attained a dominant position in the market for these yarns,
but it was a narrow market, and in the present state of the hosiery
trade it seemed unlikely to expand. The prospect for cotton yarns,
Hollins' original line, offered no encouragement, for cotton hosiery
was now quite out of favour, except where cheapness mattered. The
demand for woollen hosiery was increasing and Hollins took advantage of this in expanding their production of worsted yarns. But it was
the merino trade that they wanted to revive and expand. In the end
they solved the problem by developing an entirely new line of manufacture, which, as time went on, absorbed a rapidly increasing
proportion of merino yarn output and eventually became the main
basis of its trade.

Pigott's 'History' gives an interesting account of the origins of
Viyella, based largely on the recollections of those who assisted in
its introduction and development. It appears that, as early as 1889,
Hollins were spinning small quantities of yarn for weaving into

cloth. This was done in the normal course of trade with hosiery manufacturers. At that time, underwear garments, especially men's vests and pants, had cloth facings, and makers of high quality goods knitted in Hollins's yarn began to ask for facings woven from the same material. These were produced by certain Yorkshire weavers and the cloth proved very acceptable for its purpose—so much so that Hollins decided to experiment with a general purpose cloth woven for themselves.

This, however, was more difficult than it sounds. Hollins's knitting yarns were fine and also soft; softness was no disadvantage in a loosely woven cloth for facing underwear, but it was quite another matter to ensure that the properties peculiar to Hollins's high quality mixture yarns were retained in a yarn which would weave well into a close cloth. It was here that the technical knowledge of the Sisson brothers played such an important part. They had visited the Paris Exhibition of 1889 and returned with many new ideas for processes and machinery. Working separately, James at Pleasley and Robert at Radford, the search for the ideal yarn became a matter of intense rivalry. Different proportions of wool and cotton, different ways of mixing, different refinements of carding and spinning were tried until the right formula was found.

Meanwhile, various firms of commission weavers were put to a similar test with samples of yarn. Their chief difficulty was in devising a satisfactory method for treating the warp yarn. Wool and cotton were normally sized to the required stiffness by the use of different agents, and a mixture cloth was made with a cotton warp and a woollen weft. But in Hollins's case the mixture was in the yarn itself and the problem was how to size such a yarn without harming either of its component materials. Of the several firms engaged in these experiments, the most successful were two Glasgow weavers: Renison McNab & Co, of Boden Street Mills, and John McMath & Co, of Brookside Mills. It was the latter firm, directed by the young and energetic John Park Douglas, which eventually produced the first acceptable samples.

The experiments, both in spinning and in weaving, continued all through 1890 and for most of 1891. But before that year was out, the first small orders for what was in fact Viyella cloth had been completed at Brookside and the new material was ready to be offered to the public. But now a further problem arose. Hollins, as spinners, had no experience of the cloth market. They might have used wholesalers as the medium of distribution, but as yet their output was small and they wanted to test the market through direct contact with selected retailers before embarking on large-scale production. The difficulty was overcome with the help of Frank Hollins, second son of Edward Hollins and brother of Henry Ernest and Claude. Frank Hollins had had a highly successful career as a cotton manufacturer and was now directing the large combine of Horrockses, Crewdson & Co Ltd. Some years before, this firm had adopted the then novel system of selling its famous cotton piece goods direct to retail shops, and Frank Hollins now came forward with the suggestion that his travellers should introduce the new cloth to its customers among the retail bespoke shirtmakers.

The idea of test-marketing in this way was readily accepted and the results were sufficiently promising for Hollins to go ahead with the new product. The decision was taken at the board meeting on 23 November 1893. In the rather dull record of business transacted on that day there is one minute that stands out. 'Resolved,' it reads, 'that up to £2,000 be risked in the cloth trade.' The commitment was modest enough, but it marks the beginning of a new phase in Hollins's history.

For the first year or two cloth production was only about fifty pieces[1] a week in a very limited range of men's shirtings, and it was reckoned that output would have to be doubled before a profit could be shown. In 1896 the cloth department just about broke even, but the accounts for 1897 recorded a profit of £1,381. The trade was now 'progressing steadily and satisfactorily', which was

---

[1] It is not known what yardage this represents. A piece can vary in length between 50 and 100 yards, according to the type of cloth.

*Plate 7. Wm Hollins the Elder
as a young man*

*Plate 8. Wm Hollins the Elder
in later life*

Plate 9. The last 'stockingers' shop

Plate 10. Stockingers shop—interior

the more gratifying in view of the rather poor results in some of the other branches. By this time a policy for the promotion of the cloth trade had been decided.

The first step was the appointment of a specialist to be responsible for designing patterns and planning production. This was Archie Brown, a Scotsman. To him the success of the new venture was largely due, and when, thirty years later, the output of Viyella was running at the rate of 3,500 pieces a week Archie Brown could be proud of his achievement.

But the development of a marketing policy backed by an appropriate sales organisation was equally important. Hollins had always been strong on the technical side; they had consistently striven to give their products distinctive qualities and they had won for them a high reputation. This was supported by the adoption of the 'Wheatsheaf' trade-mark bearing Hollins's name: for yarns supplied to manufacturers and also for domestic use; it was registered in 1877, but had been used for at least twenty years before that. Branding ensured that the product was identified with the manufacturer and the name of Hollins had in this way become well-known in many households. But, in selling yarns as an intermediate product to

G

hosiery manufactures, the spinners' power to influence the market
was more limited; for the goods, if branded at all, were identified
with the hosiery manufacturer or with the wholesale distributor.
Hollins therefore decided, now that it was able to offer a new product, to give it a name and appeal direct to the final consumer as it
had done with its domestic years. Their cloth, with its unique qualities, must be recognisable as such, and clearly identified with the
firm, as sole supplier. This has since become the common practice
with many commodities, but Hollins were among the first to adopt
it in the textile trades.

The name 'Viyella' has been variously attributed to Claude
Hollins and to Charles Hill. Its derivation from 'Via Gellia',[1] where
Hill had his business, is obvious enough, but, as Pigott says, there
are as many stories about its exact origins as there are about the first
and earlier decision to make the cloth. At all events, the company
registered the trade-mark in 1894. The name was a happy choice,
particularly for the way in which it lent itself to variation as the
range of cloths was extended in later years.

In deciding to brand their cloth, Hollins had the question of sales
policy very much in mind. Their first samples had been placed by
Horrockses Crewdson, which dealt directly with retailers. But this
was no more than an experimental arrangement to test the market
and the normal practice would have been to deal with wholesalers
once the trade was established. There was much to be said for this
method of distribution, especially for a firm like Hollins, which was
launching a new product in a market where it had little experience.
If on the other hand, it decided to trade with retailers, it would need
more travellers, more warehouse and office staff to deal with
numerous small orders and accounts, and it would have to maintain
considerable stocks. It would absorb the wholesaler's margin but
also incur the costs of performing his functions. There was, how-

---

[1] The picturesque road known as the Via Gellia, linking the villages of Cromford
and Bonsall, was built in the early nineteenth century by the Gells, the local
landowners, who helped to develop leadmining in this part of Derbyshire.

ever, a further consideration which ultimately determined the issue. In branding its product it had already made a link with the final consumer. If this link was strengthened by advertising Viyella, and building up goodwill for the product, there would be an assured demand from the better-class retailers, which Hollins, as proprietor of the brand, could exploit to its own advantage. The directors were confident of their ability to make the market for Viyella cloth, where they saw themselves in a potentially much stronger position than in selling yarns to hosiery manufacturers.

The policy of direct selling, with all its implications, was quickly put into operation. Five travellers were appointed to begin with, two for London and one each for the North of England, the Midlands and the South. A Horrockses Crewdson man continued to look after Wales, and later two more men were appointed for Scotland and Ireland respectively. Before long the firm had two thousand retail customers on its books and the provision of effective service by prompt despatch of orders and dealing with complaints began to strain the organisation.

It was not easy for a firm hitherto dominated by the manufacturer's interest to adapt itself to the commercial outlook and the needs of a marketing organisation. Claude Hollins was the director with general responsibility for the new department but he still managed the coloured mill and the silk mill. There are hints in the board minutes of his having too much to do, though according to Pigott he was inclined to get absorbed in details. 'He was also parsimonious; he steadily resisted the extravagance of buying a typewriter and all letters were answered by hand.'[1] The cloth department operated first from Radford, where a new warehouse was opened in 1897. From there orders for weaving were sent to Glasgow and, since all book-keeping was now done at Pleasley, there were plenty of opportunities for confusion and delay. In order to give better service to his London customers the sales representative there insisted on having his own stock, supplied direct from Glasgow. There was

[1] Op cit, p 107.

really no case for having the main cloth warehouse in Nottingham; it should be either in Glasgow where the cloth was made or in London, which was at that time the chief market. In the end the choice fell on London and in 1899 the cloth department moved into premises in Friday Street. This was Hollins's first London office, and Claude Hollins, now relieved of all conflicting duties, was sent to manage it.

By this time the cloth trade was well established. Each year the board minutes record its steady and profitable growth which, in certain years, is in marked contrast with the depressed state of the old, and still larger, trade in hosiery yarns. The successful launching of Viyella owed much to advertising, particularly in the better magazines. The range of cloth too was rapidly extended, and the adoption, at Mrs Claude Hollins's suggestion, of the 'Day and Night Wear' trade-mark in 1896, emphasised the variety of uses for the cloth. Viyella became as popular with women as with men. In 1897 Viyella was awarded a gold medal at the Brussels Exhibition, and there is evidence of its increasing sale abroad in the decision to protect the trade-mark in the USA, in South America and in Japan.

The success of Viyella within such a short time of its introduction is indeed remarkable. One of the company's travellers, W. B.

Furley, who covered the South of England was moved to express his enthusiasm in verse:[1]

> 'For Hunting, for Shooting, a luxury real,
> For Cycling and Tennis, the long sought ideal,
> For Bathing and Fishing, for Sea side and Boating,
> For Tailor-made Dresses and smart Winter Coating,
> For Layettes and Lingerie, Gowns, Frocks and Trousseau,
> Once buy it, and try it, for ever you'll do so,
> From torture to comfort it leads, so we think
> Our "Viyella's" unrivalled, because it Don't Shrink!'

Although the trade had started with orders from shirt makers, hosiers and women's outfitters who made up garments for individual customers, sales through drapers' shops soon became more important. There was, as yet, little readymade clothing and cloth was bought by the yard for making-up at home or by private dressmakers. A sharp stimulus was given to the shirt trade, however, by the South African War, when the British army went into khaki. Khaki Viyella was soon on the market for making into officers' shirts. This extended further the reputation of the product and won for Hollins many customers who maintained their loyalty to the brand.

The brand stood for quality. Viyella was never cheap; it was bought, by those who could afford it, because it was distinctive and good. Hollins consciously catered for this kind of custom and they took some care in selecting their retail outlets. Retailers who undertook to maintain stocks and promote sales were allowed a fairly generous margin. But soon price cutting began in certain shops, including some of the new department stores. Hollins saw this as a threat to the stability of their market and of their relations with the general body of retailers. They reacted quickly, and as early as 1895 announced minimum retail prices for Viyella cloths. Resale price maintenance, as it came to be called, was almost unheard of at this time, and it required a good deal of courage and determination on the part of Henry Ernest Hollins, whose idea it was. The policy could only be enforced by signed agreements with individual shops,

[1] Quoted by Pigott, op cit, p 108.

and while this was easy in the case of new accounts, existing customers could be coerced only by threatening to cut off supplies.
Most retailers accepted the conditions as operating in their own
interests as well as Hollins', but there were one or two large stores
that refused to co-operate and did not offer Viyella for many years.

Then a somewhat similar problem arose with some of Hollins's
yarn customers in the hosiery trade. The goodwill built up for
Viyella represented a considerable investment for Hollins and their
yarns benefited from this too. But now certain hosiery manufacturers began trying to attach some of the benefit to themselves by
offering goods made from Hollins' yarn as Viyella products. Claude
Hollins protested against this at a board meeting in 1898. The yarn
trade was not too good at the time and no immediate action was
taken. Later on, however, Hollins adopted the practice of buying
all hosiery made from their branded yarns and selling it themselves
under their own trade mark.

Such were the principles on which Hollins based their marketing policy in the early days of Viyella. In a highly competitive industry it had won for itself a position that was, at all events for the time being, unassailable. So long as these conditions lasted, the policy served the firm well, but it became consolidated into a tradition and, when circumstances changed, tradition was to become a hindrance to adaptation.

VIYELLA IN THE WASH

CHAPTER SEVEN

The Modern Business Takes Shape

HENCEFORWARD the fortunes of Hollins became more and more closely linked with the success of Viyella. What had begun as an experimental side-line, designed to supplement the firm's traditional trade in hosiery yarns, eventually transformed the nature and scale of the business. It was a gradual process but by 1903, ten years after the decision to go into weaving, Viyella cloth sales had reached £145,000. Including unbranded lines, cloth now accounted for 47 per cent of Hollins's total sales.

The board minutes give the impression that the early success of Viyella exceeded expectations. The new line was profitable almost from the start and by 1899 Hollins felt sufficiently confident to make a bid for one of the Glasgow weaving firms which had been making their cloth on commission. This was John McMath & Co, owned by J. P. Douglas, whose co-operation had been a vital factor in the launching of Viyella. The business was bought for £15,000 and agreement was reached with Douglas whereby he received £10,000 of Hollins's ordinary shares and a seat on the board; in addition, he was to be paid a salary and commission on profits. In the following year Douglas negotiated the purchase of the other Glasgow firm which had been weaving for Hollins, and which was now trading as Alexander McNab & Co.

With these two mills Hollins had more than enough weaving capacity to satisfy the existing demand for Viyella, and a variety of other cloths was produced. To distribute these, Alexander McNab was retained as a supplier of unbranded goods to wholesalers and garment manufacturers. In this way Hollins was able to use both mills and at the same time keep control of the Viyella trade through direct selling. The McNab outlet also provided a useful means of testing the market for different qualities of cloth, some of which were eventually branded and sold direct. The dual system of cloth marketing continued until after the First World War when, for a time, Hollins went in for merchanting in a big way, but with unfortunate results. On the manufacturing side, a major reorganisation took place in 1907 when Brookside Mill was sold to James Templeton & Co, the carpet manufacturers, and the whole of Hollins's weaving was concentrated in the Boden Street Mill, formerly owned by Alexander McNab, in which modern Northrop looms[1] had now been installed.

In acquiring their own weaving plant Hollins's objective was to improve co-ordination between spinning, weaving, designing and selling, and also to ensure the maintenance of quality in their branded cloth. Most of the cloth, was bought by the yard for making-up at home, or to customer's order by dress and shirt makers. But the demand for ready-made clothing was growing and retailers were now being asked for Viyella garments. Hollins' first response was to make agreements with a few making-up firms to produce Viyella shirts and sell them under the brand name. But the proprietors of the brand had no control over the garment maker and any fault in the garment would reflect on the reputation of Viyella. Hollins therefore decided that they must have their own garments factory. With their own weaving plant they could control the quality of Viyella cloth; similarly, they must be able to control the quality of Viyella garments by designing and making-up themselves.

Garment-making began in one of the rooms in the Radford mill with a few girls working treadle-driven sewing machines. By 1904, however, the machines had been connected to the mill shafting and production was so speeded up that an extensive range of garments could be offered for the autumn trade. *The Drapers' Record* reported favourably.

---

[1] The Northrop loom was an American invention, patented in 1894 and introduced into Lancashire in 1902. Its main feature was automatic shuttle changing. It cost three times as much as an ordinary loom but doubled the output per weaver. Single. *History of Technology.* 1958.

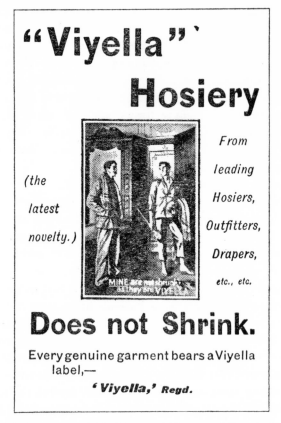

In nightdresses, for which this material is so specially suited, some extremely pretty models have been brought out. Drapers who have not yet seen these tasteful productions of the new department should do so at once. . . . Now that elegance of design is added to durability, Viyella for nightwear will be more popular than ever. Some of the latest designs in blouses and shirts have already sold well for the autumn.[1]

As the garments trade grew and the contracts with outside makers-up were ended, the department expanded and in 1910 a new garments factory for 200 operatives was opened on the Radford site. Nine years later a further move became necessary, this time to

[1] Quoted from Pigott, op cit, p 113.

There were three tiny Tots in Viyella—
They were Eleanor, Elsie, and Ella.
"Oh, Mummy," they said, as they snuggled in bed,
"We're *so* comfy and warm in Viyella."
"So am I, too,"
said Mummy.

a new location in Castle Boulevard, Nottingham. Here a large, light and airy building was constructed; eventually the head office of the company and its main warehouse were accommodated on the site.

With its extension into garments manufacture Hollins had become an outstanding example of vertical organisation in the clothing trade. Only certain of the finishing processes were done outside. Textile finishing was a highly specialised technique and Hollins, like other textile manufacturers, relied on commission finishers. The great problem with Viyella was to ensure against shrinkage; the yarn had a high wool content, but the manufacturers believed they had succeeded in producing a stable yarn by meticulous care in the mixing and spinning processes. 'Viyella does not shrink' had been a constant advertising theme from the beginning and it was from this quality that much of its popularity derived. But in 1910 the company began to get more and more complaints of shrinking. The trouble was due to a change in washing methods; instead of being carefully hand-washed at home, more garments were being sent to laundries. The solution of the problem rested with the finisher and eventually Hollins found a firm in Paisley, the Seedhill Finishing Co, which was able to produce it. Seedhill thus came into close association with Hollins, but it was not until 1928 that it became a subsidiary.

In Hollins's original trade of hosiery yarns developments took a different course. One might have expected that the same process of vertical organisation would have occurred here, for much of the yarn supplied to hosiery manufacturers was now Viyella and some of these were offering their goods under this name. In the circumstances Hollins might well have gone into hosiery manufacture as they had gone into weaving and garment making from cloth. But there is no evidence that such a course was considered, and the reasons for this are fairly clear. Despite their growing trade in cloth and garments, Hollins's main trade was still in hosiery yarns. The trade was highly competitive, and in setting up its own hosiery plant Hollins would have risked antagonising many of their customers. This would not have mattered so much if Hollins could have absorbed most of their yarn output in their own hosiery department. But such a department would have to be very large and capable of producing goods in great variety. It would have added considerably to the difficulties of managing what was already a complex business.

Yet there remained the problem of ensuring that hosiery goods made from Viyella yarn, and described as such, maintained the high quality standards that had come to be associated with the brand. There was also the question of the terms of trade in such goods, which derived much of their selling value from the proprietary brand name which Hollins had created and publicised. The issue had been raised by Claude Hollins in 1898. A few years later a system was introduced whereby a number of hosiery firms who had long been customers for Pleasley yarns entered into a licensing agreement. Their goods made from Viyella yarn carried the appropriate label and Hollins advertised to the trade and the public the fact that Viyella hosiery and underwear, 'made from the same yarn as the celebrated cloth', was available. In 1909, however, Hollins went a step further in the control of Viyella hosiery by setting up their own hosiery warehouse in London. Now all Viyella knitted goods were made by approved manufacturers to Hollins's orders and distributed through their hosiery department. Through this arrangement a measure of vertical integration was achieved in Hollins's hosiery trade, but it was never so complete as in the case of cloth and garments.

These changes in organisation and, of course, the growth in the scale of operations following the introduction of Viyella, involved considerable investment. Much of the money came from profits retained in the business but debentures were issued amounting to nearly £100,000 by 1907 and there was also a bank overdraft of £83,000 at the end of the year. Profits averaged £48,115 a year over the nine years 1899–1907 and, after the establishment of a dividend reserve fund in 1896, the distribution on ordinary shares was usually 10 per cent. In 1901, however, the company's capital was raised to £350,000 by the issue of 5,000 more ordinary shares of £10 each. These were taken up by the existing shareholders, of whom H. E. Hollins was the biggest subscriber. It was at this time that a proposal was made to convert the firm into a public company. It came from the Cockrofts but found no support among the other shareholders. There is no record of the discussion on this occasion, but it was evidently felt that the company had sufficient resources for the time being, in view of its accumulating dividend reserve fund. Under the original arrangement this had been invested outside the company, and it was now agreed, on the managing director's proposal, that it should become an ordinary reserve to be used in the development of the business.

In the light of subsequent events, it is clear that the proposal for

a public company in 1901 was rejected as being premature rather
than undesirable in itself; for only six years later definite steps were
being taken to this end and the firm's accountants were instructed
to prepare a scheme. Thus, in March 1908, the private company
was liquidated and its assets sold to a new public company of the
same name.

The company's authorised capital was £800,000, half in £1
ordinary shares and half in £1 5 per cent cumulative preference
shares, but 40,000 of each class of share were left for future issue. In
part payment of the purchase consideration the vendor company
took 120,000 of each class of share so that only 480,000 shares altogether were offered for public subscription and some 80,000 of
these were taken up by the directors and their associates. The issue
was a complete success and Hollins' shares were soon being transferred at a small premium.

The value of the assets being acquired by the new company, as
stated in the prospectus, was £702,000, which included £315,000
for premises and plant and £245,153 for stocks of materials and
finished goods. Goodwill was valued at £50,000, which was largely
attributable to the name and reputation of Viyella. 'Very large
sums' had been spent on creating this asset, 'with the result that
Viyella is now a household word and both the yarn and cloth and
made-up garments enjoy everywhere a very extensive sale.' Many
of the new shareholders were employees of the company or had
trading connections with it, and the success of the issue is a measure
of their confidence in Henry Ernest Hollins, who now became
chairman while continuing also as managing director. He was
joined on the board by his son, Arthur, and William and Claude
continued as directors. The Hollins family were thus well represented. W. B. Paget had retired on the liquidation of the private
company and was succeeded by his cousin E. L. Paget. The other
two directors were Hill and Douglas, both members of the former
board. All but William Hollins were full-time managers, and an
important newcomer to the senior management team was Marcus

Hare, a chartered accountant, who now joined the company as secretary. Hare, the first professionally qualified man to be employed by Hollins, was destined to play an important part in the firm's affairs.

The new company's record, from its formation until the outbreak of the First World War, was one of steady prosperity. Annual gross profits averaged about £84,000 as compared with £50,000 over the preceding six years and the dividend on ordinary shares reached 7 per cent. These results were not unsatisfactory, but they hardly fulfilled the hopes that had been expressed when the company's capital was increased by public issue. Indeed, the chairman warned the board in 1911 that it was employing too much capital for the volume of business done and that the position in this respect compared unfavourably with that of six years before.

Hollins had based their hopes for expansion on the new trade in cloth and garments. Viyella was already well established and in 1908 a cheaper cloth called Aza had been introduced. Garment making had also begun in that year. Much enterprise was shown in extending the range of goods, especially those bearing the Viyella trade mark. Each year new patterns appeared. There were double-width Viyella costume cloths for women, lighter dress Viyella, tropical Viyella and nursery Viyella. The garments factory turned out men's shirts and pyjamas and women's blouses and nightdresses, and increasing attention was given to fashion trends and even to influencing them through such garments as women's robes. Among Viyella hosiery novelties were articles made in club colours, and outside the clothing range there were Viyella sheets. From time to time new brands were introduced—Hollinta was one, Plesella another—to fill a gap in the range, and, though few survived for long, they are an indication of alertness to market opportunities.

These goods were marketed through a sales force which had grown to ten by 1911, and in this year Charles Warren[1] was

[1] Much information on the marketing of Viyella was supplied by Mr Warren when interviewed in 1963.

appointed as the first manager of the travellers' department, operating from London. The travellers, paid by salary and commission, called on selected retailers with their patterns and samples, not merely pushing sales, but advising, receiving suggestions and complaints, building up an intimate relationship with their customers and seeking their goodwill and co-operation. In all this they were strongly supported by the firm's advertising. From the beginning Hollins had recognised the need for advertising as a corollary of branding and direct selling. Now they had an advertising department at the London office and by 1912 its expenditure on Viyella alone had grown to £8,000 a year.

Like most firms at this time, Hollins did its own advertising; it was many years before an agency was used. Space was taken in newspapers and magazines giving a national coverage and also in the provincial press, where the advertisements mentioned local shops selling Viyella. Point-of-sale advertising and display, involving close co-operation between manufacturer and retailer, was particularly important. In some of the bigger shops display weeks were organised, with entire departments devoted to Viyella goods. Hollins' goods were also shown at many exhibitions at home and abroad.

Through all this publicity a definite image was created. 'Viyella does not shrink', 'Specially suitable for sensitive skins', 'Economical because durable'—such were the qualities that 'Viyella' stood for. They were solid qualities, designed to appeal to solid people, whose loyalty to a brand, once secured, was likely to remain.

With the early success of Viyella in the home market, Hollins soon turned their attention to exports. They had, of course, been exporting yarns for many years, their agencies in Chemnitz and Berlin being particularly important. Now they began to export Viyella yarn to Australia, where it was made into hosiery under a licence system similar to that operating in England. For overseas sales of Viyella cloth, however, Hollins made an agreement in 1898 with I. & R. Morley, the big Nottingham hosiery manufacturer and wholesale

Plate 11. Pleasley Works Cricket Club 1899

The Captain of the Eleven
DOES NOT SHRINK

in her **'Viyella'** Regd.

For TENNIS and BOATING SHIRTS, PYJAMAS, &c.
LUXURIOUS AND COMFORTABLE.
From Leading Drapers and Outfitters—or name of nearest sent by
'VIYELLA,' (C. L.), 55, FRIDAY STREET, LONDON, E.C.

Plate 12. Viyella advert:
girl playing cricket

Plate 13. Viyella advert in
The New Yorker

UP and DOWN the AVENUE in

Viyella

Viyella

washable and colorfast

THE LABEL FOR MERCHANDISE EXPORTED TO GERMANY, *c.* 1900

merchant firm, which was widely represented abroad. This arrangement continued until 1918, except for the USA. There sales of cloth were handicapped by very high tariffs and Hollins's idea was to export yarn for weaving into Viyella cloth. This proved an expensive failure, for the Americans could neither weave Viyella properly nor give it the required finish. In the end J. P. Douglas had to go out and arrange for the disposal of the inferior cloth in cheap, anonymous lots, the unused yarn being returned to England. But a market of such potential importance could not be abandoned and eventually Hollins established itself through an agency in New York, which was superseded, in 1919, by William Hollins & Co Inc. However, the American trade was to be a persistent source of trouble.

In the meantime Hollins were developing an export trade in

H

cloths to other markets. The Morley agreement applied only to Viyella but the Glasgow weaving mills produced a variety of un-branded mixture and cotton cloths which were sold either in Hollins's name or through the Alexander McNab subsidiary. Hollins were also free to export Viyella hosiery. It thus built up an exporting organisation far more extensive than that created for the yarn trade, with agencies in Paris, Melbourne, Sydney and Toronto as well as in New York. In the years just before the First World War several members of the firm visited overseas markets and brought back favourable impressions. The need for a single export system was apparent and when the Morley agreement expired Hollins set up an export department in their London office to handle all overseas business.

Yet despite all these vigorous efforts in sales promotion at home and abroad, only moderate success was achieved in the early years of the public company. Sales of Viyella cloth had been £145,000 in 1903; ten years later they were still only £147,000, though £165,000 had been reached in 1911. Aza, one of the cheaper cloths introduced some years before, made only a modest contribution of £16,000. Other cloths added £40,000 to total sales. These were unbranded woollens and cotton Zephyrs for shirtings, which Hollins sold for W. & J. Anderson & Co Ltd along with their own goods. The expansion of garment sales from £55,000 in 1908, when production began, to £70,000 in 1913 was more encouraging, and the increase here partly accounts for the stagnation in Viyella piece goods. More cloth was being sold in the form of garments.

But the success of the new trade cannot be measured merely by sales. What did it contribute to Hollins's profits? The accounts for 1913 show total profits of £77,000, of which only £9,800 is directly attributed to cloth and garments. This, however, is somewhat mis-leading. A profit was charged on all yarn transferred to the weaving section, as though it were an outside sale, and an independent analysis of the costing system carried out some years later showed that the spinning mills were treated generously at the expense of weaving and making-up. On the other hand, the selling costs of cloth and garments were much heavier than those of outside yarn sales to hosiery manufacturers. It thus appears that the new trade was, to some extent, subsidising the traditional yarn trade.

There is no doubt, however, that the relatively poor returns on the new trade were due to heavy selling expenses, not matched by a corresponding growth of sales. For instance, in 1903 £4,000 was spent on Viyella advertising, and other selling expenses amounted to £17,000, giving a total percentage on sales of fifteen. Under the public company, annual advertising expenditure was doubled and other selling expenses increased; in 1912 the total reached 21 per cent of sales. Exporting was particularly costly. The USA was the principal overseas market, taking about £60,000 worth each year, mainly of cloth, but the profits were small and fluctuating and were replaced by losses in 1912 and 1913. Canadian and Australian sales were much less and it was some years before the costs of establishing Viyella in these markets were recovered.

The outbreak of war in 1914 brought little immediate change in Hollins's business; no sense of emergency is apparent in the board minutes. The old-established trading link with Germany was, of course, severed, leaving frozen assets of about £15,000, but exports to the USA, Canada and Australia increased. In the home market there was an all-round improvement in sales, especially of woollen cloths, though Viyella cloth and garments also did well. Yarn sales increased too; for the war stimulated the hosiery industry and started a boom in home knitting. It also reduced supplies of imported yarn, and Fairfield Mill, which had at times seemed a doubtful asset, benefited by turning to the production of Belgian-type yarns. By the end of the war Hollins's total sales had almost doubled in value. The growth and distribution of sales by product is shown in Table 4. (See page 116.)

It will be seen that throughout the period Hollins continued to rely on yarn for more than half of its total sales and that the war brought very little change in this position. Cloth sales were about the same proportion in 1917 as in 1913 but the detailed accounts show big changes in the content of these sales. Viyella cloth sales at £145,000 in 1917 were no higher than in 1903 and slightly less than in 1913. In view of the general rise in prices this represents a substantial fall in quantity. If the proportion of cloth sales was maintained it was due to the cheap Aza cloth, to Zephyr shirtings (not made by Hollins), and above all to the big expansion in unbranded woollen cloths, sales of which grew from £27,000 in 1913 to £109,000 in 1917.

TABLE 4

Sales of Yarn, Cloth and Garments 1903–1917*

	YARN		CLOTH		CLOTH		GARMENTS		
	Sales	% of Total	Home Sales	% of Total	Export Sales	% of Total	Sales	% of Total	Total
	£		£		£		£		
1903	220,000	53	175,000	43	17,000	4	—	—	412,000
1908	270,000	50	175,000	32	45,000	8	55,000	10	545,000
1913	390,000	54	200,000	28	65,000	9	70,000	9	725,000
1917	730,000	52	390,000	28	140,000	10	140,000	10	1,400,000

* The 1918 accounts are missing.

The war thus brought a setback to Viyella. It had always been a rather expensive article, and it was not well suited to the pattern of wartime demand, particularly to the demand for mass produced army clothing—which, incidentally, is reflected in Hollins's increased sales of woollen cloths and, to some extent, of garments. In overseas markets Viyella did better. The USA, by far the most important market, took £85,000 worth in 1917, as compared with £52,000 in 1913, and Canadian and Australian sales, though much smaller in amount, showed a bigger proportionate increase.

As well as this setback to the firm's distinctive product, on the promotion of which so much had been spent, the conditions of wartime brought other factors unfavourable to profits. Firstly there was the rise in wage rates. Before the war there is no record of any dealings with trade unions and, like many other employers, Hollins had presumably fixed their wage rates according to their judgment of the local labour market; but, soon after the war began, they decided to pay a war bonus, as a concession to the rising cost of living, and they also made allowances to employees on war service. Then, in 1916 trade union demands were encountered for the first time, and strike threats too. The union, the National Union of General Workers, was asking for a 15 per cent increase, which, the directors were told, would mean a rise of 30 per cent in wages since the war began. On this occasion the dispute was settled by an arbitration award of a 7 per cent increase but there was further trouble in the following year, resulting in a three weeks' strike at Boden Street. Unrest was reported from Pleasley too, and further concessions had to be made.

The second unfavourable factor was the rise in the prices of cotton and wool, but all these adverse effects were offset to some extent by the fact that most of the plant in the various mills was working to full capacity, with favourable results on the incidence of overhead charges. In so far as unit costs rose, prices were put up—with no fear of spoiling the market under the prevailing inflationary conditions. Moreover, goods sold at these higher prices embodied materials bought when prices were lower.

On the whole, war conditions, with their accompanying inflation, were inevitably favourable to profits, and Hollins was no exception to the general rule. Between 1909 and 1914 the average gross profit, before charging management commissions, was about £73,000. Average net profit was £64,000. In 1915 gross profit was £186,000, but excess profits duty had now been introduced, and this charge, with management commissions, left £106,000 as the net amount. By 1918 gross profits had risen to the record level of £538,000— seven times the 1914 figure—but this was drastically reduced, by excess profits duty and management commissions, to a final net profit of £134,000.

The firm's results for the whole period from the formation of the public company to the end of the war are shown in the following table.

TABLE 5

Year	Dividend declared	Net Profit	Management Commissions* (and EPD during war)	Gross Profits
	% of Total	£	£	£
1908	5	45,000	7,500	52,000
1909	6¼	64,000	10,500	74,000
1910	7	63,000	10,000	73,000
1911	7	60,000	8,000	68,000
1912	7	67,000	12,000	79,000
1913	7	66,000	11,000	77,000
1914	7	66,000	10,000	76,000
1915	10	106,000	80,000	186,000
1916	10	86,000	71,000	157,000
1917	10	89,000	105,000	194,000
1918	12½	134,000	404,000	538,000
1919	12½	225,000	238,000	463,000

* During the war most of the amounts charged as management commissions were paid into a reserve against the liability to excess profits duty.

Throughout the war years the membership of the board remained unchanged. In 1916, however, Henry Ernest Hollins gave up his post as managing director, though retaining his office as chairman. The complex organisation which he had done so much to create allowed considerable autonomy to the directors in charge of the individual units, but co-ordination was the managing director's responsibility, and this, combined with the duties of company chairman, had become too heavy. Unlike William Hollins, Henry Ernest had a son who, by virtue of his training and experience, seemed well qualified to succeed him in the firm. Arthur Hollins had been appointed to the board on the formation of the public company and had special responsibility for Pleasley mills. Now, at the age of thirty-seven he became managing director and deputy chairman. Early in 1919 his father, whose health was failing, relinquished the chairmanship and Arthur Hollins was unanimously chosen to fill his place. Thus the two offices of chairman and managing director were again combined.

Henry Ernest had proved himself a worthy successor to William Hollins. Like his uncle, he devoted himself to the firm's affairs and to directing its further expansion, and his outside interests were mainly confined to the Mansfield area. He continued William Hollins's work for the Mansfield hospital, where he was chairman of the board from 1886 to 1916. He was a leader of the local Liberal party and a Free Trader and for some years a member of the Nottinghamshire County Council. William Hollins had been a Unitarian, but his nephew attended the Pleasley Parish Church. He died in 1920 and was buried at Barbon in Westmorland, where he had spent his brief retirement.

CHAPTER EIGHT

The End of the Hollins Dynasty

HOLLINS emerged from the war years in a prosperous condition and with seemingly bright prospects. The immediate task was to develop the market for its branded lines, as government orders fell off, and as capacity became available for the requirements of normal trade. A new and very promising cloth had been introduced during the war; it was called Clydella, and was designed to sell at a price between Viyella and Aza. Advertising of this and older-established lines had been maintained on a modest scale but, with the end of the war in sight, a big effort in sales promotion was planned. In October 1918 £33,000 was voted for advertising, £10,000 of which was for spending overseas.

The growth of exports during the war encouraged hopes of a big expansion in overseas markets when normal trading conditions were restored, and Hollins had sent out Charles Warren and other representatives to explore the ground. Their reports gave an optimistic account of prospects in North and South America and in Australia. It was recommended that Hollins should open offices and warehouses of its own in New York, Toronto and Melbourne, and the possibilities of setting up subsidiary companies for manufacturing were considered. The first of these recommendations was acted upon in 1919 when the American agency arrangement was superseded by the establishment of a small company, William Hollins & Co Inc, with a warehouse in New York to handle the sale of goods sent from Glasgow. Offices and warehouses were also set up in Toronto and Melbourne.

Hollins's sales in 1919 were nearly £3½ million. The firm's experience was typical of British industry in the first year of peace when, for a short time, the demand for most kinds of goods exceeded supply. Prices rose and profits soared. Hollins's net profits reached £225,000 and a 12½ per cent dividend was again paid, this time free of tax, while £75,000 was appropriated to a contingencies fund. But with trading at its present level, and raw material, wages and other costs rising, more capital was needed. In 1918 the bank overdraft fluctuated between £29,000 and £70,000; in the following year it touched £419,000. The value of the company's fixed assets had, of course, risen with the higher level of earnings, but there was a shortage of cash for trading requirements and for re-equipment. The directors therefore resolved to recommend an increase in share capital.

In putting the resolution to the shareholders, Arthur Hollins, as chairman, placed particular emphasis on the prospects of the export trade. Besides providing for direct representation in the principal overseas markets, the company had its travellers visiting most European countries as well as India, China, Africa and South America, and the results so far had fully justified its policy. But trade expansion entailed the carrying of much larger stocks and would necessitate an increase in productive capacity. The directors had no doubt that the additional capital could be profitably employed, and their confidence was endorsed by the shareholders. They were impressed by the firm's progress in its first decade as a public company and this, as one of them declared, 'makes it quite easy for us to acquiesce in the proposal, being satisfied that the business is in good hands and prudently and efficiently managed'. The proposition for an increase in capital was carried unanimously.

The additional capital was raised by creating a further 400,000 £1 shares, 382,500 of which were offered to existing holders at par and the balance to employees.[1] These were attractive terms, the market price of existing ordinary shares being about 30s, and the response was satisfactory. Thus, at the end of 1919, Hollins's issued capital

[1] Some of the employees' shares had been allocated under a profit-sharing scheme started in 1917. The scheme lost its attraction in the post-war slump and was wound up in 1923.

was represented by 360,000 £1 preference shares and 761,118 ordinary shares, giving a total of £1,121,118. However, this soon proved insufficient and early in 1920 the chairman reported negotiations for bank overdraft of up to £500,000. Accordingly, another rights issue was undertaken, on a one for four basis, and this time the price was 25s. The new issue added 186,767 ordinary shares. At the same time the managers who had been remunerated partly on a commission basis received 190,790 ordinary shares in lieu of such payment. The total ordinary shares capital was therefore increased to £1,515,528.

However, by the end of 1920 the boon had passed and Hollins's declared net profit fell to £179,758. But provision had been made for short term fluctuations; for the firm's policy, as stated in 1909, had been to make liberal additions to reserves in good years, so as to maintain dividends as far as possible, and protect the market price of its shares. By 1919 it had built up a general reserve of £140,000, a capital reserve of £42,000, and a contingencies fund of £101,000. Thus, despite the unfavourable trading results of 1920, a dividend of 10 per cent was paid by drawing on reserves.

At the time it seemed reasonable enough to regard the experience of 1920 as a readjustment to more normal trading conditions after the unhealthy boom of the previous year. But far worse was to follow; what had seemed a mere recession in 1920, now turned into a major depression, which brought disaster to many firms and severely tested even the soundest. In the slump year of 1921 Hollins suffered a trading loss of £378,000. This was not disclosed in the published accounts, which, in fact, showed a profit of £103,300; the loss was made good by the return of excess profits duty, paid in more prosperous years, and by certain reserves being appropriated to profits. Out of the profits so ascertained, a 5 per cent dividend was paid.

The handling of the accounts in this bad year is open to criticism. When, in circumstances to be related later on, the true position came to light, *The Economist* commented: 'we are here provided with a striking example of the way in which the true results of a company's trading can be obscured by the abbreviated form of profit and loss account which has become so popular in the last decade'. But there is nothing to suggest financial mismanagement. Very large reserves had been built up in the good years and the excess profits payments, now returned, also represented past earnings. The directors could therefore claim that they were pursuing the policy laid down in 1909, and indeed practised long before then. Their prudence had enabled the firm to survive the slump which forced so many into liquidation. There is further evidence of prudence in the form in which new capital was raised. At one stage it was suggested that part should be obtained by issuing more preference shares; in the event only ordinary shares were issued, giving a low-geared capital structure. Furthermore, in 1920, goodwill, which had stood at £80,000, was written off, and a stock reserve of £50,000 was created.

The trading losses of 1921 were largely due to the suddenness of the change from inflation to deflation. Hollins, like so many firms, particularly in the textile and clothing trades, were caught with big stocks, bought at high prices or manufactured at high cost, while facing a falling market. The value of Hollins's stocks of raw materials, as shown in the balance sheet, increased from £649,026 at the end of 1918 to £897,519 a year later. By the end of 1920 the figure had reached £1,206,860, and, although it had been reduced to £872,151 by December 1921, the sales for that year were only £2,538,403, as compared with £3,467,819 for 1919.

A large part of the sales for this period consisted of goods, mainly cloth, bought from other manufacturers. Such purchases amounted to £992,141 in 1919 and to no less than £1,498,471 in 1921. Hollins had done a certain amount of trade in bought-in goods before the war, but this was regarded as supplementary to its main interests as a manufacturer; it had been undertaken where it was considered useful to extend the range of goods carried by travellers and as a means of testing the market for possible new lines. The trade, which had now grown to such proportions, was inspired by different motives. The post-war boom provided opportunities for speculative transactions on an unprecedented scale, and Hollins, like many other manufacturing firms, set out to exploit the situation, as merchants. Even when prices started to fall they continued to buy, for there were now many weak sellers about, anxious to liquidate their stocks, and a firm like Hollins with plenty of cash, could pick up supplies at what seemed 'bargain' prices. Unfortunately, prices continued to fall through 1921 and 1922, with serious consequences for profits.

By the end of 1923, however, the worst of the trade depression was over. It is true that Hollins's turnover for the whole year was 25 per cent below that for 1922, but recovery was now setting in. Raw material costs had fallen substantially and there had been some reduction in wages and salaries. Profit was still low, but this reflected the conservative policy for valuing stocks. From the accounts it would seem that Hollins had weathered the storm, but in these difficult years a crisis had been developing in the firm's direction and in the latter part of 1923 this came to a head.

A break had occurred in 1919 with the retirement of Henry Ernest Hollins from the chairmanship of the company. He died in the following year. But his son, Arthur, who succeeded to the chairmanship, was already managing director and before that he had had considerable experience as the director responsible for Pleasley Mills. He was the inevitable choice as the new head of the firm, and there appears to have been no question as to his continuing also as managing director. Indeed, his powers as managing director were extended, or, at least, made more explicit, when he became chairman. Hitherto they had not been formally defined; now the board resolved that, in addition to the general powers of management deriving from the office, the managing director should act on behalf of the board in appointing and dismissing staff and in fixing salaries and determining duties.

Arthur Hollins was thus placed in a seemingly strong position, but he had to reckon with his fellow-directors, and the composition of the board was changing. William Hollins the second had died in 1918, and Claude four years later. J. P. Douglas had agreed to resign in 1920, on the payment of substantial compensation for loss of office. Only Charles Hill and Edgar Paget still remained from the board which Arthur Hollins had taken over. The new directors were H. A. Dowson, a solicitor, whose firm had acted for Hollins over many years, S. F. Peshall, manager of the hosiery department, Marcus Hare, the company's secretary, and Charles Warren, the sales manager. The last two appointments were particularly significant. Hitherto the board had consisted of men whose interests were mainly in manufacture; finance and sales had been underrepresented. Now there were specialists in these fields, whose views on issues of policy might well clash with those of their colleagues, including the chairman.

In a complex concern, such as Hollins had now become, conflicts of interests and ideas were inevitable. It was Arthur Hollins's responsibility, as chairman of the directors, to resolve the conflicts and to develop a balanced policy through his own powers of leadership. In this his father had been conspicuously successful; but the task, of course, had been less difficult at a time when the firm was doing well, in a favourable economic environment. Continued expansion had provided opportunities for able and vigorous members of the management team to satisfy their ambitions, and successful expansion, in turn, enhanced the prestige and authority of its leader. The post-war situation was very different. Under the stress of depression, conflict was sharpened to a degree that would have tested many a wiser man, more experienced in leadership, than Arthur Hollins.

It is never easy for a man trained in one department of a firm to assume the responsibilities of general management. Hollins is remembered as a man of great ability on the technical and manufacturing side of the firm's operations. But unfortunately his outlook on the many-sided problems of general management was always conditioned by his particular experience, and he seems to have shown scant respect for the experience and outlook of others. The minutes of the board meetings are less informative than one would wish, but there are various hints in the early 1920s of the growing dispute between Hollins and his fellow directors.

From 1921, the worst year, profits recovered to £125,000 in 1922, but they were down again in 1923. Throughout this period there was general concern about the high level of stocks in all departments, to which the big cloth purchases had contributed. Wool, too, which had been very scarce during the war, was heavily bought. These transactions were undertaken, of course, with the chairman's agreement, though whether he initiated them is uncertain. If he did, he was certainly not alone in the excessive optimism from which he acted in 1919–20.

When the depression began, much of the raw material bought at high prices had been converted into yarn for the hosiery trade and for weaving in the firm's own plant. But yarn supplies were now greatly in excess of the current demand for cloth, whether for sale in the piece or for making up in the garments department. In an effort to relieve the position, the sales director was asked to advise on making garments for stock. But, unless there was a prospect of an eventual improvement in sales, this would merely shift the burden of stocks to the garments department and, indeed, the overall situation would be worse, since the additional cost of conversion would be incurred. All this pointed to the need for a reduction in final selling prices; in the opinion of the sales representatives a substantial cut was called for. The only concession reported in 1921, however, was a reduction in the price of Clydella. Hollins opposed price cutting on principle. The price of cloth, he insisted, must reflect the cost of the yarn, and that of garments the cost of cloth, and on this basis no further reduction in selling prices could be conceded.

There was trouble too, over dealings with hosiery manufacturers. The peculiar feature of this trade was that, where branded yarns were concerned, Hollins bought back the goods made from its yarn and sold them through its own hosiery department. But, with the onset of depression, many of these orders to hosiery manufacturers were cancelled on Arthur Hollins' instructions, with obviously damaging effects on the firm's goodwill. Relations with the hosiery trade became so strained that Hollins seriously considered setting up their own knitting plant. But the risk was too great; in the present state of the trade the firm could not hope to operate profitably on a scale sufficient to absorb its whole output of hosiery yarns. It would thus still need the custom of hosiery manufacturers, and this might well suffer further damage if Hollins set up in competition.

Another bone of contention was the buying of yarns and cloth from outside the firm. Those responsible for sales emphasised the advantage of buying supplies in the cheapest market. For instance, the hosiery department claimed that under prevailing conditions it was more profitable to deal in goods not made from Hollins's yarn. The cloth department contended that it could get cloth made from Hollins' yarn more cheaply from outside weavers than from Boden Street. The point was also made that the sales organisation was unduly restricted if its representatives could offer only the range of goods determined by the firm's manufacturing interests. Hollins's goods were too dear for some markets, and unsuitable for others, for instance where lighter fabrics were preferred. This was particularly true of some overseas markets. Thus we find the New York company complaining that it was unable to make a profit on Hollins's goods and asking permission to go into certain lines of domestic products. From Australia too, it was reported that most consumers found Hollins' goods too dear; the branch had to be able to offer cheap cotton goods if sales were to expand. Another point emphasised by the sales department was the seasonal character of the trade in Viyella cloth. It was mainly an autumn and winter trade and additional lines were needed to take up the slack at other times.

These examples illustrate the difficulties of trying to run the firm as a self-contained vertical organisation. It made for rigidity, which must have exasperated those concerned with the commercial, as distinct from the manufacturing, side of the business. There might be merit in being self-contained so long as supplies were scarce; but, in the buyers' market that had now developed, weavers spinning their own yarn and garment makers using their own cloth might be at a disadvantage. For yarn and cloth could often be bought from weak sellers below the cost of manufacture within the firm. On the other hand, buying outside meant idle capacity in the firm's own manufacturing departments. This was the point re-iterated by Arthur Hollins. The firm was essentially a manufac-turing, not a merchanting business, and its first responsiblity was to keep its plant as fully employed as possible. It was not in the firm's interests to buy outside when it had idle capacity of its own.

In the face of such arguments the board was induced to agree that orders for cloth should be kept within the firm whenever looms were available. A similar policy was agreed for the hosiery department, which should order nothing from manufacturers that was not made from Hollins's yarn. Moreover, such goods were to be bought only when the terms allowed a margin of not less than 25 per cent on Hollins's resale price.

These attempts to reassert the firm's traditional policy were un-likely to succeed, however, unless Hollins strengthened its market position. There would be no advantage in keeping orders for cloth within the firm, if the orders were inadequate because of excessive prices. As for yarn sales to hosiery manufacturers, these would de-pend on the price charged by Hollins, and also on the ultimate demand for the finished hosiery goods. This again depended on Hollins's selling prices.

In 1922 price policy was becoming a major issue at board meet-ings. All but the chairman had become convinced that Hollins's prices must be brought into line with the downward trend in their markets. It was revealed that some price cuts had already been made, despite the known opposition of the chairman. Eventually, after lengthy discussion, all-round reductions in cloth and gar-ments prices were agreed upon. The chairman was apparently still

sceptical about the response of the market; he seems to have regarded the price reductions as experimental and referred to the
chances of increasing prices again 'to ensure a profit on possible
additional sales'. He was also concerned about the loss to retailers
who had bought at higher prices, and it was agreed that some
compensation should be allowed.

The root of the controversy on pricing seems to lie in Hollins's
reluctance to write down the value of stocks. Other directors saw the
necessity and Paget, in particular, protested against the current
method of stocktaking, which was 'not based on a correct interpretation of market value'. It was only after Hollins's eventual departure, in 1923, that the position was fully remedied, and in the
following year the directors were able to announce that 'in order to
place the future trading on a proper basis the board has found it
necessary to write down the old stocks by over £36,000 out of the
profits for 1923'.

The concessions to price competition succeeded in giving some
stimulus to sales, although Hollins's selling policy had never relied
on mere cheapness. The emphasis had always been on quality,
rather than low prices, and this required investment in various
forms of sales promotion, especially advertising. Until 1923 advertising expenditure was based on turnover. This is a common practice, but it has the effect of reducing sales promotion at the very
time that a stimulus is needed. In 1921 the amount spent on advertising was a mere £6,036. Next year it was decided that the
advertising appropriation should be voted by the board, instead of
allowing the various departments to spend according to their sales.
But judging from the amount voted for the second half of 1922,
£3,000, it looks as though the change was designed for more strin-
gent control rather than for expansion. If this was the intention, it
was fortunately overruled in the following year, when the advertising budget shot up to £24,000.

From the record of the meeting on this occasion it is clear that
the chairman had misgivings. Only on the assurance that advertise-

I

ments could, if necessary, be cancelled at short notice, did he agree
to let the proposed budget go through. Hollins's anxiety about selling
costs was shared by other directors on the manufacturing side. For
instance, the London warehouse had charged the hosiery department 25 per cent as selling expenses, subsequently reduced to 15
per cent, including transport costs. There had also been complaints
about the wide margins on other goods attributable to selling costs.
Such complaints were of course justified, if selling costs were in-
flated by inefficient organisation and methods, but it should have
been recognised that, for a firm whose sales depend on prestige
rather than price, it might be false economy to save on sales promotion.

On all the issues we have discussed so far agreement had been
reached, at all events on the board, though it is clear that the chairman usually found himself in opposition to most of his colleagues.
But it has to be remembered that Arthur Hollins was also managing
director and with unusually wide powers. These gave him scope for
independent action in matters that, if only in the interests of good
relations, should have come before the board. Moreover, even when
decisions had been taken by the board, the chairman, in his capacity
of managing director, might refuse to implement them or, worse
still, reverse them.

It was on one such case that the conflict came to a head. For
some time the firm's overseas branches had been in difficulties
owing to trade depression and the restriction of their activities by
the parent firm. At the end of the war, the New York subsidiary, in
particular, had been encouraged to place large orders, and now,
with unsold stocks piling up, it was unable to pay, and sought to
cancel further deliveries. The New York manager saw no prospect
of early improvement in Viyella sales, but, in his opinion, the
company's profitability could be restored, if it was allowed further
capital for developing trade in cheaper American goods. Eventually
the board agreed to grant £20,000. The chairman was instructed to
decide upon an appropriate arrangement in conjunction with Hare

(the company's secretary) and the latter informed the American management of the decision.

This was in April 1923. At a board meeting in the following September Hare had to report that the transfer of capital had been vetoed by the chairman. Hare had already consulted his colleagues and secured support for his proposed line of action. Accordingly, when the American company's accounts came up for discussion, Hare made his protest and tendered his resignation as a manager, though not as a director. His reference to 'other matters which had occurred during some considerable time' suggests that the matter at issue was the culmination of a growing conflict between him and Hollins.

It was soon made clear to Hollins that Hare had the support of the other directors. He was, by all accounts, an able man of great integrity, and generally respected, and he had been placed in an intolerable position. Warren, as sales director, had often clashed with the chairman on issues of commercial policy. Paget too, despite the long connection between his family and the Hollins, had become estranged. It was Paget who now led the opposition and who, at the September meeting, proposed the motion, seconded by Hare, 'that A. R. Hollins be removed forthwith from office as managing director and that he cease to be chairman of the company'. The motion was carried and Hollins left the meeting, whereupon C. H. Hill, as the senior member of the board, was elected chairman and Hare became managing director.

This was not the last of Arthur Hollins, however. As an important shareholder, and, with some support from others, he was able, in accordance with the articles of association, to call for a shareholders' meeting. They were asked to consider the board's policy in providing further capital for overseas branches, in view of the losses incurred, its policy in continuing to make 'speculative' purchases of goods 'outside the scope of the company's business as mill owners and manufacturers', and its action in removing Arthur Hollins. The shareholders were also asked to elect two additional directors nominated by Hollins.

An independent investigation followed, directed by Sir William Plender, an eminent accountant. His report was less comprehensive than might have been expected, but, on the two issues of policy specifically referred to him, Plender upheld the board's decisions in opposition to Hollins. He accordingly recommended that capital should be provided for William Hollins & Co, New York, 'within reasonable and proper limits' to support its business in Hollins's goods and such other goods as could be sold at a fair profit. This policy should also apply to other overseas branches, except that in Toronto, which the board had already decided to close. As regards the home market, the firm should not restrict its sales to its own products, but, again 'within reasonable and proper limits', should through its travellers, sell, at a fair commercial profit, goods of other manufacturers which were found to be in demand by its customers.

On the removal of Arthur Hollins, Plender found the board's action justified on the evidence; but it had been effected in an 'abrupt and unfriendly manner' which made it 'unnecessarily harsh'. It was in the company's interests that Hollins should continue as an ordinary director. It would also be desirable to retain his services as a joint managing director, but with clearly defined responsibilities, and subject to control by the board.

The report's most important recommendation concerned the composition of the board. There were 'too many employee directors'. In particular, the chairman should be independent of departmental interests. He should be a man of wide business experience, brought in from outside the firm. At least two other independent directors, not employed in the management of the firm, should be appointed. Arthur Hollins' own nominees for these posts were not considered suitable, however, and Plender offered to assist in the selection. Finally, he expressed the opinion that the board should meet more frequently than in the past and that it should be supplied with much fuller information.

This insistence on the need for a large independent element in the company's direction—at least three out of eight directors—was said to be based on extensive evidence, obtained from the directors and fourteen other witnesses. With the board reconstituted as proposed, it was expected that managerial duties and responsibilities would be more clearly defined and activities more closely controlled. Further, it was hoped that the presence of independent directors would ensure a more objective approach to the problems of policy making.

It is unfortunate that no record has survived of the evidence obtained by Plender. All we have are the board minutes and the firm's accounts. The minutes are less informative than one would wish; they record the decisions taken, but reports of argument and discussions are generally scanty. However, one gets a clear impression of the growing conflict between Hollins and his colleagues, which made a break inevitable. Yet we cannot doubt Hollins' concern for the long-term interests of the firm which his family had founded; and in the difficult post-war years it was not easy to see what was best for the firm.

On the issue concerning the American company, which precipitated the crisis, Hollins had a case. The company was losing money and, despite the assistance ultimately provided, accumulated losses, amounting to £65,930, had to be written off at the end of 1925. Then, after a brief recovery, losses were again recorded. As regards trading in bought-in goods, he also had a case, but it was a matter of degree; should such trade be regarded as marginal, or should it become a major activity? Plender's advice to keep it 'within reasonable and proper limits' suggests some sympathy with Hollins's attitude; and it is worth noting that after Hollins's departure the proportion of cloth and garments bought outside did in fact decline. There is also evidence in the accounts to show that the gross profit margin on bought-in cotton goods, for instance, was substantially less than on Viyella and other proprietary cloths.

When all is said, however, there remains the fact that, on controversial policy issues, Hollins was generally found in opposition to his fellow directors. He failed to persuade them and then tried to use his wide powers as managing director to frustrate them. Eventually the leading personalities rebelled and combined to depose him.

The Plender report was accepted by the majority of the directors, who proceeded to act on it in the expectation that their decisions would be confirmed at the next annual general meeting of shareholders. In the meantime both parties issued circulars to shareholders explaining their positions and asking for support.

The first step was the appointment, on Plender's recommendation, of an independent chairman in the person of Sir Ernest Jardine. He was head of a well-known Nottingham firm of lace-machine builders, which was now developing as a diversified group, extending into typewriters and even concrete. Jardine also held directorships in other textile firms. Charles Hill, who had reluctantly assumed the chairmanship on the dismissal of Hollins, now became deputy chairman.

Hare was confirmed in his appointment as managing director, though without the wide powers conferred on his predecessor. Nothing more was heard of the compromise proposal for sharing the office with Arthur Hollins. In furtherance of the report's recommendation to reduce the executive element on the board, two departmental managers, Shaw and Clark, who had recently been added, agreed to resign and become assistant directors without votes. Only one independent director was brought in besides the chairman. He was Charles Pain, a local accountant. The other newcomer was H. W. Benskin, who joined the board, after his appointment as manager of the wool department, with responsibility for wool buying.

Hollins remained on the new board for only a short time. He protested against the changes, in advance of the shareholders' meeting, and, after this had confirmed them, his opposition continued on matters of policy. Soon he ceased to attend and so lost his seat on the board. His departure brought to an end the Hollins dynasty extending over five generations, although another member of the family, Henry Hollins, served for some years as an executive, until he resigned in 1935.

Another link with the past was severed by the departure of H. A. Dowson. He had only recently joined the board when he became manager of the legal department, but his forebears had been trustees of the old partnership and were closely associated with the Hollins family. In the conflict culminating in Arthur Hollins's dismissal from the chairmanship, and in his continuing opposition afterwards, Dowson had been his consistent supporter. His agreement with the company was cancelled in 1924.

Of those who had been members of the former private company, only Hill now remained on the board. Edgar Paget also stayed on— the last member of the family which had been so long associated with the Hollins. There were, however, two others who had been schooled in the old traditions: Hare, now managing director, who had been appointed as secretary in 1908, when the public company was formed, and Charles Warren, whose service went back to 1911.

CHAPTER NINE

The Seedhill Acquisition

THE year 1924, in which Sir Ernest Jardine took over the chairmanship of Hollins, was one of restrained optimism in the business
world. The boom and slump of the immediate post-war years had
run their course, though there was still much unemployment.
Prices had settled down at about 65 per cent above the 1913 level
and the national income in real terms was about the same as in that
year. The return to the gold standard in 1925 handicapped exports,
but the next few years were on the whole a period of modest expansion.

For Hollins, external conditions were in several respects favourable. As regards raw materials, there was no longer any fear of depreciating stocks; the price of wool, especially merino, was rising,
and there was a welcome improvement in the cotton trade. On the
demand side too, prospects were encouraging. The firm's traditional product, hosiery yarn, was still important, accounting for
about one-quarter of total sales. The hosiery industry was now re-
suming its pre-war growth and in the next few years was to expand
remarkably. A boom was developing in hand knitting also, bringing
an increasing demand for coloured yarns. Viyella cloths were still
pre-eminent in their own field, and the wartime introduction,
Clydella, was doing particularly well, as a lower-priced but high-
quality fabric. Again, the growing market for ready-made garments
offered good opportunities to the firm which had been a pioneer in
the field.

Hollins now had substantial liquid resources with which to
finance expansion. Bank cash fluctuated considerably with the
seasonal buying of raw materials, but it was generally substantial.
At the end of 1925 it reached a peak at £309,000, of which £59,000

was on deposit account. Net profit improved in 1924 to £131,055 but the dividend on ordinary shares was prudently kept to 7½ per cent.

One of the first moves of the new board was to increase advertising expenditure. This was no longer tied to turnover; it was directed so as to give a stimulus where it seemed to be needed, to assist the introduction of new lines and to enable the firm to break into new markets. Thus in 1926 the advertising appropriation increased to £30,000. In 1927 the vote was for £50,000, including £10,000 for overseas, and a further £13,000 was authorised for emergency, or special advertising. Two years later total expenditure on advertising and patterns was £87,848. For a firm selling under its own trade marks, and largely dispensing with wholesalers, advertising expenditure was still quite modest; even the highest figure represented only about 5 per cent of total sales. But some members of the board were still sceptical about the value of advertising as a means of creating demand. They stressed the advantages of direct personal selling, and Hollins continued to rely heavily on this method both in the home market and overseas. Advertising and personal selling were, of course, complementary; sales representatives, and their retail customers, needed to be backed by advertising, and advertising needed to be followed up by salesmen. These also provided a market intelligence service. Although no systematic market research was undertaken, the sales department was well supplied with market information. The practice of direct selling to shops kept the firm in close contact with the retail trade at home, and it had regular reports from its overseas branches and agencies.

Hollins's trade was now more dependent on piece goods and garments than on yarn sales. The latter were still important, and yarns for hand-knitting were doing particularly well, but the trade with hosiery manufacturers began to suffer from foreign competition. Among established lines of piece goods, Clydella continued to do very well in both home and overseas markets. In Viyella cloth, new designs in line with fashion trends were introduced and Viyella sheets were again offered. At the same time a new cloth, made from Viyella yarn and rayon, appeared under the name of Visylka. In the garments branch there were several innovations including Viyella socks and a widening range of children's wear. Total net sales of all lines reached £1,789,206 in 1929. This was still much less than in 1921, but it will be remembered that in this year prices were higher, and more than half the value of sales was offset by cloth purchases; in 1928 cloth bought was less than a quarter of total sales.

At meetings of the reconstituted board, price policy in relation to sales was not often discussed. When it was, the emphasis was usually on the virtue of stability. However, a few concessions were made to representations from the sales department on the need for more competitive prices. For instance, a considerable reduction was sanctioned for knitting wools, and demand soon responded. There was also the case of Aza cloth, for which a reduced price was fixed after reports that it was not selling well. But, for established lines, firm prices were the rule. It was even suggested in 1925 that the Viyella price should be raised, though this was rejected by the board. In 1930, when trading conditions everywhere were again deteriorating, the chairman, in his speech to shareholders, re-affirmed the policy of maintaining the prices of standard lines so as not to jeopardise the goodwill of their retailing customers.

Apart from the reluctance to reduce prices, there seems to have been no lack of commercial enterprise and yet the improvement in sales was less than might have been expected under the fairly favourable conditions we have described. The record for the years 1926-9 is shown in Table 6.

It will be noted that home sales, after improving in 1927, had a disappointing setback in 1928, and that this occurred in the field of finished goods where Hollins had, for many years, directed their main efforts. On the other hand exports did surprisingly well, in view of the difficulties experienced by British textiles generally. Indeed the firm's dependence on overseas trade increased over the period, so that exports accounted for nearly 40 per cent of sales.

TABLE 6

Cloth, Garments, Hosiery and Knitting	*1926* £	*1927* £	*1928* £	*1929* £
Home	727,427	756,726	711,551	791,517
Overseas	491,216	537,471	558,486	566,082
Mechanical Yarns				
Home	302,784	314,375	306,318	306,012
Overseas	112,537	132,166	108,032	125,595
	1,633,964	1,740,738	1,684,387	1,789,206

With no marked increase in sales there was little justification for expanding productive capacity. There was, in fact, persistent short-time working at Pleasley throughout the 1920s, reports on which were regularly supplied to the board. Nevertheless considerable investment was undertaken, particularly in the second half of the decade. This was largely in the form of improved machinery and equipment. New looms, mules and ring spinning frames were installed and more electrical equipment was introduced. £70,000 was spent on a new power plant and extended sidings at Pleasley mills. More sewing machines were bought for the garments factory and the offices were mechanised to an increasing extent.

Some of these improvements in plant involved new buildings. For instance, important extensions were made to the wool department at Pleasley. The new sorting room was claimed to be the finest in the country and the same unit accommodated a new scouring and carbonising plant and improved drying and blowing equipment. These developments were designed to reduce costs and to give better control of the blending on which the quality of yarn and cloth depended.

Attention was also given to the needs of the London warehouse and salerooms. In 1925 Hollins' sales centre was still at Newgate Street, where it was supplied with hosiery, garments and knitting wool from Nottingham and Pleasley, and with cloth from Glasgow. The location of commercial activities in London was considered

essential and, until 1924, board meetings were often held at Newgate Street. Now the sales department pressed the claim for more
and better accommodation. There was some talk in 1925 of buying
part of the old post office site, at an estimated cost of £200,000, but
the board failed to agree on the proposal. Shortly afterwards, however, the firm bought the lease of a building in Old Change, just
east of St Paul's and in 1926 the London office and warehouse were
moved to these much bigger premises. The sum of £22,000 was
spent on structural alterations and equipment, bringing the total
cost to some £46,000.

This development emphasised the dispersal of activities which
had long been characteristic of Hollins' organisation; two years
earlier, however, another move had taken place, which, though it
was never planned as such, turned out to be the first stage in a
process of centralisation. In 1924 the head office, which had remained at Pleasley since leaving Warser Gate, Nottingham, in 1891,
was transferred back to Nottingham, where it occupied the top floor
of the garments factory building on Castle Boulevard. It was here
that board meetings were now held until a new building was
erected on the frontage of the site in the early 1930s.

The firm's total capital expenditure over the period from the end
of 1924 to mid 1929, and the main items involved, were as follows:

TABLE 7

Nature of Expenditure	Amount (£)
Land	11,371
Warehouses	76,181
Other Buildings	57,411
Machinery	72,607
Engines	26,453
Electrical Plant	27,473
Utensils	25,924
Fixtures	8,091
Total	305,511

It is hard to say how much of this represented increased production capacity. A good deal of it was clearly for replacement—for

instance, the item for utensils; and much old machinery, some of it dating back to 1876, was replaced. The installation of new power plant too, was partly replacement expenditure but the substitution of new equipment, for what was old and technically obsolete, did, in itself, increase capacity, apart from any additions to plant. It was also calculated to reduce manufacturing costs and, given full employment, the results might have been very favourable. But with no marked increases in sales revenue the depreciation charges imposed a heavy burden. The biggest item, investment in warehouses, is open to criticism. The greater part was attributable to the London office and it seems strange that no one at that time appears to have considered an alternative location in Nottingham. When this was decided upon, only five years later, it made the London warehouse largely redundant.

An investment decision in which the issues were much clearer, concerned the acquisition of the Seedhill Finishing Co Ltd in 1928. For many years Hollins had been a remarkable example of vertical integration in the textile trades. Its activities included spinning, weaving, and garment making, as well as direct selling to retailers; but there was one stage in the manufacture of most of its products, of vital importance to quality, which it did not include; most of the dyeing and finishing were still done by independent firms, one of which was Seedhill of Paisley.

The origin of Hollins's connection with Seedhill has already been described. There is no doubt that the success of Viyella owed much to the technical competence and enterprise of this small family firm, constituted as a private company.[1] The connection was broken in 1912 when a fire put Seedhill temporarily out of business and Hollins turned to another Paisley firm, Wm. Fulton and Sons, which had also introduced an unshrinkable finish. Some of Hollins's dyeing was placed also with a member of the Bradford Dyers Association.

[1] The account of Seedhill given in this chapter is based on a memoir written by James Ross.

Within a year Seedhill was back in production with a new plant
under the able and energetic direction of James Ross, to whose
efforts the reconstruction of the business was mainly due. But its
approach to Hollins was disappointing and only a portion of the
former trade was retrieved. One reason for Hollins's attitude accord-
ding to Ross, was their desire to take over Seedhill as their own
finishing plant and the possibility of getting it at a bargain price if
the reconstruction failed. The war, however, put Seedhill on its
feet. Moreover it became a member of the newly formed Flannel
Finishers' Association and, though prices were government controlled, they were rising. Hollins now decided, in 1916, to make a
cash offer for the company. The Seedhill shareholders would have
been willing to accept £48,000, though James Ross was reluctant to
agree; but the negotiations produced no more than £38,000 from
the other side and this ended the matter at that time.

During the war, and in the brief post-war boom, Seedhill did
well, but the slump of 1921 convinced Ross that they must rely
more on dyeing than on finishing. More capital was raised, a new
dyehouse was built, and the firm soon acquired a high reputation as
a dyer of piece goods; it was particularly successful with the new
artificial silk. Then it went in for calico printing, using the nearby
Arkleston Works, which had been acquired at the end of the war,
and installed a new stean-raising and electricity-generating plant
with a loan of £25,000 from the Trade Facilities Board. The
Arkleston business continued to grow, and in 1927 the question of
additional investment arose. But before going further in this
direction it was important to ascertain the intention of Hollins, on
whom Seedhill was still heavily dependent. Could it hope to get
more of Hollins' finishing work? Might Hollins still be interested in
buying Seedhill? Or were they planning to set up their own finishing
plant, as had been hinted from time to time?

In 1928 this uncertainty was resolved. A Scottish Dyers Association was being formed to amalgamate a number of firms, including
Wm. Fulton & Sons, and the syndicate made an offer for Seed-

hill. The move promised a rise in finishing prices and Ross was now able to press Hollins for a decision on their relations with Seedhill, a matter which he had already raised without result. At first Hollins offered to place all their business with Seedhill on condition that it remained independent; but this was too indefinite. The syndicate had made a cash offer of £3 a share and the Seedhill directors were tempted to accept. Hollins thereupon came forward with a counter-offer to take over all the 50,000 Seedhill shares at £2 17s 6d a share in exchange for 115,000 of Hollins ordinary shares at 25s. This offer was accepted, the transaction involving an increase in Hollins's issued ordinary capital.

Under the agreement Ross joined Hollins's board while retaining his position as chairman and managing director of Seedhill. The new Seedhill board included Jardine and Hare from Hollins. For a time the agreement worked well. Ross with his technical ability was a considerable acquisition to the Hollins's board and he himself valued the new relationship with a firm which, as he afterwards recorded, he had always looked upon 'as having the possibilities of being the foremost textile concern in the country'. Soon after the take-over the relationship was further consolidated by Hollins deciding to pay off the Seedhill debentures, the balance of the Treasury loan, and the bank overdraft, amounting in all to some £70,000. On this sum Seedhill now paid interest to Hollins.

It was not long, however, before dissension appeared. The Seedhill Company's activities were, of course, distributed between Seedhill itself and the subsidiary works at Arkleston, a mile or so away. Although each unit specialised to some extent, there was a good deal of to-and-fro movement between them. Hollins favoured concentration at Seedhill, and when a site adjacent to the main works became available this was bought for £10,000. Plans were made for a new works to replace Arkleston and also for a warehouse from which finished cloth could be despatched to customers, instead of being sent back to Glasgow. However, with the deterioration of trade in 1930 and their commitment to the Viyella House project in Nottingham, Hollins became more cautious about capital expenditure, and, when it turned out that the Seedhill scheme would cost £60,000, it was promptly dropped. This left the £10,000 already spent as an addition to Seedhill's loan from Hollins, on which Seedhill had to pay interest.

During 1931 and 1932 relations between Ross and his colleagues on the Hollins board were further strained. At the time of the take-over Hollins seem to have had no clear idea about the use of Seedhill and its subsidiary. Ross assumed that besides getting more, if not the whole, of Hollins's finishing he would be free to develop in any direction in which profitable business could be found. But as the trade depression worsened it became difficult to get other business. Ross claimed that he was handicapped by shortage of capital; he needed improved plant to reduce his costs. Hollins for their part were opposed to any investment not connected with its own trade. It had, in Ross's view, 'come to regard Seedhill far too much as being merely a finishing shop for Hollins' products'. This was not his idea of how the subsidiary should be run; it was too big and its resources were too varied for this limited purpose.

One proposal made by Ross was certainly worth more considera-tion than it appears to have received. In connection with his work on artificial sink he had set up a small research department in the charge of a graduate chemist. This soon proved its worth and when in 1933 the Hollins board were discussing the possibility of a re-search department for the whole organisation, Ross suggested that a nucleus already existed at Seedhill, and that he had the man to develop it. However, before anything was decided, the chemist left to serve a competitor, and no more was heard of the matter.

By this time no proposal emanating from Ross was likely to find much favour with the Hollins' board, which was becoming increas-ingly critical of the Seedhill management. Two years before, the subsidiary had been told that no capital expenditure should be authorised for the finishing plant unless required by Hollins for

Plate 14. Staff photograph of Hollins

A. R. Hollins	Claud Hollins	H. E. Hollins	Charles Hill	W. H. H. Shaw
Director	Director, Radford	Chairman and Managing	Director	Manager, Radford
		Director		

Second row, fourth from right: Charles Warren, Sales Manager

Plate 15. Viyella House, Nottingham

processing their own cloth. As regards investment for developing outside trade, this would only be allowed to the extent of any surplus after Seedhill had paid a 20 per cent dividend on its nominal capital, equal to $7\frac{1}{2}$ per cent on the purchase price. This $7\frac{1}{2}$ per cent was the return Hollins had anticipated from their investment, but the dividends received had been less than 4 per cent a year. A low return might have been tolerable if Hollins had benefited from low finishing prices. But trade depression had intensified competition and Hollins found their own subsidiary more expensive than independent finishers. Eventually it secured a 10 per cent reduction; but this threatened to make Seedhill still less profitable, so Hollins instituted a critical survey of Seedhill's costs; these were found to have risen, and Hollins insisted on a still tighter control, on current, as well as capital, expenditure. According to Ross, however, the increased cost of finishing was mainly due to reduced volume of work, including that from Hollins. The printing trade with outside customers was increasing but prices were very poor.

The story of Hollins's relations with Seedhill during this period is an interesting illustration of the problems of vertical integration. Hollins's motives in acquiring Seedhill were quite plain. Finishing was the only important stage in its manufacture which was outside their own organisation. So long as there were several firms competing for its orders Hollins were safeguarded against excessive charges and inferior quality and were assured of prompt service. But in 1928 their interests were threatened by a combine which was to include the two firms on which Hollins mainly depended. Hollins might have set up their own finishing plant and the possibility was considered. But there were difficulties. A new finishing plant would have required a big investment not only in buildings and equipment but in expert staff. The existing finishers had proprietary rights in the processes used on Hollins' goods. Then there was the question of scale: what size of plant would be appropriate to Hollins' capacity, making allowances for the varying demands of the cloth department? Moreover, would such a plant be less than the optimum size

K

for the finishing industry, so that unit costs would be higher than in specialist firms?

There was evidently a strong case for acquiring a going concern of proved ability to meet all Hollins' requirements in high-class finishing. But Seedhill, with its Arkleston subsidiary, was more than this; it was a diversified business adapted to a wider environment than that offered by Hollins, whose trade represented only about 20 per cent of Seedhill's turnover. Ross, who had built up the business on these lines, wanted to keep it so. His ideas were quite incompatible with those of Hollins, yet he seems to have been regarded as indispensible for running Seedhill. Then again, the circumstances in which the take-over occurred were not the most favourable from Hollins's point of view. Although they had been considering the possibility for some years, in the end it had to decide quickly and under pressure. It was not easy at this time to determine the present net worth of Seedhill, but the price in Hollins's shares seems rather high.

What weighed with Hollins, however, was the prospective value of Seedhill as part of their organisation. Hollins were not without experience in this kind of transaction and it was not unreasonable to suppose that the success with which weaving firms had been absorbed thirty years before would be repeated in finishing. But before this could be proved there came the great depression of the early 1930s. In trade depression, when competition is intensified and price cutting is rife, vertically-organised firms are at a disadvantage compared with those which are free to buy materials and services in the open market. After 1929 Hollins would have been in a strong position in dealing with outside finishers. As it was they had to do the best they could with the firm to which they had committed so much capital. Nor was it easy to see what was best for Seedhill. Ross thought he knew, but his ideas usually involved still more investment. The Hollins directors, and particularly the managing director, insisted that expenses must be cut. They also tried to liquidate part of the assets by selling the Arkleston works, but it was not possible to reach agreement with Ross on the terms of the proposed sale.

It was not until many years later than the full value of the Seed-hill acquisition came to be appreciated. All through the 1930s there was friction between the Seedhill management and the Hollins board. James Ross never ceased to regard Seedhill as his own business and he claimed the right to run it in his own way. Highly competent on the technical side, and an enthusiast for technical training, he had little time for office work. He knew his costs, he would say, and had no need for fancy costing systems. He believed in close personal supervision; if this was efficient, the costs of production would take care of themselves. His methods were in marked contrast to the sophisticated techniques that Hollins began to introduce, and with which Seedhill was expected to conform, but in the difficult years that lay ahead, Seedhill was by no means the least efficient part of Hollins's organisation.

Another investment decision of this period, which was less fortunate, was the establishment of a manufacturing plant in the USA. Reference has already been made to the American subsidiary formed to act as a sales organisation in 1919 and to the losses sustained by this enterprise. There had always been trouble with customs regulations, which discriminated against finished cloth. Then, with the onset of trade depression in America in 1930, the tariff was sharply raised. Hollins's export trade had already suffered severely and the decision to start making cloth in America was prompted by the desire to alleviate the position. Forestdale Mill, Rhode Island, was bought in 1931 at what seemed a very favourable price, £4,300, but a further £20,000 had to be spent on weaving and finishing plant. As might have been expected, it proved difficult to delegate responsibility to the local management, while supervision by the remote parent company was equally difficult. The maintenance of quality was a particular problem. Finally, with the start of the New Deal programme, labour costs rose substantially. Over the two years to the end of 1933 trading losses amounted to £31,193 and it was then decided to cease production and retain the works on a maintenance basis. Taking into account the depreciation of the assets which this decision involved, the net losses sustained by Hollins in America were computed at £68,523.

Throughout these years of trade depression and increasing stringency there was one project that was pressed forward with determination. When the decision was taken to develop the Castle Boulevard site in Nottingham as Hollins's headquarters, the depression had already begun. Nevertheless a contract for £42,000 was placed early in 1932 and Viyella House, as the new premises were called, was ready for occupation in July 1933. Much of the building was used for warehousing and this seemed to settle the question of where the merchandise department and sales direction should be located. But among the sales people themselves there was still opposition to so much concentration in Nottingham as against London—an issue which was to be disputed for a considerable time. If concentration in Nottingham was the right policy, the board's decision to go ahead with Viyella House, in the current state of trade, was commendable. It obtained an impressive building at a reasonable price; and, although premises are not always a reliable indication of a firm's standing, the appearance of Viyella House certainly contributed something to Hollins's prestige, at a time when it needed support.

CHAPTER TEN

Marketing Problems

THE world-wide depression of the early 1930s was particularly severe in the textile trades where so many firms were heavily dependent on exports and for Hollins it brought troubles that persisted in one form or another throughout the entire decade. The change in the firm's fortunes came abruptly. In his review of the year 1929 the chairman told the shareholders that conditions in the textile industry generally had been far from satisfactory and business had been difficult. Hollins' sales had increased, however, and although net profit was £15,000 less than the average for the past six years, investments in improved plant, calculated to reduce costs, were expected to at least restore the position. But 1930 brought no relief; on the contrary, sales revenue fell sharply and for the first time in the history of Hollins as a public company a loss was recorded on the year's trading, amounting to £67,190.

This loss was partly due to excessive stocks accumulated in London. The Viyella stock, for instance, was 24,890 pieces at the end of 1929 as compared with 9,488 pieces in 1922; for cotton goods the figures were 34,059 and 9,899 respectively. Much of the cloth was in old patterns and the losses attributable to it should have been cut earlier. Now, with sales prospects worsening, these stocks were heavily written down. For the next two years a modest profit was shown, though sales declined still further. Then in 1933 another loss, of £5,381, was sustained on a yet lower turnover.

Of course, part of the fall in profits was attributable to the experience of Seedhill and the American subsidiary but a further item was the exchange loss on the transfer of a substantial bank balance from Australia after the currency had depreciated. The main cause however was the decline of Hollins's sales revenue in relation to costs. Some costs naturally fell, under the same conditions as were depressing sales. Wool, for instance, became very much cheaper. In 1924 the 2,095,000 lb stock of lambs wool and tops was valued at £342,500; in 1928 2,456,000 lb were worth £287,500; at the end of 1933 the stock amounted to 4,600,000 lb while its value was only £265,000. Wages could be, and were, reduced, as were also some salaries. But capital charges were less flexible; indeed, the investment decisions of the 1920s had increased these charges, for depreciation rates were prudently maintained.

How to restore the comapny's prosperity was a many-sided problem and in 1933 some shareholders were beginning to doubt the capacity of the directors to solve it. At the annual general meeting in April 1934 they proposed the appointment of a committee to investigate the position of the company and its future policy. Although this was heavily defeated on a poll of shareholders, the board nevertheless invited the co-operation of a consultative committee, consisting of the larger shareholders' nominees and having the power to co-opt a representative of the smaller shareholders. This committee of six persons, with an independent accountant as secretary, presented its report to the directors in January 1935.

Much of what follows is based on this report. It will be understood that specific criticisms of individual members of the board and management cannot now be verified, but there is plenty of evidence in the existing archives of the firm to support the committee's general findings.

In reviewing the recent history of the business, the report naturally gave prominence to the decline in sales revenue. In accordance with the usual practice of public companies the figures had not been published to shareholders; they are reproduced as set out in the report in Table 8.

The sales figures in themselves provide ample justification for the shareholders' anxiety about the way things were going with the firm. The sharp drop in 1930 and the further fall in 1931 could be explained in terms of the great depression which affected business

Table 8

	1929	1930	1931	1932	1933
	£	£	£	£	£
Viyella					
Home:					
Pieces	23,240	19,411	18,146	17,228	21,322
Sterling	168,952	136,832	125,750	109,880	108,814
Export:					
Pieces	22,440	16,411	15,294	12,977	10,567
Sterling	156,620	112,531	102,908	86,693	67,855
Other Piece Goods					
Home:					
Pieces	49,244	43,668	43,951	33,819	30,703
Sterling	267,679	215,748	176,616	121,534	90,787
Export:					
Pieces	29,715	21,309	19,464	16,234	13,609
Sterling	112,971	73,376	60,694	50,199	40,449
Knittings					
Home:					
Sterling	79,804	107,211	127,432	243,171	163,549
Export:					
Sterling	8,447	10,432	17,499	29,799	29,654
Yarns					
Home:					
Sterling	321,227	193,272	141,489	127,534	149,778
Export:					
Sterling	125,592	44,262	32,887	33,609	32,879
Hoisery					
Home:					
Dozens	106,453	114,756	120,405	108,811	124,310
Sterling	139,478	139,470	136,129	117,597	130,528
Export:					
Dozens	39,008	30,656	26,902	23,463	22,271
Sterling	44,334	34,297	28,320	23,854	22,644
Garments					
Home:					
Dozens	19,987	20,844	23,455	22,839	25,712
Sterling	132,865	134,783	146,352	132,855	137,962
Export:					
Dozens	1,400	1,180	898	784	655
Sterling	8,436	7,034	4,414	4,283	3,393
Sundry Sales					
Home:	13,355	7,800	6,900	13,670	40,409
Export:	262,979	227,964	123,393	126,247	121,695
Totals					
Home:	1,123,360	935,116	860,668	866,241	821,827
Export:	719,339	509,986	370,115	354,684	318,569
GRAND TOTALS	1,842,739	1,445,012	1,230,783	1,220,925	1,140,496

everywhere. Hollins was particularly vulnerable because of its heavy dependence on exports. It was here that the decline was most marked, amounting to 55 per cent of the 1929 value. The fall in the purchasing power of overseas markets, higher tariffs and exchange restrictions were obvious causes. Hollins's experience with exports of piece goods and garments was very much in line with that of other British manufacturers. But it is hard to account for the disastrous fall in yarn exports to only a quarter of the 1929 figure; for total British exports of woollen and worsted yarns never fell much below half of the 1929 value and recovered to well over half in 1933. Home sales fell by 30 per cent over the period; and what was especially disturbing was the set-back in 1933, after the slight improvement of the previous year. For by 1933 the worst of the depression was over in Britain; moreover protective tariffs had been introduced, which should have helped some branches of Hollins's trade. Sales of some lines did indeed improve; garments and hosiery remained buoyant throughout the period, while sales of knittings and sundries increased substantially. But home sales of piece goods reached their lowest level in 1933. Yarn sales, which were already falling before the depression and slumped heavily after 1929, recovered somewhat with the improvement in the hosiery trade in 1933.

Turnover statistics, however, have only a limited significance in assessing the health of a business. What matters is the profit on sales and this depends òn costs, including selling costs. Much of the fall in turnover, on which the committee put such emphasis, is a reflection of the general fall in values, including those of raw materials. Some reduction in selling prices could therefore have been conceded without encroaching on profits. For piece goods, hosiery and garments, the table shows quantities as well as values. It will be seen that the volume of hosiery and garments sold increased substantially over the period, while the number of cloth pieces sold fell far less than their value. But, except for Viyella, the quantities still relate to broad categories, so that no firm conclusions about price policy and its effect on sales can be drawn. In the case of 'other piece goods' particularly, it looks as though the trend was towards the cheaper lines in the range. Viyella, however, is in a class by itself and the comparison between quantities and values has more significance.

Until 1932 hardly any change was made in Viyella prices, and export prices were practically the same as home prices. The fabric had always been rather expensive and in view of the general state of trade it is surprising that Viyella sales held up so well. The experience does perhaps provide some justification for the policy of firm prices which was declared in 1930 and 1931. When prices were reduced in 1932 and particularly in 1933, the response of demand was hardly encouraging. This, however, was partly due to inefficient sales organisation and failure to give adequate support through advertising. The consultative committee made no references to price policy but it was very critical of selling methods.

By 1933 it had become clear to most members of the board that a general revision of price lists must be undertaken. But before this could be done the costing system had to be overhauled. Under existing practice goods were transferred from one department to another in the course of manufacture at prices that often bore little relation to their true costs of production; and there was a similar arbitrary element in fixing selling margins. It was thus impossible to determine the relative profitability of the various lines. In more prosperous times it might have seemed satisfactory that a good profit was earned on the firm's operations as a whole. But now total profit was small, or even negative, and a detailed analysis of operations was called for.

When this was undertaken, on the advice of the firm's auditors, it was found that the true cost of producing certain lines was far less than had been assumed. For instance, on the new cost basis certain knitting wools would show a gross profit on sales of 50 per cent. Here was an obvious opportunity for reducing prices to stimulate sales. The increased sales would then react favourably on costs, by reducing idle capacity in the mills and giving better recovery of overheads.

By the end of 1933 revised costings had been generally adopted and a thorough revision of selling prices agreed upon. Not all prices were reduced; for certain patterns of Viyella they remained unchanged and there were a few increases among other lines; but the new prices were generally down. These reduced prices were not always a reflection of lower costs attributed to manufacturing processes; some were made possible by cutting the margin on sales, which was often 40 and in some cases 50 per cent, The policy of resale price maintenance was still adhered to and generally the retailer's margin was left at between 30 and 33 per cent, in fixing the new minimum retail prices.

This revision of prices had taken place before the appointment of the consultative committee but its full effect had not yet been seen. The committee, however, did not believe that mere passive response to market pressures would restore sales. Hollins was faced with 'the difficulty of selling an expensive article in a world that (was) becoming more and more accustomed to mass production and cheap substitutes'. It needed to strengthen its sales organisation and adopt a vigorous sales policy.

There was undoubtedly much justification for the committee's criticisms of sales organisation and policy. In June 1931 Warren the director with general responsibility for sales had resigned following a dispute with Huskisson (recently appointed as managing director)[1] over the function of the London office. The managing director had thereupon assumed control of sales policy and endeavoured to maintain contact with important customers. Executive responsibility was delegated to a sales manager, but there was disagreement over his proposals for sales organisation and he resigned after two years. In 1934 the company's secretary, a chartered accountant, was prevailed upon to take over the post of sales manager, with the rank of assistant director, but all important

[1] See p 160.

matters were apparently still referred to the managing director. Thus during this critical period there was, as the committee said, no firm control of sales policy. The sales function was inadequately represented on the board and there was a lack of continuity at the executive level.

One result of the change in sales direction had been the shift of the centre of activity from London to Nottingham. The committee criticised this move as tending to diminish active contact with the market. More important, however, was the hesitancy in sales policy and in particular the lack of effective sales promotion. In the search for economies prompted by the trade depression, advertising expenditure had been cut, until in 1933 it was no more than £35,000 as compared with £60,000 in 1929. In submitting the proposed appropriation to the board the managing director explained that he had endeavoured to cut advertising to the absolute minimum figure. It was £14,000 less than the amount advocated by their advertising agents. The allowance for overseas markets, £12,000, was relatively generous; but the total effort was timid for a firm selling branded goods and depending so heavily on retailers. Its effectiveness was further diminished by faulty disposition of resources. New lines needed support, but too often it seems to have been given at the expense of established lines which the firm could not afford to neglect. The committee also heard complaints about lack of continuity in advertising effort and lack of co-ordination between design, sales and the advertising agents.

Apart from the overriding need for economy which, in the board's view, justified a reduction in advertising expenditure, there was the question of advertising versus personal selling. Even at the reduced figure Hollins were spending more on advertising than on salesmen, and whenever the advertising appropriation was discussed some directors had doubts as to whether the firm got enough value for its money. It is of course impossible to measure the effect on sales of a given amount of advertising; for the impact of this one factor cannot be isolated among all the influences that affect sales.

In contrast, personal selling seems to produce definite results. But in a trade like Hollins's, both methods were needed. Advertising prepared the way for the traveller. If advertising was reduced, retail customers were less willing to stock the goods. If travellers were reduced, the advertising was not properly followed up and part of its value was lost. It was a matter of getting the right balance between the two methods of sales promotion.

After the resignation of the sales director the emphasis shifted to personal selling, the organisation of which was changed. Formerly the home market had been covered by about thirty travellers, each carrying a full range of goods and serving a wide area. Now, on the advice of the new sales manager, the country was divided into a greater number of areas and the number of travellers increased to over one hundred. Further, the travellers tended to specialise in different lines of goods. These changes, with the prospect of a fall in earnings, were naturally resented by the established sales representatives. Some were retired with compensation, others found new employment, and within a short time the personnel of the sales force had been transformed. The younger men now brought in started at much lower salaries. The consultative committee found that the average remuneration of travellers in 1934 was £210 a year as against £700 in 1929. The reduction was of course partly due to the reduced value of sales on which commission was earned; but the committee certainly had reason to doubt whether the company could attract the kind of representative needed at this rate of pay.

Despite its increased size the cost of the sales force was almost exactly the same as before. This hardly supports the argument accepted by the directors that because they had more travellers they should spend less on advertising. The fact was that total expenditure on selling had been reduced at a time when, in 1933, the home market at least was becoming more responsive. This partly explains Hollins's failure to share in the revival that was setting in. A further factor was the disruption of personal relationships between travellers and customers. It was a temporary disturbance, but the transition to the new system would have been smoother if the directors had taken care to secure the co-operation of the older travellers, as the sales manager had advised.

In the opinion of the committee further damage to the firm's goodwill with customers had been caused by faulty liaison between sales and production. When trade was steady, prompt delivery could be ensured by maintaining ample stocks, though with fashion goods this policy always involved some risks for the manufacturer. But, with the onset of depression, mounting stocks naturally caused anxiety. Much of these had to be sold at a loss, and it was clear that making for stock must be watched very carefully in the future. Economy in stocks, however, can lead to delay in deliveries to customers. Though desirable in itself, as saving working capital and reducing risk, it does make increased demands on co-ordination between sales and production. This aspect of the firm's organisation was strongly criticised by the committee. According to its report there had at one stage been a breakdown in deliveries accompanied by many cancellations of orders. The managing director was in America at the time looking into the affairs of the subsidiary company and the sales manager lacked the necessary authority to improve relations with the production departments. It was soon after this that he resigned.

These developments in sales organisation involved no fundamental changes in Hollins's traditional marketing methods. But one innovation was tried which, though it failed, is of some interest. Through their practice of selling direct to shops Hollins were already in close touch with the retail trade; their selected outlets, supported merchandise displays with point-of-sale advertising, and controlled resale prices. But should the firm go further and acquire shops of its own, or at least a financial interest in retailing? At a board meeting in 1930 the managing director persuaded his colleagues that they should. Soon afterwards negotiations were opened with Griffiths Bros (Brentford) Ltd, which had a chain of nineteen shops in the London area. This firm was short of working capital and Hollins undertook to provide £6,000 in the form of debentures. In return Griffiths was to push the sale of Hollins's goods. However, the venture was very short-lived. Within two years Griffiths was forced into liquidation through inability to reduce stocks to meet the demands of creditors. The member of the Hollins board who had advised them on the transaction now tendered his resignation and it was accepted. He was replaced by a director of a Nottingham department store. Efforts were also made to strengthen relations with large retailers by arrangements under which Hollins allowed a rebate on purchases of their goods when the retailers' turnover exceeded an agreed amount.

In the midst of all this concern with sales there was another aspect of the firm's commercial activities that demanded attention. Hollins's profits depended to a considerable extent on successful buying of raw materials, especially wool. Nearly all the wool came from Australia where Hollins was the main buyer of lambswool. Wool buying was a specialised business, requiring technical knowledge for assessing quality, and ability to judge market trends. Since 1924 Hollins's wool-buying department had been in the charge of a part-time director who was also a partner in a firm of wool merchants.

Although the raw materials position was frequently reviewed by the board and instructions were occasionally given to the wool buyer, his advice seems generally to have been followed until 1933. Towards the end of this year, however, the board's attitude became more critical. Wool stocks had grown to about 4,600,000 lb; this was nearly double the 1928 figure and was sufficient for eighteen months' requirements at the current rate of consumption. Lambswool accounted for rather more than half the stock and it was customary to hold a large stock of this material because it was essential for Viyella yarns and supplies were uncertain. But the present stock was certainly excessive, while the stock of other wools, which could always be bought as and when required, was grossly excessive. In the course of an inquiry into the valuation of the company's assets the firm's accountants were informed by the manufacturing departments that wool stocks could with safety be reduced by 50 per cent. This would release about £130,000 which, invested in gilt-edged securities, would produce £4,500 a year.

Further investigation ordered by the board showed that wool had been bought at unduly high prices and, moreover, that much of it was unsuitable for Hollins's products. In the face of these criticisms the wool buyer resigned from the board. But this was not the end of the matter. It appeared that the director, though employed by Hollins to buy for them in the open market, had been supplying wool through his own firm at a profit. Hollins claimed compensation and to avoid litigation a settlement was reached.

It is significant that the period with which the consultative committee was concerned, contains a number of features very similar to those of the crisis of ten years earlier. That crisis had been investigated, criticisms of the firm's management had been made, and recommendations offered. Yet the report sent to the directors in January 1935 makes the very same points: 'We have had evidence from a number of sources of what can only be described as cliques among the directors and senior employees. The cliques were not, in our opinion, altogether actuated by personal motives; but, however unwise in the methods adopted, they appear to have been prompted by a desire to forward the interests of a particular department or to remedy the unsatisfactory state of the general management. As a result, the board in fact did not exercise its prime function as a board, which should be to consider and decide upon the broad lines of general policy.' These words might well be a description of conditions in Arthur Hollins's time.

The main recommendation of the report on the earlier crisis was for the appointment of an independent chairman, and this was adopted. In Sir Ernest Jardine Hollins acquired, as chairman, a man of wide business experience and considerable personal prestige. But he was already sixty-four years of age when appointed in 1924 and, as time went on, ill-health often prevented his attendance at board meetings and even necessitated long absences abroad. The deputy-chairman, E. L. Paget, who had served on the board since 1908, and was a full-time executive on the production side, was generally respected, but was reluctant to assert himself in the absence of the chairman. Thus the company was weak at the very centre, and this, as the consultative committee reported, 'resulted in the absence of any definite and consistent policy being formulated and pursued either on the sales or production side. Coupled with this general lack of direction, there was an avowed constant cleavage of opinion and even personal disagreement amongst the various directors.'

Next to the chairman the most influential member of the board was the managing director. From all accounts Marcus Hare, who had been appointed in 1924, had just the qualities required for this office. His untimely death in 1929 was undoubtedly a grievous loss to the firm. His successor, A. Huskisson, brought in from outside, was an able and energetic man with considerable experience of the textile trades. But he seems to have been handicapped from the start by lack of support from a united board. In exasperation he took on more and more of the responsibility for running the firm. He had assumed general responsibility for sales in 1931 but he became heavily involved on the production side too, and in a critical period he had to make several visits to the USA in an endeavour to sort out the problems of the American subsidiary. Inability or unwillingness to delegate was his main fault, according to the consultative committee. It did, however, point out the difficulty of delegation in a firm that had no system for training efficient seconds-in-command.

In concluding its report the committee expressed the unanimous opinion that the business of William Hollins & Co Ltd was in the main sound. Its recent adverse fortunes were attributable primarily to lack of proper leadership and control on the part of the board. The directors had failed to formulate and pursue a consistent well-founded policy. As a board they had failed even to control the acti-

Plate 16. Weaving Shed, Boden Street, Glasgow

Plate 17. Garment factory, Hucknall, nr Nottingham

vities of their own members. Information on departmental activities was often inadequate or completely lacking; and though some improvements had recently been made, in particular the reform of costing methods, there was still not enough insistence on the need for regular and accurate records to measure efficiency.

The committee felt that the deficiencies in organisation could be remedied by a 'satisfactorily constituted directorate'. At an early meeting of the committee Sir Ernest Jardine had intimated his willingness to resign as the company needed a 'younger and more energetic man' at its head. The board accepted this resignation, and also the committee's recommendation for a new chairman. This was Sir Frederick Aykroyd, a prominent figure in the West Riding textile industry, who agreed to accept the chairmanship for a period of not more than three years.

The appointment was confirmed by the board in August 1934 and a few months later Douglas Hamilton was brought in as a part-time director. This strengthened the independent element; for at the time when the committee was set up, the board had, besides the chairman, only one independent member, and he was a newcomer. Moreover, Hamilton had the experience which, since the departure of Charles Warren, had been lacking on the board. He had for many years been engaged in textile exporting and was familiar with overseas markets.

Thus the principle of having an independent chairman and other part-time directors was reasserted. It had been strongly insisted upon at the time of the 1923 crisis; now however, it was given only a qualified approval. A more vigorous chairman might have been able to drive the executive directors as a team. But in any case an independent chairman, with other interests, had only a limited amount of time for Hollins' affairs. Further, these affairs were now in such a state that 'root and branch reforms' must be undertaken. The committee therefore insisted on the 'urgent need for the appointment of a vice-chairman who shall devote his whole time to a thorough and minute examination of all the company's activities'.

L

It was on this condition that Sir Frederick Aykroyd agreed to accept the chairmanship of the board. The committee had a candidate for the office they proposed, E. D. A. Herbert, and at a board meeting in July 1935 he was duly appointed. As Sir Edward Herbert he became, in later years, the dominant figure in the company.

CHAPTER ELEVEN

Depression and Reorganisation

WHEN, in April 1934, the board invited the co-operation of a shareholders' committee, it stated in a circular letter to shareholders that it 'welcomed any criticism of the company's policy which might advance the prosperity of the business'; moreover, the directors gave full facilities for the investigation, and they themselves had discussions with the committee. But, in fact, the board was not committed to accepting the report. Its attitude to the committee's findings is clearly indicated in the new chairman's letter, acknowledging receipt of the report on behalf of the board. 'In view of the fact that practically the whole of the report deals with matters prior to my appointment as chairman,' he writes, 'I have asked the various members of the board and the staff referred to in the report to submit to me, in writing, their observations. I am now in possession of these and find that in many cases their version of events is very much in conflict with the report itself.' The chairman of the consultative committee was informed that the board would 'fully consider all the suggestions of the committee', but no further undertaking was given.

Furthermore, the committee was to report to the directors, not to the general body of shareholders. For the latter a circular letter was produced, summarising the main recommendations in very general terms. Reference was made to the committee's criticism of the board's constitution and certain of its decisions, but for obvious reasons no specific criticisms were publicised. The shareholders were assured that in the committee's opinion the company was 'in the main, sound, and that deficiencies which it is of opinion have existed are capable of being remedied by a strengthening of the board'.

In these circumstances it is hard to assess the committee's influence on subsequent developments. The board was strengthened, or so it was hoped, by the appointment of a new chairman and a full-time vice-chairman. But it was for the board to decide what measures to take and how far to go in reorganising the company's activities and its management.

Certain organisational changes had been made, particularly on the sales side, before the committee's appointment. Expenditure had been reduced in many directions and the management's efforts to economise had been commended by the auditors. Then, in the early part of 1934, the board began to consider more fundamental changes. When the company had shown a loss in 1930, it had been possible to attribute this to the world-wide trade depression. The partial recovery in the next two years fostered the hope that the set-back was temporary, and that normal profitability would eventually be restored. But when 1933 again showed a slump, so that no dividend could be paid on the ordinary shares, it seemed that the idea of normal profitability might have to be revised. Further, if a lower amount of profit had to be accepted as normal, devaluation of the company's capital must be contemplated.

Accordingly the board instructed the accountants to make a complete survey of the company's assets and to consider whether their values should be brought more into line with prospective earnings. The accountants were also asked to report on the individual departments, and the subsidiaries, with a view to the possible concentration of existing units and the elimination of unprofitable activities.

As a basis for estimating prospective earnings of the assets as a whole, the accountants took the average of the seven years 1927–33, a period which included three good and four bad years. They then had to determine the rate of interest at which an annual revenue, equal to this average, should be capitalised to give the current value of the fixed assets. Two factors entered into this. Firstly, there was the rate of interest that an investor would expect to earn from capital invested in a business such as Hollins. Secondly, account had to be taken of the need to replace fixed assets as they reached the end of their useful life. Taking the two factors into consideration, the accountants decided that a capitalisation rate of 10 per cent was required.

On this basis the value of the company's fixed assets would be £152,087 as against a book value, at the end of 1933, of £552,299, a reduction of £400,212. The value of current assets, mainly stocks of raw materials, work in progress and finished goods, stood at £846,003, and the accountants were satisfied that this fairly represented their worth. Similar calculations were made for the two subsidiaries—Seedhill and the New York firm—and for outside investments. These brought the total reduction to £475,060. If the new valuation of the company's fixed assets were accepted as a basis for writing down the value of the issued capital, the ordinary shares would need to be reduced by at least one-third, £1 ordinary shares becoming 13s 4d.

Having completed the exercise, the accountants made no definite recommendation on the general question of capital reconstruction, but it is clear from their report that they had grave doubts as to the wisdom of the proposed scheme. 'In order that a scheme involving a reduction of capital shall be fully effective, it is of the utmost importance that the board should satisfy themselves in the fullest possible manner that the company will continue to earn profits commensurate with the values it is proposed to place upon its assets, and sufficient to pay reasonable dividends on its written-down capital after placing a sufficient proportion (say from 25 to 30 per cent) of its profits to reserve. The board should also satisfy themselves that there is a reasonable prospect of the present trading conditions of the company being maintained or improved, and if there is the slightest doubt as to this the scheme should be held in abeyance, as probably a great deal of harm would be inflicted on the company's reputation if it became necessary within the next few years to again write down the capital of the company.'

This warning evidently impressed the directors, and it was reinforced by the steady fall in the market value of the shares. In June 1934, when the accountants were producing their report, the average price at which Hollins's ordinary shares were being transferred was 12s 4d—substantially below the figure suggested for revaluation. A year later the price had fallen to its lowest level at 7s 9d. By the beginning of 1936 it had recovered to 12s 9d, although dividend payment was still suspended. The test of the market thus gave little indication of what might be regarded as a realistic basis for valuing the company's capital. In view of this uncertainty, the directors decided to take no action on the writing down of capital, though they were prepared to reconsider the proposition after the accountants' other recommendations had been acted upon. The first thing was to restore the company's ability to earn profits; when this had been done and the level of prospective earnings could be estimated with some confidence, the value of the assets could be ascertained by applying the accountants' formula.

In dealing with the question of capital reconstruction the accountants had been concerned with the current earnings of the company as a whole. But they were asked also for recommendations designed to improve earnings in the future. This required them to investigate 'the capacity of the various departments to earn profits, taking into consideration the percentage of activity for several years past and stating what steps are necessary to concentrate the various production units and, by elimination of overhead charges and the increase in the percentage of activity of the concentrated units, what savings and economies could be effected'.

Hollins's productive capacity had been built up over many years partly by development on the original Pleasley site and partly by the acquisition of other units, in some cases involving the take-over of existing businesses. The company had thus come to control a varied range of activities carried on in a number of widely separated plants, most of which were now operating considerably below capacity. Moreover some of this capacity was in lines where Hollins was no longer able to compete with bigger and more specialised units. The distribution of activities, in terms of employment, is shown in the following table relating to 1934.

TABLE 9

	Total Employed
Head Office and Warehouse, Nottingham	206
Hosiery Department, Nottingham	25
Garments Factory, Nottingham	369
Via Gellia, Waste Processing	30
Weaving Mill and Warehouse, Glasgow	586
Fairfield Mill, Huddersfield	66
Lower Mill, Pleasley	498
Combing Shed, Pleasley	137
Worsted Mill, Pleasley	345
Coloured Mill and Dyehouse, Radford, Nottingham	380
London Office and Showroom	59
Travellers:	
Home	120
Export	7
Demonstrators	6
Seedhill Finishing Co, Paisley	718
William Hollins & Co Inc, New York	12
Australia (Sydney & Melbourne)	6
Canada (Toronto)	6
Total	3,708

In the early 1930s many firms, and indeed whole industries, were engaged in schemes for what was called rationalisation: the elimination of surplus capacity and the concentration of production in plants which had a reasonable prospect of full-time operation. This was the problem which Hollins now faced and on which they sought their accounts' advice.

The accountants produced their report in 1934 'after careful consideration and detailed investigation of the revenue accounts for the past five years and after long and detailed discussion with senior officers of the company'. Their first proposal was for the closing of Fairfield Mill. It will be recalled that this Huddersfield concern had been acquired in 1898 as a means of safeguarding Hollins's position as merino spinners. But Fairfield's share of this trade had long since been transferred to Pleasley. Then the plant was mainly employed on coloured cotton hosiery yarn until Hollins abandoned the trade in 1931. The remaining production was very small; only sixty-six people were employed, and the mill had shown a loss during the past six years. Structural alterations and new machinery would be needed to put the mill on a competitive basis and in view of the precarious state of the market for cotton yarns this investment could not be recommended.

The Via Gellia mill was a similar case. As with Fairfield, the business carried on there had been acquired to strengthen Hollins's hold of the merino trade. The mill, employing thirty workers, was now used for processing waste from Hollins's other mills, and also from outside. As a semi-autonomous, isolated unit, it yielded little or no profit to its parent company, and the present manager was willing to buy Hollins out on suitable terms. It was recommended that a sale be negotiated.

More important than either of these cases was that of the Radford mill. Hollins had been established in this Nottingham district for many years. Beginning with the acquisition of a silk mill, they had greatly enlarged the premises, making Radford the centre for worsted spinning. It was here that the first Viyella yarn was spun, and the dyehouse established. But Radford had suffered severely in the trade depression. For some time half the spinning capacity had been idle and it was recommended that spinning should now be concentrated entirely at Pleasley, where there was also considerable excess capacity. Much of the Radford plant was old and due for scrapping; the remainder should be transferred to Pleasley and most of the Radford premises should be sold or let. Only the dye-house would be retained; it was obviously desirable to have this at Pleasley too, but there were difficulties with regard to effluent disposal. The accountants estimated that at least £4,000 a year would be saved by closing the Radford spinning mill, apart from what might be realised from the sale or letting of the premises.

Another aspect of reorganisation concerned the location of stocks. Raw material stocks were, of course, held at the point of manufacture; but for stocks of finished goods there were three widely separated locations. Until 1931 the London office had been the main centre for stocks and distribution. Then it was decided to retain most of the cloth stock near the weaving factory in Glasgow and to despatch orders from there, though the final control of production rested with the head office in Nottingham. However, despite its diminished function, the London office retained its warehouse and a considerable staff, incurring direct expenses of about £18,000 in 1933. The London management argued that this was necessary for the convenience of the west-end trade and of overseas buyers. But the accountants were not convinced. They recommended that the whole of the warehouse be closed down, except for a showroom to be retained under the charge of the manager and with one or two assistants. The stock should be transferred to Nottingham where room was available in the new Viyella House and where stocks of garments were already held. With the increasing emphasis on Nottingham as the centre of the firm's trading activity, it was clearly desirable that the cloth stock should also be held there. The company would thus have a central warehouse for all its products and for the receipt and despatch of orders.

The net gain from all this redistribution and concentration of manufacturing and commercial activities was problematical. It would depend on the sale or letting of released premises, and the saving on salaries and wages, taking into account any compensation that might be agreed upon for long-service employees. Moreover, the further centralisation of activities in Viyella House would add to head office expenses. These had already increased from £25,264 in 1929 to £37,427 in 1932, excluding depreciation and an internal rental charge for the building itself. The biggest increase, from £10,755 to £18,067, was in salaries and wages and, although the figure was reduced to £15,625 in 1933, it called for critical comment. Part of it represented the cost of various specialist services now being introduced. The most important of these was cost accounting and there was no doubt about the need for this development. Another innovation was the installation of Hollerith equipment to assist the analysis of records and particularly of sales data for use by the sales promotion department in market research.

Much of the increased cost of head office administration was the result of measures intended to improve the firm's efficiency. But away from headquarters there was scepticism about this. 'During the course of our investigation,' the accountants reported, 'we have received from heads of the various mills and departments serious complaints of the time and clerical labour required to prepare the large number of returns and statistics required by various departments at head office. Doubts were expressed either as to the usefulness of the purposes served by many of these returns or as to the efficient application of the information contained therein.' These attitudes were partly a result of bad communications. But there was always the danger that the clues to increased efficiency would be lost in a proliferation of paper work.

The survey of Hollins's assets and their productive capacity was completed by a review of the two subsidiaries: the Seedhill Finishing Co and Wm. Hollins & Co, New York. In the past, both these enterprises had presented problems and, in view of the somewhat strained relations between the Hollins board and the Seedhill management, the investigation of Seedhill was particularly emphasised in the instructions to the accountants.

Like the parent company, Seedhill suffered in the trade depression. Work for Hollins, accounting for about one-fifth of the turnover, fell off and so did the outside trade in shirtings, woollen cloth and artificial silk. Prices to Hollins were already 10 per cent less than those charged to outside customers and in 1931 these other prices had to be reduced. Yet the cost of finishing rose, owing to increased prices for dyestuffs and other chemicals. The firm still made a profit in 1933 but it was only £9,291 against an average of £23,277 for the period 1927–33.

The accountants were impressed by the efforts made to reduce costs, partly by new investment, and quoted Ross's opinion that with certain additions to the plant other kinds of finishing work could be undertaken. They also suggested that the possibility should be explored of transferring the dyeing of Hollins's yarn to the Arkleston works owned by Seedhill. The Arkleston dyehouse needed reconstructing and with the prospect of additional work from Hollins the outlay might be justified. On the whole, Seedhill came out well from the investigation. It was clearly a viable enterprise; but its place in Hollins's organisation was still not clarified, and this handicapped its development, since the parent company controlled investment.

The case of the American subsidiary was very different. Heavy losses had been sustained over the three years 1931–3, mainly on manufacturing. The mill was now closed down and the efforts to dispose of it had so far been unsuccessful. It was proposed to write down the value of the fixed assets by $60,000 provisionally. Then there was the question of the company's trading stocks. Part of the yarn supplied for weaving had been shipped back to England, but the stocks of cloth were suitable only for the American market and there appeared to be little hope of selling them at a profit. Exports from the parent company were handicapped by the increased tariffs, which had been the main reason for starting manufacture in America, and it was doubtful whether the subsidiary should continue even in its original function as a merchanting concern. If it did continue there was the prospect of further losses for some years to come.

The report of the accountants' investigation was presented to the Hollins board, meeting under the new chairman, on 23 August 1934, and at the same time a copy was supplied to the shareholders' consultative committee. The latter's own report was not yet completed and it was agreed that discussion of a possible capital reconstruction should take account of both reports.

In the meantime steps were taken towards the concentration of production and the cutting of expenses on the lines recommended by the accountants. Fairfield mill and the Radford spinning mill were closed down, as was the greater part of the London warehouse; but the disposal of the various properties and redundant equipment proved difficult. The one exception was the wool-combing plant at Pleasley. This had been under-employed for some time and the new chairman had emphasised the economy of buying combed wool (tops) from specialist firms; when Hollins decided to offer the plant for sale, it was readily disposed of to the Woolcombers Association for £20,000. As for the American company, it was decided, since the Forestdale mill was still unsold in 1937, to resume weaving and finishing as an experiment.

The transfer of the cloth stock from Glasgow did not take place until the middle of 1936, since this involved the removal of the garments factory to the top floor of Viyella House. Some rearrangement and structural alterations were also needed at Pleasley before the Radford equipment could be installed there. However, by the end of 1936, the physical redistribution of resources appears to have been accomplished. The effects on personnel cannot easily be traced. Hollins employed about 3,500 people in its various units in 1934 and some reduction certainly occurred about this time, particularly at Radford, where 380 people had been employed. Reduction was effected partly through the retirement of long-service employees, and it was the firm's custom to give a small pension in such cases. Some staff were transferred from London and Glasgow to Nottingham. But the reports of dismissal notices show that some employees were forced to leave.

The last stage in the pruning and concentration of the company's resources was a capital reconstruction at the end of 1935. While the accountants had not recommended a writing-down of the ordinary share capital under the prevailing conditions, it was evident that something should be done about the preference share capital. For some years it had not been possible to utilise, safely and profitably in the business, anything approaching the whole of the company's financial resources. The balance sheet for 1934 showed a total of some £254,000 in cash at various banks, and £50,000 in municipal short-term investments, and during 1935 these amounts increased by nearly £100,000. Interest rates on these liquid resources were now extremely low. Thus the company was unable to cover the preference share dividend, either by using the capital in its own business, or by investing it elsewhere, and during the past three years £65,000 had had to be transferred from the general reserve to meet it.

The directors therefore decided, after consultation with the auditors, that it would be in the best interests of the company and of both classes of shareholders to repay 15s for each £1 share of the £360,000 issued preference share capital, thereby reducing the total capital by £270,000. At the same time provision would be made for restoring the total authorised capital to £2 million, so as to permit the replacement of the repaid preference share capital by ordinary shares, if it should be desirable at some future date.

This transaction would benefit the ordinary shareholders by the reduction, amounting to £13,500, in the annual cost of the preference dividend. The preference shareholders would suffer some loss of income, if they failed to secure as good return from the reinvestment of the repaid capital. But they would at least get repayment at par and have the satisfaction of knowing that the dividend on their capital remaining with Hollins was more secure. At all events, agreement was reached with both classes of shareholders and the capital reconstruction was confirmed by court order.

CHAPTER TWELVE

New Methods of Management

THE developments which took place in the mid 1930s have been described as a process of rationalisation, designed to produce a more compact structure of viable units. But rationalisation implies more than this. It implies the introduction of sophisticated methods in the planning and control of all the operations of business.

Hollins was typical of many businesses in the older manufacturing industries. Its goods had a high and distinctive quality, the result of what might be called superior craftsmanship rather than elaborate scientific research. In the development of its selling methods it had been in advance of its time. But in management the methods of 1930 were not noticeably different from those that served before 1914. There was no means of measuring accurately the manufacturing costs of individual lines, no means of assessing the efficiency of particular departments, no market research or sales forecasting, no budgeting and, apparently, no regulation of capital expenditure in terms of prospective return. On the personnel side the definition of responsibilities was often obscure and the delegation of authority uncertain. Moreover, the frequent changes of recent years must have disturbed confidence and, at times, caused confusion.

These conditions were by no means unusual in British business; but a wind of change was beginning to blow. New ideas of management were being discussed, new techniques and specialists in their application, were appearing. Hitherto, management so far as its nature was considered at all, had been regarded as an art. Success depended on being able to form a judgment on information that was necessarily inadequate; it depended on flair. Now, in the more progressive firms, management was becoming more sophisticated. It was being recognised that the methods of science, which had contributed so much to productive efficiency on the technical side, had many applications on the administrative side of industry.

A basic characteristic of scientific method is measurement, which implies the careful recording of data and its interpretation in terms of some standard or objective. In business the objective is profit. But with the scientific approach to profit-making, it is not sufficient to know what profit, or loss, has been made on the total operations of a business. Techniques for ascertaining this had long been available in the form of financial accounting, but its further development was an important step in progress towards scientific management. Financial accounting merely records what has happened; it does not show whether the business's resources could be used more efficiently, or how this might be brought about. This is the task of cost accounting, or management accounting as it was coming to be called. With the introduction of this new technique, management was provided at once with a more rational basis for decision-making and a more effective means of control.

The reform of the costing system, on the lines of management accounting, appears to have started at Hollins as a by-product of the accountants' investigation of 1934. One purpose of the inquiry had been to ascertain the capacity of the various departments to earn profits, and this naturally led to an inquiry into existing costing methods. A separate report on the subject was produced and although, unfortunately, this cannot now be traced, it is evident from what is said in the main report that existing methods were far from scientific. Hollins was a vertically organised concern and, in the course of manufacture, goods were transferred from process to process and department to department at 'transfer prices'. These prices, the accountants found, were 'based on a formula, which in its turn was based to some extent on the market prices of the raw materials used in manufacture. The formula had the effect of giving a large proportion of the profits to the manufacturing departments to the detriment of the selling departments, which in bad years showed losses. Although there had lately been a change in the formula to include interest on capital employed and a bigger charge for depreciation, the transfer prices still included 'arbitrary percentage additions for margins'. The underlying theory was that each manufacturing and warehouse department should recover its costs; but in view of the arbitrary element in the allocation of costs and in the fixing of transfer prices, it was impossible to measure the true contribution of each department to the firm's total profits or to assess the profitableness of the various lines.

The reform of the costing system was begun in 1933 with the firm's accountants acting as consultants, and the revision of selling prices in the latter part of that year was influenced by the results. The secondment of a specialist in cost accounting, to work with the management and reporting to the board, was evidently a valuable educational experience for the directors. It was their introduction to scientific management. From about this time the board minutes become fuller and they are supplemented by the reports of a newly established executive committee. The records become much more informative and more systematic and contain the results of various analytical exercises designed to provide a basis for rational decision making.

Acting on the advice of their accountants, Hollins appointed their own cost accountant in 1935 and set up a central department for this function. The first task was to secure the co-operation of the various sections, which had hitherto produced their own costings, and to ensure that information was supplied to the cost office on a uniform basis. But this was intended to prepare the way for an entirely new approach to costing.

When he began, the cost accountant had only recently investigated the techniques of standard costing and budgetary control. This is hardly surprising; for management accounting, as it came to be called, was still in its infancy and few firms had adopted the new approach to costing. However, Hollins' cost accountant soon became an ardent advocate and, in their present receptive mood, the directors were prepared to let him go ahead.

The essential character of the new approach is in the formulation of a plan for the firm's operations over a defined period. Since the scale of operations depends ultimately on sales, the sales budget is taken as the starting point. On the basis of past and current sales statistics, and likely future trade, as indicated by market research and salesmen's reports, a sales estimate is produced, built up from the quantities and values of sales in the various markets. Some assumptions as to prices must be made at this stage, but prices depend on costs, and these depend on conditions in the production departments.

A production budget is thus complementary to the sales budget, and it is also built up from the budgets for individual departments. In the estimation of total production costs, standard costs are used; these are calculations of what each unit of output ought to cost under given conditions. Here again assumptions must be made about prices of materials and labour for the budget period; but costs depend also on the usage of materials and labour. Ideally, each manufacturing process should be studied, so as to ascertain the minimum input of materials and labour-time, and also the mini-mum use of machine time, required to produce a given result. This involves time study, and in 1936 Hollins decided that a man must be appointed for 'this most important work'.

In this way the standard direct cost per unit of output is deter-mined. But there is a further assumption that must be made in calculating the total standard cost. Each unit must carry its appro-priate share of fixed charges, and the burden of these charges de-pends on output volume—on the number of units over which the fixed charges are spread. The standard cost is therefore the cost per unit assuming that standard conditions, including a standard rate of output, are maintained.

The rate of output is not necessarily fixed at full capacity work-ing. But the nearer this position is approached, the lower will be the costs of production. Thus, up to a point, the bigger the sales the lower the prices at which profitable sales can be made; and the

M

lowering of prices will, in turn, help towards the achievement of the sales budget.

Standard costs, as the term implies, provide a basis for measuring the efficiency of operations for each process or group of processes selected as a cost centre. Actual costs may be higher or lower than the standard and, in analysing the variances, a distinction is made between internal and external causes. The latter are due to factors outside the firm's control, such as an unforeseen change in raw material prices during the budget period. But where variances can be traced to internal factors, remedial action is called for. The setting of standards thus provides a test of efficiency, and the study of variations from the standard indicates the means of maintaining efficiency at the desired level.

This, in outline, is the system that Hollins were working towards in the later 1930s. But progress was slow. As might be expected, the setting up of a central cost office was not particularly welcome to the production departments. Moreover, the cost accountant was himself in a rather difficult position. His authority for securing the production departments' co-operation derived from the company secretary, who had to be convinced of the necessity for any proposed change in costing methods and organisation. The accountant's relation with the secretary on the one hand, and the production director on the other, is clearly illustrated by the correspondence which passed between them. Much of it concerns points of detail, but on the more general question of co-operation the following extract from one of the accountant's letters to the secretary is revealing. 'Once the system is operating,' he writes, 'no one must be allowed to alter the forms or methods without your permission. By this safeguard the cost system will be saved from being wrecked by clerks who do not understand the purpose of the records, and who may be only interested in their particular mill. At the same time the production and cost departments will be kept in harmony with each other. As it is of absolute importance that the maximum of team work should prevail, clerks handling any of the cost system records should be responsible to the cost office through you as secretary to the company.'

The production departments were also concerned about the investigation of their costs and the reallocation of certain items which the new methods implied. They had already had their transfer prices reduced in 1933 when it was decided that the basis should be manufacturing costs (assuming production at 75 per cent of capacity), plus 5 per cent interest on fixed assets, plus 5 per cent departmental profit. Now they were required to provide information about direct costs in much more detail. The production manager at Pleasley was inclined to question the value of some of the information asked for and detailed explanations had to be supplied. He also questioned the additional work involved in providing the information and one can imagine his reaction to the accountant's suggestion that the existing office staff at the mills were 'not fully occupied and could increase their output quite easily'.

Then there were arguments about what items should be treated as variable and what as fixed costs, and as to how the latter should be allocated. For instance, the accountant proposed to charge head office expenses as a proportion of production hours in each manufacturing department. But the production manager disputed this; he contended that head office expenses should be charged 'strictly in accordance with what the expenses have born in connection with each department'. The allocation of advertising expenditure was another source of controversy. Here the firm's practice had been notably inconsistent. In the 1920s advertising had been charged to the trading accounts for the various lines, but on an arbitrary basis which resulted in under and over-allocation. Then for a few years the total advertising expenditure had been simply debited to the profit and loss account. In 1932 the original practice was restored. Now, in 1935, an effort was made, for the first time, to allocate expenditure according to the amount spent on advertising particular lines.

The object of these reforms in costing methods was to ascertain, as nearly as possible, what each item in the firm's output cost to make and to sell. This information could then be used as a guide to pricing. It was not until 1936 that the directors could claim the establishment of 'a sound and comprehensive costing system'. 'For the first time,' it is then recorded, 'we know accurately what every one of our lines has been costing to produce, and we also have valuable information as to the possible effect of well organised, increased production on our costs'.[1]

It is evident from this statement that the methods of standard costing were coming to be applied. For standard costs allow for the effects of changes in the volume of production on unit costs. There is also a reference, in the same statement, to a concept which is a corollary of standard costing. 'In the case of every department a standard margin of profit has been determined, this figure taking into consideration the value of the buildings, machinery and equipment concerned in the production of the various goods handled by that department, as well as the length of process time, so that an adequate return on the capital involved may be provided for.'

This was followed by a declaration of price policy. The selling prices of certain lines had already been reduced in 1933, following the institution of new transfer prices on the basis recommended by the firm's auditors, but these reforms were only a beginning. The new policy was apparently to be based on what is now called the full-cost principle. 'It is our endeavour to secure exactly this standard margin of profit, neither more nor less, in the cost of every line we handle, for only by pursuing such a policy can we ensure that our goods are truly competitive and that they yield us an adequate margin of profit.' There is, of course, a certain ambiguity here; for a price sufficient to cover the full cost, including standard profit, might be too high for the market.

However, the management was by now more keenly aware of the need to be competitive on price. It expressed the firm opinion that the business could only expand by the desired amount if the policy

---

[1] This quotation and much of the following material is from the minutes of the Executive Committee, established in 1935 with Herbert as chairman.

of offering to the public the maximum possible value were extended to every line marketed. 'Whatever may be the temptation to adhere to the high margins of profit—which, in some instances, are as much as 40 to 50 per cent—that we have been attempting to secure, we must abandon them in favour of acceptance of the realities of our position.'

In certain cases selling prices on the new cost basis were found to be too low to yield the required standard profit and a few prices were raised. But this was rarely possible in the present state of markets and such lines were usually eliminated. Only those lines were kept where the estimate of sales prospects indicated that the minimum profitable level of production could be attained. There is now, for the first time, a clear indication that account was taken of the elasticity of demand, the response of sales to a reduction in price. The management recognised that 'in most instances the margin of gross profit reflected in prices was dangerously high'. Unless prices were reduced sales would continue to decline; but if prices were brought down to levels which the new knowledge of costs showed to be feasible, an expansion of sales could be confidently predicted. A general reduction of prices, it was felt, would 'do much to remove the feeling in the minds of both the trade and the public that Viyella is dear'.

Accordingly, most garment prices were reduced for the autumn of 1936; men's Viyella pyjamas went down from 25s 6d to 21s, and shirts from 15s to 12s 6d. These were the fixed retail prices to the public; in all cases Hollins's prices to the trade allowed retailers their 'full customary margin of profit', generally 33⅓ per cent of the resale price. The retailer's profit per sale would of course be less, but his total profit could be expected to benefit from an increase in turnover. It was also hoped that garments of Hollins manufacture would now be competitive in price with those made up by other firms from Hollins cloth, and which had been selling at much lower prices.

It was the declared intention to reduce cloth prices in the following spring. But this does not appear to have been done. By this time raw materials were becoming dearer and wages had risen somewhat. Moreover, production in some departments was now approaching full capacity and any further stimulus to sales might mean delay in delivery. The main exception was knittings, of which the 1936 turnover was less than half that of the peak year 1932. The deputy-chairman expressed the belief that the knittings department ought to be capable of a turnover of £250,000 a year if prices were made competitive. They would not be competitive if costings were based on the present turnover of £105,000, or even £150,000, and he suggested that knittings prices should be reduced by means of a temporary subsidy from other departments. Then, as turnover was built up to the desired level on the basis of lower unit costs and selling prices, the knittings department would be able to earn the standard profit on its increased output.

This example again shows the growing awareness of the relation between costs, prices and turnover. But the volume of business is ultimately dependent on market conditions. Production must be co-ordinated with sales and the successful planning of production requires a forecast of sales. Every firm, in so far as it produces in anticipation of orders, makes some kind of sales forecast. Hollins, with its direct contacts with retailers and numerous representatives overseas, was well equipped for getting the 'feel' of the market; and it was not lacking in experience of sales promotion methods. But until 1935 there had been no consistent effort in market research and no systematic sales forecasting. The technique of sales budgeting which was now introduced was an essential part of the new system for planning all operations in accordance with defined objectives, and for measuring achievement in terms of standards.

The first step in sales planning has already been mentioned. This was the elimination of all lines which seemed unlikely ever to reach a profitable level of production. Over the years many new lines had been introduced, often on the initiative of the manufacturing departments rather than the salesmen. This is not necessarily a ground for criticism—Viyella itself began as such an experiment. But what had appeared as promising novelties had often disappointed; the Aza and Visylka fabrics and the Viyella sheets were examples. In the process of rationalisation now begun, such items were discarded. At the same time, efforts were made to develop lines that might fill in the troughs in the seasonal fluctuations of orders and so help to reduce costs, by evening up the loading of productive capacity. A particular need was to increase the summer trade and it was hoped that the new Aerolite fabrics for sports and children's wear would help to meet it. It was, however, established as a guiding principle that 'the utmost possible use should be made of Viyella in all its forms'. It was felt that there were 'enormous possibilities' in developing the applications of Viyella. For any new line suggested, it should be asked 'can we make it in Viyella?' Most of the ten new lines of garments introduced in 1936 were described as Viyella.

When the pattern of merchandise to be offered had been decided in this way, estimates were made of the likely sales of each line in the various home and overseas markets. These estimates were then incorporated in an annual sales budget, divided into months, and actual sales were compared month by month with the budget. In 1937 an even closer check was instituted, requiring the preparation of weekly sales statements.

Simultaneously with the introduction of sales budgeting in 1936 considerable changes were made in the marketing organisation. Four product divisions were created—Men's and Boy's Wear, Ladies' and Children's Wear, Piece Goods, Knittings—each under a sales promotion manager. The number of sales representatives was further reduced from 102 to 79, and they were attached to divisions instead of carrying the full range of goods as before. This made for a better concentration of selling effort. At the same time the reduction in numbers gave each salesman wider scope and improved prospects, making a worthwhile job for a good man. The changes resulted in a net saving of between £3,000 and £4,000 a year, but it was claimed that the firm now had a more effective and more stable sales force.

In the same year, the first series of half-yearly conferences in London, Birmingham and Manchester was held, at which members of the higher management discussed with the sales representatives the relevant points of the company's policy, the formulation of sales estimates and the strategy designed to fulfil the sales budget. Special efforts were to be made to secure distribution of standard lines through the chief accounts for each line in all the important towns, which it was hoped would give a lead to smaller shops in each neighbourhood. Lists of the 'key' accounts for each type of merchandise were being drawn up and the full force of the sales organisation would be directed towards them. Full use was to be made of sales aids, such as special displays and co-operative point-of-sale advertising, whereby the cost was shared between the manufacturer and the retailer. The first conferences were reported as being very successful. 'Representatives were enthusiastic over the new merchandise and the new sales policy generally, and they returned to their grounds in no doubt as to the strength of purpose behind the company's intention to progress and to provide them with an opportunity to progress.'

The sales budget was a statement of the quantities of the various lines which the sales department undertook to sell during a given period. The logical implication of this was a production budget drawn up in consultation with the heads of production departments. The administrative link between sales and production was provided by the recently appointed executive committee, meeting under the chairmanship of the deputy-chairman of the company, and including the managing director, the secretary, and the assistant directors for sales and production respectively. This committee assumed the entire responsibility for all orders to the manufacturing departments, so that sufficient stock of all standard lines could be built up to the requirements of the sales budget, and delivery of orders by return could be guaranteed throughout the season. The executive committee was confident that this procedure would overcome the criticisms concerning the lack of co-ordination between sale and production made by the shareholders' consultative committee.

As with sales, meetings were held with the managers of production departments for explaining and discussing the new policy. Then a production planning section was formed, responsible for ensuring that the mills and garments factory were supplied with a steady flow of orders so as to reduce, as far as possible, the amount of short-time and overtime working. This, of course, could effect a considerable improvement in productive efficiency and help to keep down costs to the levels prescribed in the production budget.

The introduction of management accounting, budgeting and budgetary control necessarily involved making many changes in the general administration of the firm. Responsibilities had to be redefined, or at least clarified, new functions came to be recognised and had to be provided for. In all this Herbert, the new deputy-chairman of the company, played a leading part. The executive committee over which he presided had been given wide powers, and its recommendations were generally accepted by the board of directors.

Most of the new posts created at this time were filled by recruits from outside the firm. The shareholders' consultative committee, had pointed to the lack of systematic training for promotion within the firm, and this, no doubt, partly explains the need to bring in new men. But the methods of planning and control now being introduced demanded a break with tradition, which men brought up in the old ways would find it hard to make. The appointment of a cost accountant and the establishment of a central cost office had been followed by changes in sales personnel, although the former chief accountant, now an assistant director, remained in general control. Another new post on the sales side was that of export secretary, whose duties were to maintain supervision and control in the absence of the export managers abroad, and to ensure that overseas representatives were supplied with up-to-date information about merchandise and prices. Stocks of finished goods, and responaibility for the despatch of orders, were placed in the hands of a merchandise manager. The post of merchandise development manager was also created to introduce new lines and improvements in existing lines, in conjunction with both sales and production. The department included stylists for garments.

An appointment of a different kind, and an interesting sign of the times, was that of a staff adviser with general responsibility for the welfare of employees. It provides a further illustration of the tendency to centralise functions hitherto performed, if at all, by individual departmental heads. In their relations with their workers, Hollins had a good reputation, according to the tenets of authoritarian management. The firm looked after its people, and long service employees, of whom there were many, received a small pension on retirement. The board minutes record, from time to time, the presentation of a gold watch to an employee with fifty years' service. But there was no formal organisation of labour-management relations, and little trade union activity. It was regarded as an innovation, worth recording in the board minutes, when the deputy-chairman addressed senior employees at Nottingham and Pleasley 'with a view to increasing their interest in the company's work and progress'. He outlined the firm's plans and hopes for the future and 'this taking of the staff into the board's confidence appeared to be much appreciated by all present'.

It was in this spirit that the post of staff adviser was created. The adviser, a retired naval captain, was required to keep personal records of all employees, with notes on character, ability, education and progress. Heads of departments were to consult him before taking action affecting any employee. The adviser was also to be available for consultation by any employee and it was his duty to help the staff in every possible way. Soon after his appointment it was reported that 'steps were being taken in many directions to improve the general standard, welfare and morale of the staff throughout the company'.

As might be expected, these changes in organisation and in personnel were not made without criticism or friction. There are hints of this in the correspondence between heads of departments and particularly between the 'line' and 'staff' members of management. But on the whole they appear to have been accepted as being in the best interests of the old firm, which needed new men, new ideas and new methods. One notable resignation occurred however, that of Henry Hollins, a son of the second William Hollins and great-great-grandson of Henry Hollins who had helped to set up the mill at Pleasley Vale 150 years before. Hollins's work as assistant director in charge of production had been commended by the shareholders' consultative committee and the reasons for his resignation are not clear. It is evident, however, from the correspondence quoted earlier, that he had some difficulty in reconciling himself to the new order; and the reference to his resignation in the board minutes suggests a dispute with the senior members of the board. The vacancy was filled by E. C. Pollit, who was to serve the firm for many years to come.

CHAPTER THIRTEEN

Disappointing Results

THE great depression of the early 1930s had been a testing experience for Hollins, as for many other old-established firms in the
textile trades. It had precipitated a crisis in the company's direction
which delayed reaction to the changing economic environment, so
that sales continued to decline to 1935. The continued fall of exports
accorded with the general trend of world trade; but conditions in
the home market were improving in 1934 and 1935 and Hollins's
poor performance in these years must be attributed partly to the
weaknesses revealed in the report to the shareholders' consultative
committee. Home sales in 1934 were only about two-thirds of the
1929 figure and the results for 1935 were little better. Some allowance must be made for price reductions, in comparing the figures;
but as evidence of the severity of the depression we have the
auditors' statement that in 1934 no more than 55 per cent of the
firm's spinning and weaving capacity was employed.

However, in 1935 it did seem that the crisis in Hollins's affairs was
being overcome. A new chairman had been appointed, albeit on a
short-term basis, and also a full-time deputy-chairman. The latter
acted as chairman of a newly constituted executive committee and
the minutes of this body provide evidence of his vigorous leadership. For the first time there are clear and concise statements of
policy, and there are indications in the correspondence with heads
of departments of energetic action towards the fulfilment of policies.
The whole administration begins to take on a new look. There are
signs too of efforts towards creating a stronger sense of common
purpose and co-operation between higher and lower levels of
management and between management and the general body of
workers.

It was in 1936 that the effects of reorganisation really began to be felt. There was some difficulty in bringing Seedhill into line and in inducing its management to produce accurate figures based on the new costing principles. Indeed, as the chairman confessed at the shareholders' meeting in 1936, the administrative work involved in the parent firm and its subsidiary had been far more than he had at first supposed. But it could be claimed that much had been done and that the current year should see the process completed. The new financial year had in fact opened with an improvement in sales and, although there were no hopes of a spectacular recovery, the board 'hoped to show shareholders some results of their efforts before very long'.

The improvement of sales continued throughout the year. Home sales reached £858,072 as compared with £782,186 in the previous year, and the corresponding figures for exports were £314,477 against £273,136. The only disappointment was in home sales of knitting wool, which fell again after the slight recovery of 1935 and were now little more than two-fifths of the 1932 turnover. Sales budgeting had not yet been introduced, but the current trend of sales for each main product was now being compared with the average of the past years in preparation for the exercise.

Discussions on procedure for sales budgeting appear to have been initiated by the managing director before the end of 1935, with the suggestion that the deputy-chairman, the secretary and himself should meet each January and July to review the turnover in each main line for the previous three half years, and estimate whether an increase or decrease was likely for the next half year. The sales director would be consulted about the prospect of increasing turnover and the position in manufacturing departments would be reviewed with the production manager. Sales forecasting would impose a heavy responsibility on the sales director who, though well versed in sales statistics, was not in direct contact with markets. His requests for a specialist in market research, or for a temporary sales consultant, were deferred by the board and he was therefore very much dependent on the opinions of the firm's sales managers and representatives in the field.

This apparently was the way in which sales budgeting developed and in June 1936 we find the executive committee reporting that it was 'planning for an increase in 1937 of not less than 75 per cent, and not more than 100 per cent, on the total sales turnover, as compared with the 1935 figure'. It added that the closest consideration was being given to all matters concerning production, including supplies of wool and cotton, in the light of its objective.

The budget as eventually approved was for a sales turnover of £1,692,500—a 64 per cent increase over 1935. Even so it was optimistic to a degree that is hard to understand. But the executive committee appears to have had no doubt about the continuing increase of demand; its only anxiety was whether the firm had the capacity to supply it. 'It is important to note,' it says in October 1936, 'that our problem today is one of production, not of sales, and that we could sell appreciably more cloth, garments, and hosiery between now and the end of the year than will in fact be the case, had we the goods to deliver.' It reported that steps were being taken to obtain supplies of garments from outside makers-up. Yarn production was also at the maximum of existing capacity and the question of increasing it was receiving very careful consideration.

The section with the best sales prospects was apparently garments. Many new lines had been introduced, including Viyella socks, lighter-weight shirts, styled outerwear for women and a wider range of children's wear. Prices had been made more competitive and sales promotion strengthened. Garments sales increased from £109,120 in 1935 to £164,964 in 1937, and productive capacity was expanded by moving the garments factory back from Castle Boulevard to Radford where the former spinning mill was still without a tenant. But even in the case of garments the sales achieved fell far short of the budget. Hosiery sales also did well; for many of the articles described above were knitted; they were made by outside manufacturers from Hollins's yarn and sold by

Hollins. The increase in these sales was from £156,584 in 1935 to £240,782 in 1937. This, in turn, brought some benefit to yarn sales, which improved from £144,182 to £173,898. The corresponding figures for cloth sales were £223,379 and £271,968. Knittings however, though making a better showing than in 1936, were, at £118,079, substantially below the 1935 level. All these figures relate to home trade. Exports improved from £273,136 in 1935 to £367,741 in 1937, cloth and hosiery doing particularly well. But in no branch of home or overseas trade was anything like the minimum budget figure achieved. Total home sales, at £999,908 in 1937, were about 28 per cent up on 1935, while exports did rather better, recovering to £367,741, an increase of 35 per cent over 1935. The overall figure of £1,367,645 was certainly an improvement but it was £324,855 below the budget estimate.

It was in the latter part of the year that the discrepancy between budgeted and actual sales became so marked. Hollins's sales had always been subject to seasonal fluctuations. A minor peak appeared in the spring, followed by a decline to about midsummer; then orders for the autumn trade flowed in and sales reached their main peak in September; this was succeeded by a rapid fall to the end of the year. A statement produced by the firm's statistical section, shows that the monthly budget estimates followed this pattern. In June actual sales exceeded the budget, suggesting that the new lines designed to fill in the trough, as mentioned above, were having some success. But with this exception, there was a progressive divergence between plan and performance.

The excessive optimism in sales budgeting was the more serious in that all the production budgets were, as the system required, geared to the sales budget. In fulfilling the production budgets it was calculated that the limits of existing capacity would soon be reached in most sections and that expansion would be needed. Department managers were accordingly authorised to set on more workers, overtime was introduced and a night shift was started in one section at Pleasley.

Raw material requirements were similarly affected and instructions were sent to the brokers in Australia to buy up to a considerably increased maximum. Some anxiety was expressed about the supply and price of suitable lambswool, of which Hollins absorbed most of the Australian clip. It was thought that substitutes might have to be considered, provided Viyella quality could be maintained. Cotton purchases were also increased and here again it was essential to secure the customary Egyptian and Peruvian grades at whatever the ruling price might be.

It is not clear how far the possibility of increases in raw material prices and in wage rates during the budget year was taken into account in determining the standard costs of production. But budgeting required that assumptions must be made about both direct (variable) and fixed (invariable) costs of production and selling. Direct costs did not, of course, vary in strict proportion with output. For instance, if increased output necessitated employment at overtime rates, wage costs would rise relatively to output. Conversely a steady flow of work, maintained without undue strain on the manufacturing departments, would make for a fall in labour costs per unit of output. But the main significance of variations in output was naturally in the incidence of the fixed costs. It was thus possible to determine a point at which the revenue from sales, at an assumed volume and price structure, would just balance total expenditure, at an assumed volume of output and cost structure. This was the break-even point and any rise of turnover beyond this point up to the limit of existing capacity would be favourable to profits.

A series of charts based on these concepts was produced for 1936, 1937 and 1938. The 1937 chart for the firm as a whole is shown opposite; similar charts were drawn for each of the main divisions of output.

The chart obviously uses simplifying assumptions with regard to the behaviour of direct costs in relation to output; and it was not intended to take account of any change in conditions, whether fortuitous or deliberately introduced, during the budget period. It

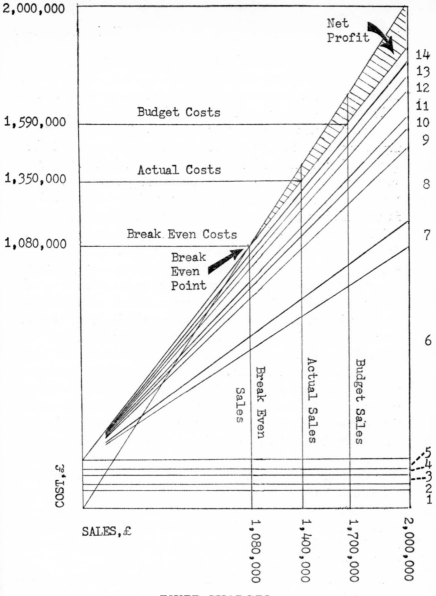

COST, £

SALES, £

2,000,000

1,590,000

1,350,000

1,080,000

Budget Costs

Actual Costs

Break Even Costs

Net Profit

Break Even Point

Break Even Sales

Actual Sales

Budget Sales

1,080,000

1,400,000

1,700,000

2,000,000

14
13
12
11
10
9
8
7
6
5
4
3
2
1

FIXED CHARGES

1. Salaries   2. Property   3. Reps. salaries and expenses   4. Depreciation
5. Miscellaneous

FUNCTIONAL CHARGES

6. Raw materials   7. Finishing   8. Wages   9. Maintenance power and stores
10. Sales expenses   11. Advertising display   12. Discounts
13. Distribution   14. Miscellaneous

may not therefore be completely accurate; but it provides a clear illustration of a technique which was something of a novelty in British industry at the time, and has since been more widely adopted. The chart shows the break-even point at a sales turnover of £1,080,000. Actual sales in 1937 were nearly £1,400,000, and according to the chart they should have yielded a net profit of about £50,000. If the year's sales target had been reached, the profit, as shown by the chart, would have been about £110,000. In view of the reservations concerning the projections in the chart, the latter figure must be regarded as no more than an approximation. But it is interesting to compare it with the actual profit in 1928, the last full year before the depression. In that year Hollins's turnover was —£1,720,483—just about equal to the sales budget for 1937—and the net profit was £153,445. Yet, according to the chart, even if the same sales total had been reached, the profit in 1937 would have been much less. The conclusion is inescapable that there had been a serious decline in the overall efficiency of the business.

Detailed analysis of the profit figures for 1937 reveals that, of the main categories of output, cloth made the best showing. For most of the year sales kept pace with the budget estimate and though the autumn peak fell short of expectations the year's turnover passed the break-even point by a wide margin. But garments, hosiery and knittings all failed to break even. There is no graph for the profits on yarn and no budget figure can be traced; the 1937 sales, at £173,898, were the highest since 1930, but the trade was keenly competitive and Hollins had to follow the market. An examination of the year's record as a whole indicates that the meagre profit earned was entirely attributable to the cloth trade, particularly the sales of Viyella and Clydella, and that other lines were being subsidised from the earnings of this trade.

The directors' report to the shareholders in the year 1936 had been cautious. It had been a year of reorganisation in every branch of the firm's activities and the benefits, it was claimed, were already being seen. Reference was made to the increased sales already achieved and expected to continue. The expectation of an increase was realised in 1937, yet the profits were less than a third of the previous year's. The reasons for this have already been described, but the shareholders, seeing only the final outcome and the failure to pay a dividend for yet another year, must have been puzzled, to say the least.

The directors' explanation of the accounts was unusually full, as it needed to be. After referring to the reorganisation still in progress, they attributed the fall in profits to five main factors. Firstly, there had been 'exceptional expenditure' on sales development. A sum of £30,000 had been devoted to the advertising and sales promotion of new lines bringing the total for advertising and display to £100,678. The increase was regarded as non-recurrent expenditure, yet experience had shown that all lines needed the continuous support of advertising. Secondly, wage increases had been conceded in the middle of the year, which had added £14,000 to the cost of output. It was hoped that the effect would be offset by the efforts being made to increase the productivity of labour. Thirdly, wool prices had been high during the last buying season and there had since been an exceptional fall, necessitating a writing down of stocks. This was met partly by drawing on the raw material reserve, but more than half the amount had to be allocated at the expense of the year's trading profit. In so far as these increases in cost could not be foreseen and budgeted for, they are of course treated as a variance according to the principles of budgetary control.

Less satisfactory, however, was the treatment of the fourth factor —the increase of stocks. The total value of stocks, including raw materials and finished goods, was now £865,000 as compared with £608,000 for 1936, and £486,000 for 1935. A considerable increase in stocks was, according to the directors' statement, essential to the satisfactory development of the business. It enabled the firm to provide prompt service to customers. Prompt delivery was, of course, important; but it had been the aim of management, as recorded in the executive committee minutes, to secure this with greater economy in stocks. In the opinion of the committee it could be achieved by better co-ordination of production and sales and by eliminating slow-moving lines. Thus the increase of stocks, as recorded at the end of 1937, could not be regarded as a planned increase; on the contrary, it indicated a failure in planning. Either the sales target had been set too high or the sales effort had been inadequate for the increased output that the production departments had been urged to achieve.

Lastly, the company's financial position had been affected by increased expenditure, amounting to £101,000, on the reconditioning of, and addition to, their factories and plant, Some of this expenditure came in for criticism later on when the expectations on which it was based were disappointed. A good deal, however, was necessitated by the redistribution of activities described in the last chapter. A new power plant was required at Pleasley. The rise in wages emphasised the need to install labour-saving machines. Particular attention was given to the garments factory; it was thought that an output three or four times the 1936 volume might have to be provided for eventually. The needs of the head office too, were considerable. Hollins' trading methods involved the handling of thousands of accounts, and the new methods of administration called for much processing of data. Efforts were made to improve efficiency by mechanising much of the office work. Altogether £30,264 was spent on machinery in 1937 and the cost of electrical plant was nearly as much.

The report on the company's results for 1937 was the more gloomy because of the high hopes with which the year had begun. But prospects for 1938 offered no relief; trade conditions generally were worsening and there were ominous signs of the approaching international crisis, which undermined confidence at home and abroad. At Hollins the course was now set for retrenchment; optimism gave place to caution, and an anxious search for economies began, recalling conditions in the early part of the decade.

The most urgent task now facing the management was the reduction of stocks. The increase of stocks, together with the capital expenditure described above, had resulted in an overdraft of nearly £324,000. Although this represented a smaller charge than the dividend on preference share capital before the repayment in 1935, it was a disturbing feature of the accounts. However, despite the urgency of the problem, stocks were as high at the end of April as in December; the spring trade had done nothing to relieve the position. The executive committee then decided to aim at a reduction of between £100,000 and £150,000 during 1938. This meant continual short-time working, which had already been resorted to in most sections. But now the cost department reported that working below capacity meant under-recovery of fixed and semi-fixed expenses at a cost of £1,250 a week.

In determining the sales budget for 1938 the same methods as before seem to have been used. But this time the basis, except for garments, was actual sales in 1937. In the outcome, the forecast again proved over-optimistic. Home sales were down to £922,368; garments did better, as anticipated, but everywhere else there was a decline, and a serious slump in the case of yarn. Exports were helped by an improvement in hosiery sales, but the total declined to £356,730. Still, in view of the general deterioration of international trade in 1938, Hollins did well in the export field.

While the sales budget was the starting point in planning the firm's operations, the success of the whole plan depended not only on the sales forecast but on the co-ordination of sales and production. A system for this had been devised when budgeting was introduced, but it is clear from the executive committee's records for 1938 that the system had never been really effective. Perhaps it mattered less, so long as it was believed that sales would tend to exceed production. Now the system must be made to work, and in the discussion of ways and means a lengthy argument developed as to whether the scheduling of production was the responsibility of the sales director or the merchandise manager. Each blamed the other for the accumulation of stocks and all the executive committee could do was to emphasise the point that there must be free and willing co-operation between the sales side and the merchandise side to ensure that the system worked smoothly.

Pricing was another problem. Much of the wool and cotton used in current production had been bought at high prices. This pointed to the desirability of maintaining selling prices, but could sales be held at these prices? There was also the effect of idle capacity on costs, and the deputy-chairman suggested that relief should be sought in the introduction of any lines that would earn their direct costs and contribute something towards fixed charges, provided that they did not prejudice future earnings on standard branded lines. They should always consider the ultimate benefit to the company as a whole rather than that of any particular department or commodity.

Investigation showed that yarn sales to hosiery manufacturers had often been made at prices which did not even cover direct costs. In view of the weakness of this market it had been the policy in 1937 to use more of the spinning capacity for Hollins's own goods. Now, however, yarn sales were to be encouraged, but only at prices which covered, at least, all variable charges and whenever possible some of the fixed charges too.

In some cases garments had been priced at an unprofitable figure, apparently through ignorance of the true cost. One example was sports shirts, offered to retail at 12s 6d. After much argument it was agreed that 14s 6d was the minimum profitable price; but at this price sales fell and there was now a surplus stock of the article. Such instances suggest that co-operation of the manufacturing departments with the cost office was still not fully effective, despite the emphasis placed upon it.

In the case of some lines held in stock production cost had no relevance in pricing; the goods had to be offered for what they would fetch. In striving for novelty as a stimulus to sales there had been excessive production of certain patterns of cloth, some of them peculiar to certain foreign markets, and insufficient regard to the disposal of older patterns. Here again co-ordination between the sales and merchandise divisions was at fault.

Price reductions, especially on lines where the price had previously been raised, were sanctioned with reluctance. Fears were expressed of the disturbing effects on retailers' goodwill, where lines had been advertised at a standard price. Manufacturers buying Hollins' cloth for making up into garments had also to be considered; it was reported that some of these outside makers-up cancelled orders when Hollins intensified competition by lowering the prices of their own garments made from the same cloth. Resistance to price cutting was naturally strongest in the case of standard lines, though it was appreciated that, in so far as demand responded to lower prices, production could still be profitable because of the increased volume.

Various devices were used to clear stocks of slow moving lines without weakening the general price structure. Special terms were offered to large stores making bulk purchases. In other cases the price fixing committee was instructed to determine 'sales' prices which retailers might adopt without contravening the fixed-price condition of trading. Another proposal was to downgrade some items of cloth and garments by including them in a range below that for which they had been intended. It was suggested that the name Sportella, already used in many overseas markets, could be adopted in the home market for this purpose.

The balance sheet for 1938 shows a reduction in the value of stocks from £865,000 to £704,000. Of this, £65,000 represents depreciation, financed by drawing on stock reserves. The rest reflects the fall in current production and in the volume of raw materials held. Production had indeed been cut drastically; from April 1938 most departments had been working at only 50 per cent of capacity. In the previous year all the emphasis was on increasing output; new workers were being recruited and trained, overtime and shift working were resorted to, new plant was being installed. Now workers were being laid off and many of those retained were on short time.

It was not only wage earners who were affected. The company's chairman asked the executive committee to consider every means of reducing expenditure and a number of staff appointments were terminated. In the search for economies it was perhaps inevitable that attention should be concentrated on the new departments set up in the process of reorganisation, such as production planning, central purchasing, merchandise development and personnel. The introduction of these 'non-productive' specialists had never been very welcome to the production departments; now they appeared, more than ever, as an unnecessary addition to costs. The sales organisation also came under critical review. Territories were re-distributed and ten representatives were dispensed with.

Nevertheless, few of these economies became effective in 1938. The cost of management and administration was only reduced from £90,000 to £85,000 and selling cost remained almost exactly the same as in 1937 at around £146,000. Advertising, however, which is shown separately in the accounts, was drastically reduced from £100,000 to £64,000. This was partly a reflection of the decline in turnover, since established lines were allowed 5 per cent on budgeted sales for advertising. But much of the special advertising mentioned in the directors' 1937 report to shareholders was eliminated, as were also some of the lines it had been intended to support.

New capital expenditure almost ceased in 1938. A capital budget was prepared showing £19,534 as 'essential' and a further £8,604 as 'desirable' expenditure; but in the outcome only a net amount of £1,430 was spent, the executive committee having determined to scrutinise every item before recommending it to the board. By ruthless cutting of capital expenditure and reduction of stocks the bank overdraft was brought down during the year from £323,818 to £144,819.

Most of the economy measures we have described were, no doubt, necessary in the emergency with which the firm was faced. But prosperity could not be regained merely by spending less. The productivity of the capital and labour employed had to be increased.

The management was well aware of the cost of working below capacity and efforts were accordingly made to offset this by reducing costs of production in other directions. An attempt had been made to fix standard costs for all operations, though there were frequent disagreements about the standards and about cases where actual costs exceeded the standard. Much of this was due to the fact that no systematic work study had been done. Very few firms in the textile trades were using this technique in the 1930s and Hollins must be commended for its enterprise in appointing a specialist in it. But he had only recently begun, and it was not until 1938 that his efforts bore fruit.

The first experiments in work study were made in the garments factory. Here much of the machinery was new and operations in the machining and assembly of garments were organised on the conveyor system, which was a recent innovation in the trade. By the use of time study, standard times were worked out for each style of garment and it was reported that the standard times adopted as a basis for costs and prices in 1936 were now actually being achieved or improved upon. Piece rates were then introduced, based on the standard times. Soon afterwards the system was applied in the Glasgow weaving plant and a new wage system was introduced, providing a bonus for output in excess of the standard.

It was reported that the new methods had resulted in much higher productivity and reduced costs; and the report concludes with a statement of conditions for the success of payment by results which is worth quoting: 'Whilst the payment by an incentive scheme does much to assist the management in its control of a factory, it does not relieve it of responsibility, but rather increases its work and tends to make it more effective by giving a pointer as to the weak links in the organisation. For a piece work scheme to operate successfully, it is necessary that the employees should have an even flow of work and that the work given to them should be so planned to make the number of changes as few as possible. The employees must continually feel that they are having a square deal since a system would be completely ruined if the incentive urge is once killed by the faintest suspicion of underhand method. I refer particularly to what happens in some firms, such as increasing the task after the rate has been set, or the secret speeding up of conveyors.'

Along with these efforts to increase labour productivity much was done to improve technical efficiency and to enhance the quality of products. A central testing department was set up, staffed by textile technologists, and the reports of its investigations covered a wide range of problems. Studies were made of the effects of dyeing on the properties of wool. There were experiments with different mixes of wool and cotton and of different grades of these materials. Possible new materials were investigated, though not rayon, which had already been discarded as not being a good commercial proposition for Hollins. Great efforts were made to ensure the quality which was a main selling point for Hollins fabrics. Shrinkage was still apt to occur under certain conditions and all complaints were investigated. Some fabrics too were liable to creasing and efforts were made to reduce this. A somewhat similar problem was the production of a semi-stiff finish for collars.

Such activities, with which Seedhill was, of course, associated, suggest that there was no lack of technical competence and enterprise. But unfortunately it did not always get the backing it needed. There was still much obsolete machinery. A report on the cotton mixing and blowing rooms at Pleasley, for instance, described the plant as quite inadequate for economical working. The machinery dated back to 1885 and its use subjected the cotton—some of the most expensive produced—to extremely harsh treatment. It was considered that with modern machinery a less expensive kind of cotton could be used to spin yarn of the required fineness. Similarly, an investigation of the weaving shed at Glasgow resulted in a recommendation for the scrapping of many looms and their replacement by automatic types with individual drive. Such evidence suggests the lack of a properly balanced investment policy. In the enthusiasm for garment making the older, and still profitable, sections of the firm had been relatively neglected.

CHAPTER FOURTEEN

The Shareholders' Revolt

IN his address to the shareholders in 1936 the chairman had emphasised the importance of confidence in determining the future of the company: 'confidence placed by the shareholders in the board, confidence placed by the staff in the board; and confidence placed by customers in the company'. Since he had taken office, eighteen months before, a lot of 'cleaning-up work' had been done and they were now on their way to better times. 'But,' he concluded, 'I must repeat that it will be necessary for you to show a little patience until this fine old company gets into smoother waters.'

By 1938 the reserves of patience and of confidence, already heavily drawn upon, were exhausted and Hollins' directors faced yet another crisis. No dividend had been paid on the ordinary shares since 1932; the hopes encouraged for 1937 had been disappointed and 1938 promised to be worse still. No explanation by the present board could excuse the failure. Something was seriously wrong and the shareholders were at the point of revolt. They demanded an extraordinary general meeting and when this was called on 25 July 1938 the following resolution, proposed by F. J. Dickens and seconded by Douglas Hamilton, a director, was passed by a substantial majority: 'That this meeting is dissatisfied with the results of the company's business and operations and with the present direction and management of the company.'

For some time before the crisis broke there had been dissension among the directors, involving, in particular, the deputy-chairman and the managing director. Then, in May, the chairman, Sir Frederick Aykroyd, had resigned. In the letter announcing this he reminded the board that the term of three years which he had agreed to serve had now been exceeded. He also expressed the feeling that the company would be better served by a man who could give more time to its affairs.

The new chairman, P. C. Cooper-Parry, was a very different type from his predecessors, who were all industrialists with experience in textiles. He was a partner in a Derby firm of chartered accountants, which meant that he brought to the board the kind of experience it had lacked hitherto and which was certainly needed at that time. Moreover, as a newcomer he was able to take an objective view of the situation and to apply, without prejudice, such economy measures as were needed to strengthen the company's financial position.

The other change, occurring about the same time, concerned the position of deputy-chairman. For the past few years the forceful personality of E. D. A. Herbert had made this the most influential post in the company, supplanting that of the managing director, which had become the most powerful position during the latter part of the Jardine era. As chairman of the executive committee, Herbert had inspired the reorganisation and the expansionist policy of 1936–7 and he was now blamed for its failure. At their meeting on 27 May 1938 the directors resolved, with one dissentient, that the office of deputy-chairman should be terminated and a letter was read from the retiring chairman expressing his complete agreement with this decision. Herbert remained on the board, but he was deprived of executive responsibility, his place as chairman of the executive committee being taken by the managing director, Huskisson, who, incidentally, had seconded the motion against Herbert.

Soon after the new chairman took office, the board received a request from F. J. Dickens, a prominent shareholder with some forty years' experience in the textile trade, for the reconstitution of the shareholders' consultative committee which had previously examined the company's affairs. Herbert and Hamilton supported him, but the majority preferred that the chairman should make the investigation and report to the shareholders before the next annual general meeting. However, Dickens secured sufficient support to

challenge this, and at the extraordinary general meeting of shareholders, mentioned above, it was resolved that a shareholders' consultative committee be appointed immediately. The directors and
officers of the company were authorised and required to give all
possible assistance and the committee was to report to the board.
It was also to make a report to the shareholders giving as much
information as might be disclosed without injury to the company.

The committee's report to the directors, issued in January 1939,
began by recalling the findings and recommendations of the previous committee. After full consideration of all the evidence now
obtained the committee was convinced that if the recommendations
of 1934 had been fully carried out most of the present difficulties
would not have arisen. No director with financial experience had
been appointed, as had been recommended, and there had been no
financial controller to advise the board until the end of 1937. Earlier
efforts should have been made to establish a proper costing system.
The optimistic budget of 1937 had been based on inaccurate costings and when more reliable data became available some selling
prices had had to be raised, with disturbing effects on customers'
confidence and loss of turnover. The committee was agreed that the
increase in stocks during 1937 was partly justified by the need to
speed up deliveries, but earlier action should have been taken to
meet the trade recession, and the fall in raw material prices towards
the end of the year. It also criticised the decision to repay a large
proportion of the preference share capital, as having been made
without sufficient consideration of the company's future policy and
possible financial requirements.

The blame in all these matters rested with the directors. Indeed,
'the board as a whole failed to appreciate their functions as directors'. They had delegated responsibility for many of the major
activities of the company to the executive committee, whose recommendations and progress reports had been accepted almost without
question. An outstanding instance was the expansion of garments
manufacture, involving its transfer to the Radford mill and the

commitment of some £45,000 for structural alterations and plant. The basic issue as to whether Hollins ought to go into garment making in a big way was never properly considered. It would require very careful consideration in the future.

The chairman of the board and a majority of its members had, tried to put the blame on Herbert as chairman of the executive committee; but this was entirely unacceptable to the investigators. 'We completely fail to understand the attitude of a board who seek to place on a chief executive officer the whole responsibility for any major act of policy, which may, or may not, have proved successful. They could not, or should not, have been in ignorance of the inception of the various policies and their development, and we deprecate the manner in which the deputy-chairman was deposed from his position.' The evidence submitted showed that when the deputy-chairman took up his appointment in August 1935 the state of the company's affairs and its reputation stood at a very low level, and the consultative committee was of the opinion 'that many of the steps taken on the deputy-chairman's advice were essential in the interests of the company and for the restoration of its reputation in the trade'.

Having said this, the committee did make certain criticisms of Herbert and the policies he advocated. He had undoubtedly been over-optimistic. This showed itself particularly in the budget estimates for 1937 and in the plans for the expansion of garment manufacture. But here again, 'while recommendations to increase stocks substantially were made by the executive committee, according to the records the board approved the policy and were at all times kept informed of the details and also of the increase in the bank overdraft'. It was easy, in the light of subsequent experience, to criticise Herbert's optimism; but, in accepting the estimates and the monthly progress reports, the board had failed to exercise any restraint; presumably it had shared the same feeling.

An important responsibility of the deputy-chairman had been to improve the firm's internal administration. The committee agreed that he had 'undoubtedly brought new life into the company'. The innovations in management, described in chapter twelve, were largely due to him. The committee found, however, that there had been a lack of willing co-operation, causing unnecessary friction and delay in the application of the new methods. This was especially true of the costing system, which was of such vital importance in budgeting, but was not fully reliable in 1937. The committee's report does not go into details, but the records show the magnitude of the task involved in reforming the costing methods. If, as the committee found, there had been lack of co-operation too, it is hardly surprising that the figures supplied for budgeting purposes and for price fixing were often inaccurate. Herbert had perhaps been too ready to accept assurances as to the reliability of cost information, but the committee were satisfied that he was 'fully alive to the importance of costings'.

In view of the many new appointments made on the deputy-chairman's initiative it is surprising that the consultative committee made no specific reference to the increased cost of administration, though it criticised the board for its failure to review the position. It found that in some cases posts had been created with insufficient consideration of the duties to be performed, so that there had been overlapping of responsibilities and friction between the persons concerned. But in the main the committee appears to have accepted the need for more functional specialists providing common services to line management and helping to co-ordinate the various sectional activities.

Unfortunately co-ordination was still deficient in many respects and, in the opinion of the committee, it was conspicuously lacking at the highest level—on the board itself. 'The smooth working of the company,' they report, 'has been greatly impeded by the existence on the board of what can only be referred to as conflicting parties. Both parties have made mistakes and neither party should be allowed to manage the affairs of the company without proper supervision by the board.'

The committee's reference to two parties on the board was not clarified in terms of personalities, but it is evident from the board minutes and other records that the chief protagonists were Herbert and Huskisson, the managing director. Huskisson had held office since the time of Jardine. An energetic and forceful personality, he had been criticised by the first consultative committee, for taking on too much, though this was brought about to some extent by the deficiencies of his colleagues. Herbert was a newcomer, brought in on the recommendation of this same committee, and as full-time deputy-chairman he enjoyed a senior status. Moreover, as chairman of the executive committee, he performed functions that would be undertaken by a managing director in many firms, and had, in fact, been so undertaken in Hollins before his arrival. Herbert was an engineer by training, but he had wide experience in administration and in marketing. Huskisson had spent all his working life in the textile and clothing trades and could also claim much practical experience on the sales side.

That a conflict should develop between these two men is hardly surprising, and their colleagues on the board, particularly the chairman, did little to resolve it. When matters came to a head, most of them came out against Herbert, and Huskisson succeeded him as chairman of the executive committee.

At the time of the investigation Huskisson produced his own version of events leading up to the crisis, and his recommendations for future policy, in an interesting report. He claimed that the improved results of 1936 were due to his recommendations. The board had then changed their policy and the effect was seen in the experiences of 1937 and 1938. 'I am convinced,' he writes, 'that had the policy introduced in 1936 and pursued throughout 1937 been allowed to continue we should ere long be facing our creditors.' There is no direct reference to Herbert, but the implication is clear that he had at this time displaced Huskisson as the dominant influence in the firm and that only his removal had saved them.

The managing-director's ideas on future policy were certainly

Plate 18. Pleasley Mills

Plate 20. Examining one of the ring frames

Plate 19. A ring frame being lifted by a crane

far-reaching, deriving, as they did, from a reconsideration of the whole structure and character of the business which Hollins had developed over so many years. He believed that the time had now come to decide which parts of the business were worth retaining and developing and which should be discarded, which methods of trading should be retained and which modified. There had, of course, been some thinking on these lines in 1934; and it resulted in some pruning and concentration of activities, although the Via Gellia mill had not been disposed of, contrary to recommendations, and the American plant had been restarted. But Huskisson's proposals went far beyond anything contemplated at that time. In general, they were in opposition to the form of vertical integration which distinguished Hollins from most of their competitors in the textile and clothing trades.

According to Huskisson, there was one section of Hollins's business in which they could rightly claim to be original, namely the spinning section, though even part of this, that producing all-wool yarns for the hosiery trade, was not essential to the main business. What was essential to the character of the business was its speciality of mixture yarns, known as Viyella and Clydella. There was no other section in which the product was not similar to those of competitors, and in which any requirements above their own capacity in warping, weaving and finishing could not be met by outside commission workers.

From these propositions it followed that effort should be concentrated on developing the trade in speciality yarns. Hollins now had access to supplies of wool and cotton exactly suited to its requirements. Mixing and spinning methods had been improved and the relatively low costs attained could be further reduced by specialisation and increased volume of output. It had been a mistake to go in for a wide range of hand-knitting yarns; in this trade the firm should cater only for those consumers who were prepared to pay for the unique qualities of Hollins' yarn and this limited market should be supplied through wholesalers.

o

As for the weaving section, this should be contracted to a modest scale which would ensure full-time working on a two-shift basis. A distinction should be made between work that Hollins had to do itself to maintain quality, and that which could be put out to commission weavers. Huskisson thought that perhaps half the work done on ordinary looms, as distinct from the Northrop type, could be put out. He recommended that the smaller plant, determined in this way, should eventually be transferred to Pleasley or Nottingham and that the Glasgow factory should be sold.

The question of the Seedhill Finishing Company was approached in a similar way. Huskisson believed that the purchase of this firm had been a grave error of judgment. It had meant acquiring responsibility for a highly technical business and for financing a trade that was mostly outside Hollins's range. Moreover, it had deprived Hollins of the opportunity to go into the open market for finishing services. What they needed was a small finishing plant in Nottingham, catering for normal requirements, any further work needed from time to time being put out to specialist finishers, including Seedhill. It was recognised that the sale of the Seedhill Finishing Company could not be undertaken in the present state of trade, but it should be disposed of at the first favourable opportunity.

Huskisson's most drastic proposal concerned the garments department. Under Herbert, the expansion of this department had been a major object of policy and a great effort had been made in sales promotion. Sales had indeed increased, but since 1930 each year had shown a loss. The source of the trouble, according to Huskisson, was in the excessive costs of warehousing, selling and distributing, involved in offering a limited range of garments to retailers. The ultimate remedy was to abandon the making-up trade and promote the sale of cloth to independent garment manufacturers. Some of these were already being supplied and they would buy with more confidence if they knew that Hollins was not competing with garments of their own manufacture. As for the argument that Hollins must make the garments itself in order to maintain the prestige of its brand names, Huskisson claimed that this was no longer valid. It would be possible to enter into contracts with a number of garment manufacturers who could be relied upon to maintain quality standards, give publicity to Hollins's brand names and adhere to fixed price lists. In this way Hollins would be able to expand its profitable trade in cloth and avoid the heavy losses incurred by making and distributing garments.

A similar organisation was recommended for hosiery. Here Hollins had never gone in for manufacture; but knitted goods made from Hollins's yarn by approved manufacturers were bought and resold by Hollins. This trade too had expanded, but it was not profitable. As with garments, the range was not big enough to justify the elaborate organisation required. Hollins should therefore confine itself to ensuring that knitwear sold under its brand names was satisfactory in quality, and price-maintained, leaving the hosiery manufacturers to distribute through wholesalers. Hollins itself should use wholesalers for distributing its hand-knitting wools, a small proportion of which were already handled in this way. Dealing with wholesalers would mean fewer and bigger orders and firms would be selected who could be relied upon to promote sales.

The effect of these proposals would be a further considerable reduction in the sales force, which had already been cut to sixty-seven representatives in the home market and five overseas. There would also be a saving in the cost of warehousing, packing and invoicing. The net saving would, however, depend on the terms which Hollins was able to make with those who were to take over such a large share of the marketing function. This point is not discussed in the report. One important factor would be the amount of advertising support that Hollins was prepared to give. Huskisson had always been concerned about the growth of advertising expenditure and he now proposed a reduction in the normal allocation to 4 per cent on cloth turnover and $2\frac{1}{2}$ per cent on that of garments, hosiery and knittings. In apportioning the allocation a distinction would be made between development lines and those to be sold simply on price and presentation. The latter would receive no direct advertising support.

The consultative committee's report makes no reference to Huskisson's proposals. It attributed the trouble with Hollins to mismanagement rather than to fundamental defects in the structure of the business. It repeated the earlier criticisms of Huskisson himself, as managing director, and recommended that he be replaced. With confidence so lacking it is hardly surprising that Huskisson's ideas on policy should carry little weight with the committee. It expressed the opinion that "the whole question of the making up of garments was inadequately considered and the policy to be adopted for the future will require careful consideration'. But it made no recommendation of its own, nor did it refer to the fundamental question of selling methods. In his advocacy of trading through wholesalers instead of selling direct to retailers, Huskisson emphasised the advantages to the manufacturer in reduced costs of selling and distribution, without considering the corresponding disadvantages in the narrowing of profit margins and the weakening of control over the market. At this time textile manufacturers, especially in the hosiery trade, were beginning to appreciate such disadvantages and were tending to favour direct selling as against using wholesalers. There was, nevertheless, a case for reconsidering Hollins's marketing methods. One aspect, at least, might have been examined. In the anxiety to increase sales, much effort was devoted to opening new accounts and the total of Hollins's customers was now about 2,500. But the cost of dealing with small customers was necessarily high and it might have been more profitable to concentrate on a smaller number of big customers.

The shareholders' consultative committee submitted the gist of its report to the directors on 27 October 1938. In accordance with its diagnosis, the recommendations were mainly concerned with the direction and management of the company. It made no criticism of the recently appointed chairman, Cooper-Parry, but it felt that the necessary reorganisation would be easier under a new chairman.

F. J. Dickens, who had initiated the investigation, was willing to act temporarily and the committee recommended his appointment as chairman of the board. Its other recommendations for the board were James Ross, chairman of the Seedhill subsidiary, who had served on Hollins' board until 1935, J. Duncan, Seedhill's managing director and a chartered accountant, J. W. Bliss, a director of the Wool Industries Research Association and a member of both the consultative committees, and Douglas Hamilton from the existing board.

The proposed reconstruction of the board made no provision for a managing director. Here the committee reiterated the recommendation of the Plender report that no full-time executives should be members of the board. This was an unusual arrangement and it had not been adopted, but the committee considered it desirable in the present circumstances. It meant the retirement of Herbert as a director, but the committee proposed his appointment as a joint general manager and he had agreed to this. The other general manager was to be Joseph Wild. He had had some forty years experience in the textile industry at home and abroad and was Board of Trade representative on the Cotton Spindles Board. Wild would be in charge of production while Herbert was to be responsible for sales.

Throughout its investigation the consultative committee had been in close touch with the directors and it hoped that the changes it proposed might be negotiated without the need for another extraordinary general meeting of shareholders, though it would, of course, require the shareholders' approval at the next ordinary meeting. However, the chairman and the three other directors whom the committee had named for replacement, Paget, Spalding and Huskisson refused to resign merely at the behest of the committee. They issued a circular to shareholders, appealing for support, which the Dickens group countered with a summary of the consultative committee's report and recommendations. When the extraordinary general meeting was held on 25 January 1939, it was reported that

Dickens had secured the 75 per cent majority of votes required to carry his proposals.

In a dignified speech, remarkably free from recrimination, the chairman recounted the recent history of the company. He agreed with the committee's criticisms of the expansionist policy embarked upon in 1937, for which he was not, of course, responsible. But he questioned the committee's assertion that the firm's misfortunes would not have arisen if the previous committee's recommendations had been carried out. In the main they had been carried out, including the appointment of a full-time deputy-chairman, which post the present committee now wanted to abolish. He also criticised the proposed new board. Of the five members, three, including the chairman, were likely to be temporary; much would depend on the more permanent appointments which were not yet in prospect.

In view of the majority already secured by Dickens, the meeting reached a foregone conclusion. There was, however, strong support for Cooper-Parry's remaining on the board. Dickens himself would have welcomed this, but his offer had already been declined and it was announced that the new board, as recommended by the consultative committee, with Dickens as chairman, would be constituted immediately. Herbert came in for some criticism, even from shareholders who supported Dickens, and he was moved to defend himself. The trouble with Hollins, he declared, went back fifteen years. In the three years of his association with the firm he had undertaken the task of reorganisation for which he was brought in. The committee had reported on the part he had played and the shareholders might judge from the summary of its findings that had been put before them.

Thus ended another crisis in the affairs of William Hollins & Co. Soon afterwards the newly constituted board was strengthened by the return of Charles Warren, who had formerly served the company for over thirty years, and by the promotion of Herbert and Wild to be joint managing directors. The latter move reversed the position as recommended by the consultative committee, but it was clearly sound in principle. At the same time the former executive committee was replaced by a smaller executive board, consisting of Herbert, Wild and Warren. There was one other change in 1939; Duncan resigned from the Hollins board though retaining his association with Seedhill.

In reviewing the financial results for 1938, which showed a profit of merely £1,725, the new chairman referred to the extremely difficult trading conditions in that year of international crisis. The directors were, however, devoting the closest attention to the company's affairs and they hoped to produce better results next year if there was no further disturbance of trade.

The hope of better results was amply fulfilled. In 1939 the net profit amounted to £167,736 and for the first time since 1932 ordinary shareholders received a dividend, at 5 per cent less tax. The whole outlook had now been changed by the outbreak of the Second World War. As the war went on, the disturbance of trade was greater than anything experienced before, and Hollins, like most firms, had to adapt to the exigencies of the war economy. But it not merely survived, it prospered.

CHAPTER FIFTEEN

The Post-War Sellers' Market

In the early months of 1939 the threat of war, which had come so close in the previous autumn, seemed to have receded. Many firms were looking forward to a trade revival and Hollins was planning its operations on this assumption. Confidence was further strengthened by the progress made in reorganisation. Several of the specialist departments which had proliferated in Viyella House were abolished or merged, with resulting savings in staff. Surplus stocks had been disposed of and bank indebtedness correspondingly reduced. A thorough review of plants had been undertaken, followed by the replacement of much obsolete or worn-out machinery, a notable example being the expenditure of over £10,000 on new blowing rooms at Pleasley.

The revival came, though in circumstances very different from what had been contemplated; for the outbreak of war in September 1939 brought such an upsurge of demand that the mills were soon working to almost full capacity. The only limiting factor was shortage of labour. In the home market demand was immediately stimulated by the expectation of rising prices and the prospect of rationing. In addition there were the growing demands of the government. The export trade, in which Hollins was already well represented, also improved; in the early stages of the war the government encouraged firms to increase exports so as to strengthen the balance of payments position, and Hollins sent out representatives to all overseas markets that were accessible.

The expectation of higher prices was soon fulfilled. Wage increases had been conceded earlier in the year and with the outbreak of war raw materials became dearer. Hollins estimated that by the middle of September 1939 costs were 15 per cent above the January level. Other firms in the trade were raising prices, and Hollins decided on a 17½ per cent increase on all lines in the home trade and abroad. There was now no danger of spoiling the market; on the contrary, it was foreseen that supplies might have to be rationed and in this event priority would be given to the firm's established customers.

As the war intensified, government control of industry and trade was progressively extended and tightened. Hollins was particularly affected by the introduction of clothes rationing and 'utility' cloths in 1941. Their cloth and garments trade had been built up on the basis of high-quality, widely-advertised branded lines, of which Viyella and Clydella were the best known. There could be no question of depreciating the quality of these, and to offer them in a 'utility' grade would be to risk misleading customers and damaging goodwill. Hollins therefore introduced a cloth which was superior to the specified minimum quality for a certain category of utility goods and called it Dayella, a name which had been registered as a trade mark in 1905. Dayella contained 40 per cent wool, yet it did not exceed the regulation price. It was so superior to most other cloths in its category that eventually the Board of Trade restricted its use to infants' and children's wear. Through Dayella Hollins became the biggest manufacturers in this trade. Dayella was never thought of as 'utility'; it sold on its own merits as a warm, hard-wearing and inexpensive cloth.

The introduction of Dayella was undoubtedly a tribute to the technical skill in which Hollins had always been so strong.[1] But the firm's success in adapting to wartime demands owed much to the efforts of the new board with F. J. Dickens as chairman. Dickens died in January 1943. At the annual general meeting that year his successor, Douglas Hamilton, expressed his gratification that Dickens had lived to see his plans for the reorganisation of the com-

---

[1] The chief credit went to Joseph Wild, joint managing director. In 1953 a bronze plaque, commemorating his achievement as 'the creator of Dayella', was placed on one of the mill walls at Pleasley.

pany, brought to fruition. Referring to their 'wonderful success' in producing Dayella, he declared that 'but for the reorganisation of our staff and the modernising of our plant and equipment during recent years, the production of such a cloth at such a price would have been a sheer impossibility'.

Production of Viyella and Clydella, which did not conform with

---

What is the
secret
of
'Viyella'
?

You are going to hear a lot about Viyella from now on, because this wonderful fabric, after an interval of ten years, is again arriving from Britain—in ever-increasing quantities. Here's the story:

1. **SUPER-BRITISH:** Viyella (rhymes with hi-fella) belongs in the top rank of super-British products. Actually, Viyella is an incredibly soft and light *flannel*. Englishmen have worn it since the turn of the century.

2. **WON'T SHRINK:** You can send Viyella to your laundry. If it shrinks or fades, we replace—and no argument. And here is the secret: Viyella is made from a mixture yarn of *lamb's wool* (for warmth) and *Egyptian cotton* (for washing).

3. **LONG WEARING:** Our venerable Treasurer says Viyella wears much *too* long. The other day a customer showed us some shirts which his papa had worn at the siege of Mafeking in 1899. The son (no chicken himself) is still wearing them.

4. **HANDLE & BLOOM:** Viyella 'handles' like nothing on earth, and keeps its luxurious 'bloom.'

5. **WELL BRED:** Viyella won't fade. It comes in authentic Scottish tartans, dressy stripes, well-bred checks and a large variety of plain shades. From $2.00 a yard.

6. **MAN & BOY:** Viyella is made by an English firm called William Hollins, who have been in business, man and boy, since 1784. Their mills are on the edge of Sherwood Forest, the home of Robin Hood.

ANNOUNCING THE RETURN OF VIYELLA IN THE NEW YORKER

'utility' standards, was drastically curtailed, though a limited supply of officers' shirts and hosiery was maintained, and efforts were made to meet the demands of overseas customers. Shipping difficulties and licensing restrictions increased in severity as the war went on, but most of Hollins' branded lines continued to be available in overseas markets, though in limited quantities. Advertising was still undertaken, though on a reduced sale; for it was important to maintain the prestige of the famous brands, on which so much had been spent, though the goods themselves might be unobtainable.

In addition to their branded lines, and to a large extent in place of them, Hollins produced much yarn and cloth on government contract and for the general trade in hosiery and made-up garments. Its plants were thus kept fully employed, the labour supply being safeguarded by the scheduling of the firm under essential work orders. Hollins was indeed fortunate in retaining most of its productive capacity. Early in the war part of the Radford mill was requisitioned; but the management had already decided to vacate the premises under its reorganisation scheme. Then, after the heavy raids on Birmingham in the spring of 1941, a section of the BSA company had to be accommodated at Pleasley, which involved the dismantling of some carding and spinning machinery. A few months before, bombing had destroyed the London showroom in Old Change, but fortunately Hollins was able to move next door into one of the few buildings in the neighbourhood that had escaped. There was some loss of space in Viyella House too, first to a department of the Ministry of Aircraft Production and later to the Army Post Office, which eventually occupied two floors; but, in the main, Hollins were able to keep their organisation and equipment intact, in contrast to many firms in the textile trades which, under the concentration scheme, had to give up their premises altogether and merge with a nucleus firm. The labour force was reduced by the demands of national service, and many members of the staff went either into the forces or into government departments. This was not always a dis-

Viyella Apologizes

We recently printed five advertisements in The New Yorker to announce the return of dear old Viyella flannel to the American market. The results have been *flabbergasting*.

But this success has been something of a nightmare to retailers, because thousands of people have been badgering them for Viyella shirts which they simply could not supply. We offer our humble apologies to all concerned. It's nobody's fault. For nobody could possibly have foreseen that the pent-up demand for Viyella could be so staggering.

Our English weavers are weaving like beavers, night and day, to catch up. We are delivering *miles* of lamby-soft Viyella flannel, as fast as we can—which isn't fast enough.

Viyella is worth waiting for and, so, it might be a shrewd idea to have your retailer ear-mark a Viyella shirt for you from his next shipment. Or Viyella pyjamas. Or a Viyella bathrobe. Or some Viyella by the yard. It's terrific stuff. And don't forget: "If it shrinks—we replace."

advantage to the firm, for staff reductions were being made when the war began.

Financially, Hollins did less well in the Second World War than in the First. This time there was no talk of 'business as usual'. The use of manpower, materials and equipment was much more tightly controlled and taxation was heavier. Excess profits tax was particularly severe for Hollins, because of its low profits in the pre-war base years. However, the war eliminated the basic causes of the depression in which the firm had floundered during most of the preceding decade. Most of the available capacity was fully employed, with favourable effects on unit costs of production, and, although both buying and selling were subject to price controls and other regulations, business was profitable.

During the six years 1939–44 Hollins earned approximately £1,509,000. Of this £1,219,000 was paid to the Exchequer, leaving a little more than £250,000 for the ordinary and preference dividends after allocations to reserves. Throughout the period the dividend on ordinary shares was maintained at six per cent less tax and a general reserve of £85,000 was accumulated. Additions to fixed assets had perforce been negligible and, despite the investment undertaken just before the war, there was still much old machinery to be replaced and some rebuilding to be done.

The end of the hostilities in 1945 brought no immediate relief from the controls of the war economy. Raw materials and most consumer goods were still rationed, prices were controlled, building was subject to licensing and much property was still under requisition. Demobilisation relieved the labour shortage, but it was a gradual process. Despite the prevailing austerity in the domestic economy it was the government's policy to increase exports, especially to North America, from which many essential imports had to be obtained.

These were the circumstances in which Hollins began to shape its post-war trading policy. The relaxation and eventual abolition of government controls was to be expected, but in the meantime the emphasis was on exports, to which price controls did not apply and for which raw material allocations had priority. The firm had maintained its connections with most overseas markets during the war and efforts were now made to strengthen and develop them.

A survey of overseas markets made in 1952 shows that Hollins exported to forty-five countries. In most of these it sold through local agents; but the firm had its own representatives in Australia and Canada and, of course, its subsidiary company in New York with its mill at Forestdale. Extensive tours of North America, Australia and Far Eastern countries were made in 1947 by Wild, as joint managing director, and Herbert visited South Africa and Rhodesia. At this time entry into many markets was restricted, not merely by the usual protective tariffs, but by licensing and quota arrangements made necessary by balance of payments difficulties. The worst instances were in South America, an important market before the war, but several European countries were affected too, and with France and Germany, in particular, Hollins was doing no trade at all. By far the most important markets were Australia and South Africa, each of which took about £145,000 worth of Hollins' goods in 1948. Exports to Canada and New Zealand were £63,870 and £61,021 respectively, but American sales were only £45,378. Total exports amounted to £697,972 in 1948, which was stated to be more than double the 1947 figure.

During the next three years a remarkable further increase in exports was achieved. In 1949 they rose to £1,039,705, more than a third of total sales. In 1950 they increased further to £1,323,204, and reached £1,770,137 in the following year. Hollins was particularly successful in the North American market, where a growth of nearly sixfold was achieved. Exports to Australia, New Zealand and South Africa doubled and there was also a marked revival of sales to Continental countries as more normal trading conditions were restored.

In the meantime the demands of the home market were growing. Clothes rationing ended in 1949 and Hollins was having difficulty in

supplying all its customers at home, while maintaining its contribution to the export drive. There was an insistent demand for Viyella
and Clydella, and for these lines export orders had priority. Once
the controls on raw materials were removed, labour became the
chief limiting factor in the effort to increase output. At the beginning of 1947 the number of operatives at Pleasley, Nottingham and
Glasgow was about 1,600, of whom more than half were employed
at Pleasley. By the end of 1948 the total had risen to about 1,900,
excluding administrative, sales and warehouse staff, but there was
still constant anxiety about recruitment. Women and girls accounted
for seventy per cent of the labour force and there was intense competition for female labour. Before the war, Hollins had been well
placed at Pleasley for drawing on the 'surplus' female labour in a
mining area. But now other firms with similar needs were establishing themselves in the neighbourhood. They were encouraged to do
so under the government's distribution of industry policy, which
was designed to relieve the pressure in congested areas like Nottingham and improve the balance of employment where there was undue
dependence on one industry, such as coal mining.

The general shortage of labour was reflected in rising wages and
it was realised in 1947 that Hollins's rates were not competitive,
especially at Pleasley. Investigation showed that low wages and
anomalies in the wage scales were the main obstacle to the recruitment and retention of workers, and a thorough reform of the wage
structure was introduced. This provided for progressive wage-for-
age scales, designed to benefit the younger operatives especially,
while older employees qualified for long service increments. The
initial cost of the scheme, which was later extended to the firm's
other branches, was estimated at £20,000 a year; but this represented
less than 2d a yard on cloth, much of which might well be absorbed
if more workers were attracted so that production could be increased.

Another means of increasing production and also of countering
the rising cost of labour was capital investment. This had been almost entirely suspended during the war, and the immediate need

was to make good the backlog of maintenance work and normal replacement that had built up. In addition, the further expansion of capacity had to be provided for, while taking account of the need to economise labour. A modernisation programme was thus agreed upon.

It was not until 1948, however, that investment was resumed on an important scale, for new machinery was still in very short supply. Much of the plant installed in the next few years was for replacement. At Boden Street many of the Northrop looms on which plain cloths were woven and also the check looms, were at least twenty years old; some of the latter indeed dated back to 1902. Between 1948 and 1954 some £150,000 was spent on looms and other machines, bringing the value of the whole weaving plant to about £300,000. Pleasley too had much machinery overdue for replacement and there also about £150,000 was spent on ring spinning frames, carding and roving machinery and wool chlorination equipment. At Seedhill, buildings were extended, a new power plant was installed and more dyeing machinery was bought. In 1952 it was reported that the replacement of obsolete equipment was virtually completed, and that some important additions to existing plants were being made, particularly at Pleasley. By the end of this year the value of the firm's fixed assets had risen to £903,000, more than double the 1948 figure, after allowing for depreciation.

Throughout this period of rehabilitation labour shortage was still a handicap in some sections. There was a high rate of turnover for women workers and total employment fluctuated considerably from month to month, so that only a general indication of the trend can be given. After the initial build-up following the war, little further increase was shown at Pleasley, but the new equipment had substantially increased the output per head. At the weaving mill, however, employment had increased by about 25 per cent and there also productivity had benefited by the installation of new plant. Garment making presented a two-fold problem. It was more labour-intensive than spinning and weaving, and female labour was parti-

Plate 21. Viyella design centre, Paisley

Forestdale, Rhode Island, U.S.A.

We, the employees of

William Hollins & Company, Inc.

on this 31st day of January Nineteen Hundred and Fifty-two, the final day of operation of the Company's Mill at Forestdale, Rhode Island, wish to express to William Hollins & Company, Ltd. our sincere thanks and appreciation for their kind consideration and generosity, not only as we leave the Company's employ, but also during the years of our happy association. We offer this testimonial with our gratitude and our best wishes for the future.

Armand B. Blanchette	George Galuza	Albert Daignault	Harry Sherboken
Anthony Olech	James Donaldson	Joseph Tessier	William Pulley
Jennie Prestnick	Joseph Vadeboncoeur	Joseph Paiva	Armand Boucher
Lydia Desrosier	Mary Romano	Robert Mowry	Manuel Freitas
George Peck	James Burke	Loretta Blanchette	Carmelo D'Angelo
Vincenzo Grossi	John Serapiglia	Edward Duprex	Eugene Jaford
Yvonne Jolin	Ida Ferriere	Mary Wronoski	Lydia Geer
John Buba	Georgianna Gregory	Harry Herman	Estelle Brunet
Omer Brodeur	Alfred Bruno	Emily Kozlik	Muriel Peloquin
Edward Swierk	George Jenckes	Martha Guertin	Edwin Buba
Arthur Plouffe	Edward Guertin	James Jaffate	William R. LaChapelle
Katherine Tringue	Manuel J. Paul	Emile Bouliane	Mildred S. Rhodes
Ovila Riendeau	Raymond Boucher	Edward Theriault	Robert L. English
Florence Paul	Joseph C. Aguiar	Frank Sudol	

Plate 22. Testimonial to Wm Hollins & Co, USA

cularly scarce in Nottingham; but in any case there was no space for expansion in the existing garments factory at Viyella House. The Radford mill which had been adapted for garment making before the war was considered unsuitable for further expansion and after investigating various possible locations Hollins secured, in 1950, a factory at Hucknall, a few miles north of Nottingham. This was particularly suitable; for the factory had been occupied by a firm of garment makers, workers and machines were available and production could start immediately. Within a short time more machinery was installed, the premises were extended and the labour force was increased to 400 by the beginning of 1953. Eventually the whole of the firm's garment making was concentrated at Hucknall, thus releasing badly needed space in Viyella House. It was stated in 1955 that the central warehouse was now handling, in quantity, 58 per cent more garments, 50 per cent more hosiery, and 20 per cent more piece goods, than in 1948.

Until 1951 the whole of this capital expenditure was financed out of profits, which by then had increased from £96,000 in 1946 to £284,000, net of taxation. Over the same period the dividend rose from 7½ to 12½ per cent, but in spite of this until 1950 the company's position was still highly liquid. One reason for the increased profits since 1945 had been prudent buying in advance of the persistent upward trend in raw material prices, particularly in the price of wool. Profits also benefited as stocks appreciated in value, and the firm adjusted its selling prices from time to time in accordance with rising costs. Following another general increase in 1948, it was stated that prices in both home and export markets were about seventy per cent above the pre-war level. But despite higher prices sales increased year by year, reaching a total of £3,620,082 in 1950. Already in 1948 and 1949 the directors had strengthened the raw material reserve against a possible recession and, as prices accelerated in 1950, they decided to add another £150,000 bringing the reserve up to £400,000. But prices still rose, until in March 1951 wool prices were between two and three times the level of June 1950, and ten

P

times the 1938 level. The value of Hollins's stocks, including raw materials, work in progress and finished goods was now £3,459,000; the raw material reserve stood at £750,000 and there was a bank overdraft of £217,438.

In the words of the directors' report for 1951, 'this situation gave rise to problems of a type and magnitude never before experienced. The most obvious was the need for increased capital to finance the higher cost of stocks.' In fact, it was something of an exaggeration to suggest that the situation was unprecedented; for it was similar to that which was faced in 1919 and 1920 and, as on those occasions, the need for increased capital was met by a new share issue. This time 508,000 £1 ordinary shares were offered at a premium of £1 per share, which brought the total issued capital of William Hollins and its subsidiary companies to £1,868,000 and immediately improved the cash position by more than £1 million. The success of the operation is evidence of the confidence felt by investors in the continued prosperity of the firm.

There was much in the post-war record to encourage confidence. Older shareholders, remembering the acrimonious disputes among the directors, the investigations and the extraordinary general meetings of the inter-war years, which had done so much damage to the firm's reputation, must have been impressed by the harmony that now seemed to prevail. Douglas Hamilton had proved a worthy successor to Dickens as chairman, and Joseph Wild had been an able and energetic managing director. Herbert was seconded to government service during the war, so that Wild assumed the chief executive responsibility. He had, however, retained his seat on the board, and with the end of the war he returned in full vigour to his post as joint managing director. For the next few years Herbert and Wild appear to have worked very well together, in marked contrast to the relations between Herbert and Huskisson before the war.

Herbert and Wild were complementary in the functions they performed, and in their personal qualities. There was between them a bond of mutual respect. Wild was essentially a production man and in the early post-war years it was production rather than selling that mattered. But raw material buying was important too and here also Wild's knowledge and foresight were invaluable. His shrewd policy had ensured that Hollins entered the war period with good stocks; and it enabled the firm to avoid the worst effects, when the post-war sellers' market abruptly ended in 1951.

It was Herbert, however, who ultimately assumed the main responsibility. In his four years with Hollins before the war he had already established himself as the dominant personality in the firm. His over-optimism was partly responsible for the mistakes in commercial policy that caused so much recrimination and he came in for his due share of criticism at the shareholders' meetings. But his influence on organisation and methods was certainly healthy. As a newcomer he had been shocked by the excessive sectionalism and cumbersome forms of communication which had developed, and he had set about the task of reform with zeal and determination. His memorandum on committees, dated 1936, is worth quoting.

> I am very disturbed indeed to note that we appear to be drifting back to the situation that existed last year, under which we had far more so-called committees than are necessary for the efficient operation of this business. I am also concerned that senior executives are attending meetings of subordinate committees. Apart from the executive comittee, I can see no permanent justification for committees other than those concerned with marketing and merchandising. As for the other committees, a number of which have sprung up during the last few months, far too much time is spent in the slavish recording of everything said by everybody on every subject discussed. I am entirely in favour of calling together all those concerned, for the discussion of any important matter, but all that is necessary thereafter is for a simple decision to be recorded, in the fewest possible words. It is unnecessary to designate the meeting a 'committee'. What matters is that some final conclusion will be arrived at, after the fullest possible consideration, and that action should be taken with the least possible delay. As to the matter of senior executives attending subordinate meetings, I can only remind you that one of the most serious criticisms made by the shareholders' investigation committee was that too little responsibility was given to individual members of the staff. I hold the view that having appointed heads of departments and sections it is the responsibility of the executive committee to satisfy itself that the individuals in question are carrying out their responsibilities. If we are satisfied that they have the right character, attitude and ability to carry out their work satisfactorily, and are in fact doing so, they must be left free from interference to do their utmost for the Company.

The latter point is made also in a letter of the same year to the manager of the New York office, who had apparently complained of interference by headquarters, and had asked for a clarification of his responsibility. 'I would say at once,' Herbert tells him, 'that it is you, and not we, who are managing our business in North America, and to you alone that we look for guidance on all matters pertaining to the territory in your charge. It is to you that we will be happy to send our congratulations if our interests in North America continue to make satisfactory progress, and it is to you that our criticism will be directed should matters not proceed in accordance with our reasonable expectations. Naturally, because we are people of reasonable intelligence and, moreover, because you and we are friends working to a common purpose, we would expect you to say more than merely "no" to any proposition that came from us, with which you found it impossible to proceed. We would expect you to send us a reasoned exposition of your views, and this, as I think you will agree, is a reasonable requirement between us. We do not ask for more than this, and I do assure you that whatever your views may be they will be regarded as those of a sincere, intelligent man, conscious of his responsibilities to those with whom he is working. If you find it impossible to proceed with any recommendations of ours, and you give us your views in the manner I have indicated, believe me, there will be no reservations whatsoever on our part, and I should be very sorry indeed to think that any of us would be prone to charge you with obstruction.'

Before the war there was little systematic thinking in British industry about the nature of management, delegated responsibility and accountability, communications, and line and staff relations. Clearly Herbert had definite ideas on these matters, and he had made some progress in getting them applied within Hollins's organisation. One of his first tasks after the war was to produce the draft of an organisation chart showing the various functions within the four main divisions of production, marketing, merchandise control and administration, including finance, and indicating the allocation of responsibilities among the staff. After consideration by the executive committee the chart was redrafted 'in such a manner as to obviate any adverse psychological effect the relative positions on the chart allocated to the various functions might have on the person concerned'. Its provisions were then put into operation on the understanding that the chart should be reviewed every three months.

This scheme appears to have settled, at least for the time being, some of the outstanding problems of organisation at the managerial level. But equally important were the relations between management and workpeople. Hitherto in this respect Hollins had been a typical example of authoritarian management tempered by benevolence. There had been a movement, after the First World War, following the reports of the Whitley Committee, for the setting up of works councils on which employees' representatives would meet with management to discuss matters of common interest. Many firms adopted the scheme, but the initial enthusiasm soon faded and comparatively few councils survived to do really useful work. There is no record of any such experiment at Hollins at this time; the firm continued to rely on welfare services, the encouragement of social and sporting activities and the provision of ex-gratia pensions and long-service awards to foster the sense of 'belonging' among its employees. It also appointed a staff adviser to look after the 'human relations' aspect of management.

But in 1940s the climate of industrial relations was changing. The experience of war had again emphasised the common interests of management and labour as participants in a co-operative activity. Joint production committees were a familiar feature of wartime industry, and personnel management came to be recognised as a distinctive function in a firm's organisation. The government had announced its determination to maintain full employment after the war, and it was recognised that with the general labour scarcity that this implied, a considerable revision of traditional management practices would be required. The attitudes and methods of authoritarian management would no longer serve; there must be organised consultation between management and labour.

Thus, with the encouragement of the Ministry of Labour, more and more firms set up their joint consultative or joint advisory committees. At Hollins, Herbert took up the idea with enthusiasm; the first committee came into being at Pleasley in May 1946 and the system was soon extended to other branches. In opening the inaugural meeting Herbert declared that, in his experience, 'full and frank consultation between the management and the people doing the job was an essential feature of all successful business'. About the same time a suggestions scheme was introduced; and in its first five years more than 200 awards of between £1 and £25 were made to employees for suggested improvements in production methods or organisation.

Another enterprise with which Herbert was closely associated was the house magazine—*The Viyella Standard*. This first appeared in a modest form in 1946, but it soon grew into an admirable publication of its kind. Of particular interest to the historian of the firm are the occasional articles on Hollins's earlier days and the short biographies of old members of the firm. The last issue for 1955 contained a Christmas message from Herbert, as managing director, reviewing Hollins's progress since the war. Using the idea of a film taken in slow motion and then shown at normal speed, he develops his theme in characteristic style. 'If such a camera had been set to work in our organisation ten years ago—when the fighting had stopped and we were all free to get back to our jobs after the long interval of war—what a perfectly wonderful film I could show you—a film packed with courage and enterprise and the running of big risks, with its full share of heroes and heroines and a "full supporting cast" of grand, steady, hardworking men and women. To us who have been straining impatiently at the leash all these ten years, it has sometimes seemed that our progress had been unbearably slow, but when we stop to consider the truly marvellous things that have been accomplished in the face of the greatest difficulties, we gain fresh heart.'

It is perhaps a little overdone, even for a Christmas message. But the story of Hollins's growth in the post-war decade is certainly impressive. It was particularly gratifying to those members of what Herbert called 'our great and growing family' who had known the stagnation and frustration of the ten years before the war.

CHAPTER SIXTEEN

The Quest for Expansion and its Sequel

THE year 1955, which marked the conclusion of the post-war decade, was not a particularly good year for Hollins. Sales, which had more than trebled in value over the first five years, had levelled off at a total of £4,419,000, and net trading profit, which had risen from £96,000 to £300,000 over the same period, was now down to £175,000. Some old problems had reappeared and some new ones were emerging, and the management was presented with difficult issues of policy.

The outbreak of the Korean war had created a serious disturbance in 1950–1 with the spectacular rise, and then sudden fall, of world commodity prices; wool was one of the commodities most affected by this, and its price rose steeply, only to collapse about the middle of 1951. As a big importer of cotton and wool, Hollins had always been vulnerable to such fluctuations and it endeavoured to safeguard itself by dealing in futures and by using its raw material reserve. The futures markets had not yet been restored, however, and in any case wool futures did not provide an effective hedge against fluctuations in the special kinds of wool which Hollins required. Accordingly, the firm suspended wool buying early in 1951 when its stocks of all kinds stood at £3,656,000, and, as prices continued to fall in 1952, stocks were written down by about 18 per cent.[1] The net profit available for distribution fell in 1952 to a mere £22,160 and the dividend was maintained at 10 per cent by transferring £75,000 from the raw material reserve, which had stood at £750,000.

From this time onwards, the high level of stocks continued to present a problem, as it had done in the 1930s. The position had

---

[1] The fall from the peak in early 1951 was much greater, but Hollins stopped buying well before the peak was reached.

indeed worsened by comparison with the pre-war period. In 1938, the value of stocks had been shown as £704,000 against a sales total of £1,279,000. In the 1950s sales varied between £3,620,000 and £4,915,000 and the proportion of stocks to turnover never fell below 62 per cent. The following table shows the position year by year:

TABLE 10

Year	Total Sales	Exports	Stocks	Stocks as Percentages of Sales
	(£'000)	(£'000)	(£'000)	
1938	1,279	357	704	55
1950	3,620	1,324	2,863	79
1951	4,043	1,830	3,656	89
1952	3,662	1,295	2,941	80
1953	4,221	1,679	2,800	66
1954	4,414	1,809	3,082	70
1955	4,419	1,728	2,957	67
1956	4,486	1,719	3,423	76
1957	4,915	1,916	3,717	76
1958	4,539	1,502	2,818	62
1959	4,909	1,802	3,141	64

The very high proportion of stocks to sales in 1951 is explained by the big holding of wool. The wool stock, valued at cost, amounted to £1,631,000, enough for twenty-two months' working, and cotton accounted for a further £278,000. But the position was little better in 1952, although wool buying had been suspended and stocks had been written down. For the first time since the war, sales had now fallen. Although sales subsequently recovered, the stock ratio continued to be much higher than before the war.

The sales decline in 1952 was due entirely to a fall in exports. Australia, the main market, was the worst hit. This country and New Zealand had benefited from the wool boom, but in its aftermath they ran into balance of payments difficulties and imposed import restrictions. Fortunately, however, Canadian sales improved, as did those to the USA,[1] except for a setback in 1954. In Africa and Asian markets demand was restricted under the policy of import substitution, as practised by most under-developed countries after attaining political independence. Sales to European countries remained fairly steady throughout the decade, accounting for about 10 per cent of total exports.

In view of the difficulties encountered by British textile exporters in these years, Hollins did well. Piece goods, sold mainly to garment manufacturers, were by far the most important category of exports. Overseas sales of made-up garments were always very small, but there was a fair trade in knitted garments made by British manufacturers from Hollins' yarn and marketed by Hollins. There were also signs of a revival in yarn exports. Nevertheless, the set-back of 1952 had emphasised the risk of being unduly dependent on exports. As for hopes of expansion, it was evident by this time that Hollins must look to the home market.

The salient feature of the home market was the growing trade in made-up garments. This was the main factor in the improvement of 1953, when net profits recovered to £274,000 and the dividend was restored to 12½ per cent. In his address to the shareholders, the chairman explained that, though exports had not fully recovered, there was a large unsatisfied demand in the home market, especially for Clydella, which had been recently reintroduced. The firm was now working to the full extent of its increased capacity and schemes for further expansion were being considered.

As the new garments factory at Hucknall was already in operation, the need now was for more spinning and weaving capacity. It had been hoped that this would be met by re-equipping the existing mills, but on visits to Pleasley and Glasgow in 1953 the chairman had expressed his disappointment that the heavy capital expenditure incurred since the war had not produced a commensurate increase in output, despite shift-working. Thus to some members of the

---

[1] The Rhode Island mill operated by Wm Hollins & Co Inc had been closed in 1952.

board, and especially Herbert, it seemed essential to set up a new spinning and weaving plant. The alternative was to buy yarn from outside spinners and use commission weavers for certain kinds of cloth.

Opinion was sharply divided on this issue, with Herbert pressing the case for expansion and Hamilton advising caution, in view of the previous year's experience, when short-time working had had to be introduced in the spinning and weaving plants. However, Herbert's advocacy prevailed, and the matter was clinched when he reported on the offer of the lease of a factory on the Newhouse Industrial Estate near Glasgow. It had been built by Scottish Industrial Estates Ltd, a government sponsored body, and the present occupants, Vatric Ltd, were giving up the tenancy. The fact that the premises could be leased, at an annual cost of about £22,000, was an advantage as regards the requirement of fixed capital. It was proposed that Newhouse should be equipped as an 'all white' mill, producing Hollins' 'bread-and-butter lines', leaving Pleasley and Boden Street to concentrate on 'coloured' lines. An economic unit would be 20,000 spindles and 500 looms involving an investment of some £600,000, and the result would be a 25 per cent increase in the firm's production capacity. It was estimated further, that, 'subject to there being no major departure from present trading conditions', an increased net profit, before tax, of some £200,000 a year would be secured.

The proposal, as presented by Herbert and his supporters certainly looked attractive, and in October 1953 the board decided to accept it. No time was lost in beginning operations. By the following May the first batch of spinning machines and looms had been installed at a cost of some £200,000 and production started. But this was only the first stage of a programme designed to create a plant of at least 25,000 spindles and 600 looms; it required further capital expenditure of over £500,000 and the employment ultimately of some 700 operatives on a two-shift basis.

The build-up of weaving capacity went fairly smoothly and by the end of 1956 420 automatic looms were working. The delivery of spinning machinery, however, was considerably delayed and consequently, yarn had to be obtained from Pleasley and from outside spinners. The position gradually improved in 1957; about the middle of that year total employment reached nearly 400 and £535,000 had been spent on the plant. As things eventually turned out, this proved to be the peak of Hollins's attainment at Newhouse.

Employment in the firm as a whole, and its distribution in the various units, is shown in the following table for May 1957.

TABLE 11

Production Units	Males	Females	Total
Pleasley	284	655	939
Radford	45	28	73
Glasgow	154	511	665
Newhouse	100	295	395
Nottingham Garments Factory	7	292	299
Hucknall Garments Factory	39	534	573
Non-Production Units	291	280	571
	920	2,595	3,515[1]

[1] This excludes Seedhill, for which complete figures are lacking. Comparison with table 9 shows that Hollins's employment was about one-third higher than in 1934.

As shown in table 10, Hollins' sales rose sharply in 1957, the recovery of exports being particularly encouraging. The only disquieting feature was the continuing high ratio of stocks. It had been recognised that the introduction of the new unit at Newhouse would involve some investment in stocks there, but it was hoped that this would be more than offset by the increased turnover of the firm as a whole. In fact the year 1958 brought another recession—less severe than the slump of 1952, but serious enough in view of the increased capacity that had been created. Exports fell and there was no compensating rise in home sales. All overseas markets, except for the Continent, were affected. In explanation, the chairman referred particularly to the American tariff provision whereby the *ad valorem* duty increased from 25 to 45 per cent, when the total weight of woollen fabrics imported into the USA in any year equalled 5 per cent of the average weight of domestic production over the preceding three years. In the important Australian and New Zealand markets too, Hollins's trade had suffered from increased import restrictions. It seemed that the pattern of British trade with Commonwealth countries was changing. There was an increasing tendency towards self-sufficiency in countries which formerly relied on British manufactures, and where imports were still bought, the tariff preference for British goods was narrowing.

The downward trend of exports was the more disappointing in view of the great efforts which Hollins had made in overseas markets. For instance, in the six years 1953–8 they spent no less than £764,000 on overseas advertising, as compared with £647,000 in the home market, the cost rising in 1958 to 10·78 per cent of exports receipts. Of other selling expenses, £856,000 was attributed to exports over the same period, while the much bigger home trade involved a cost of £915,000.

Another adverse factor in 1958 was the fall in wool and cotton prices, which necessitated a further writing down of stocks by some £260,000. At the same time, there had been a cutback in production, which meant under-recovery of overhead charges and an increase in unit costs. Altogether Hollins made a loss of about £75,000 on its operations in 1958; the depreciation of stocks was financed from the general reserve and no dividend was paid.

Underlying the depressing experience of 1958 was a continuing concern regarding the company's financial liquidity. At the end of 1953, following the increase in capital, there had been a bank balance of £303,000. It was the intention to finance the Newhouse project partly from this source and partly from retained profits. But a further £360,000 of capital expenditure was incurred elsewhere, for instance, in the transfer of the dyehouse from Radford to Pleasley and in further additions to the garment factories. Then there was the heavy cost of financing stocks and of providing for their depreciation. By the end of 1955 the bank credit had turned into an overdraft of £291,099 and a year later this had risen to £664,773. Even these figures, however, do not reveal the full extent of Hollins' dependence on bank credit. Their trade reached its peak in the autumn so that stocks were generally at their highest in July. In July 1957 the bank overdraft was about £1,416,000 and, despite efforts to reduce it, the amount rose again to £1,267,000 in July 1958. A large overdraft is not necessarily a sign of weakness, but undue dependence on bank credit exposed the firm to the pressure of the generally higher interest rates that now prevailed, and to the more drastic forms of credit restriction which the banks were required to impose from time to time at the behest of the government.

The responsibility for explaining to the shareholders the depressing results of 1958 fell to Herbert, who had been elected chairman at the end of the year. Douglas Hamilton had retired from that position three years earlier and his place had been taken in the interval by Joseph Wild. There were now three joint managing directors: Cornelius Cameron (administration), E. C. Pollit (production) and T. I. Etridge (sales and merchandise). Other full-time executives on the board were P. B. Bushell (overseas sales) and E. W. Fletcher (representing Seedhill). Sir H. Nutcombe Hume of the Charterhouse Finance Corporation, was deputy-chairman and the other part-time members were Sir Charles Hallett, Arthur Tate and James Ballard, an authority on textile technology.

The directors had decided not to recommend a dividend on ordinary shares for 1958 but to declare a special interim dividend of 10 per cent in the following April. Herbert said that 1958 had been one of the most difficult years in the last quarter of a century for the textile industry, and especially for the cotton and wool sections where raw material prices had again fallen steeply. For the special qualities of wool and cotton used by Hollins the fall was 25 per cent for wool and somewhat more for cotton. Stocks had been written down by £200,000 in 1957 and now a further £260,000 had been written off. The fall in raw material costs had made possible some reductions in selling prices, but increases in wage rates and the under-recovery of overheads due to short-time working had increased other costs, so that profit margins were narrower. The board could not foresee any substantial increase in export trade in the immediate future, but it was confident that with a continuance of its sound merchandising policies, supported by its vigorous selling organisation, turnover in the home market would continue to expand.

But could the mere continuance of present policies be relied upon to restore and maintain the firm's prosperity? The pattern of Hollins's trade was essentially that of pre-war days when the original business of spinning yarns for the market had declined and the emphasis had shifted more and more towards cloth and garments, with most of the yarn consumed internally. The expansion of capacity in the 1950s only enlarged the pattern; it did not change it, and the end products, although varied in detail, had the same physical characteristics as when Viyella and its derivatives had been first introduced.

One disadvantage of specialisation in wool-cotton mixtures was the marked seasonal fluctuations which occurred in the business. Hollins's was mainly an autumn and winter trade. Although lighter cloths had been introduced and the range of garments had been extended, the bulk of the trade was still seasonal. In the home market, where sales were made direct to retailers, customers expected prompt delivery of goods ordered when they were required. The burden of carrying stocks rested mainly on the manufacturer, and stocks had to be built up in anticipation of the seasonal rush in orders. Further, a vertically integrated concern like Hollins will usually have higher stocks than one which relies on outside suppliers. The extension into garments manufacture emphasised this characteristic because it lengthened the production cycle from the spinning of yarn to the sale of the finished product. Each successive process—spinning, dyeing, weaving, finishing and making-up—

needed to be planned so as to avoid any shortage, delay or build-up
of stocks at any stage. Moreover, the soundness of these plans was
dependent on the accuracy of a sales forecast for the end product.

Hollins had been struggling with these problems before the war.
Now, with increased commitments, they seemed no nearer to solving
them, and there was an added complication. In pre-war days some
flexibility could be obtained by reducing the labour force in slack
times and resorting to overtime and shift working when departments were busy. But labour had to be treated more carefully now;
there was continual anxiety about the supply of trained operatives,
and it was in the long-term interests of a firm to maintain continuity of employment by every possible means. Labour was becoming, like capital, a fixed cost of production.

In October 1958 Hollins's directors held a special meeting to consider the firm's future policy. They decided that selling effort
should be concentrated on the six branded cloths they were now
offering in various forms, and that each should be linked with
Viyella as a 'Viyella House' product. At the same time they should
seek to diversify their interests by association with other firms. In
the first place they should aim at firms whose products were on the
fringe of Hollins's trade, but ultimately, 'to spread the risks intrinsic
to any business engaged solely in textiles', they should link up with
businesses 'of totally different character'.

In an effort to achieve the first phase in diversification Hollins
made approaches to a number of firms, and in one case the negotiations reached an advanced stage during 1959. This involved the
well-known firm of Tootal Ltd, which, it seemed, had a similar
peaking problem with its sales, which were high in summer and
low in winter. In this respect, therefore, the two firms were complementary. In a letter to members of Hollins's staff and agents,
Herbert explained that ever since 1938 he had been seeking a
means of 'balancing up our range of merchandise, so that we might
achieve more continuous contact throughout the year with our
customers and with the public and operate every section of our

organisation more efficiently than when we are working on a seasonal basis'. Now, it appeared, the means had been found.

But it proved impossible to reach agreement on the terms of a merger. It had been contemplated that a holding company would be formed and Hollins wanted equal representation with Tootal on the board. They further proposed that Herbert, in view of his standing, should be chairman or vice-chairman. They claimed that, although Tootal was the larger firm in terms of assets, Hollins's contribution to the profits of the proposed holding company would come very close to Tootal's. But these suggestions were quite unacceptable to Tootal, which had in mind a complete take-over of Hollins. So the negotiations ended in nothing more than a promise to consider co-operation in the ordinary course of trade.

Attention was now directed to another scheme, which involved a change in the firm's commercial policy. From the time that Hollins introduced their branded lines of cloth and garments the bulk of its home trade had been with retailers, who resold at standard prices. It was an expensive method of selling. After the war the sales force had been built up again and there were now forty-four representatives in the home market visiting some 3,000 customers. The despatch of orders, the handling of accounts, the supplying of patterns, employed about 400 people at Viyella House. Then there was the heavy cost of advertising. Moreover, the flow of orders could be very erratic and was, of course, subject to seasonal peaking.

Between the wars many firms in the clothing and knitwear industries had gone in for direct selling to retailers instead of dealing with wholesalers, but they ran into many of the difficulties with which Hollins were still contending. They wanted to reduce selling expenses and, even more important, they wanted regular bulk orders to keep them fully employed. Both these advantages were offered by Marks and Spencer, which was rapidly acquiring a dominant position in the retail clothing trade.

After the war Marks and Spencer continued to expand and the number of its suppliers increased. Quite large firms, producing their

Q

own branded lines, found it worthwhile to make for Marks and Spencer too. The terms were exacting; the multiple retailer laid down the specification of the goods, which were made to sell under its own 'St Michael' brand name. The manufacturer's profit margin was cut very fine, but if his co-operation was satisfactory he got the benefit of a steady outlet for his production.

Here then was a possible solution for Hollins's problem. The firm had already done a certain amount of trade in unbranded lines through its subsidiary, Alexander McNab, and had undertaken commission work from time to time when it had idle capacity, but this trade was highly competitive and Hollins had no special qualifications for it. However, it was now very well equipped for garment manufacture. If it could be sure of working all the year round, to something like full capacity, this would reduce unit costs, not only in garment making, but in spinning, weaving and finishing. Bulk orders would also mean less selling cost.

Toward the end of 1958 Hollins approached Marks and Spencer for a trial order for children's wear and this soon developed into a regular trade. In order to avoid conflict with Hollins's traditional trade, Marks and Spencer were supplied through Alexander McNab. But the experiment was not very successful. The demands on the garment sections certainly increased, and another small factory had to be acquired; but the hope of absorbing all the surplus weaving capacity was not realized. Moreover, Marks and Spencer's price was said to allow for very little over direct costs. Thus the benefit to the traditional trade, by way of a better recovery of overheads, was negligible.

There was also the danger that the lines sold through Marks and Sp ncer would compete with Hollins's own branded lines. The two markets were not mutually exclusive; for while there were many customers who would always insist on Viyella and pay the price, there was a fringe of price-conscious consumers whose loyalty to Hollins's brands could easily shift to the cheaper St Michael article, which, being made by Hollins, had something of the Viyella quality.

Quality had always been Hollins's main selling point, and, within a certain range, the firm still enjoyed a high reputation. Besides maintaining quality it had made constant efforts to improve design and style. A notable development of this period was printed Viyella, which was ultimately undertaken by Seedhill in the Arkleston Works. But the possibilities of wool and cotton mixtures were limited. New fibres and new materials were now available in increasing variety and for many purposes they were rapidly displacing the old ones. Shirts, for instance, were one of Hollins' main products. Its shirts were guaranteed against shrinkage, but they could shrink if not washed by the prescribed method. Hollins had a special department for dealing with complaints and shrinking was one of the most common.[1] Further, there was the need for ironing. But with manmade fibres shirts could be made to 'drip-dry', with no risk of shrinking and no need for ironing.

Artificial silk, the first of the manmade fibres, was introduced by Courtaulds before the First World War. In the 1920s it became not only much cheaper than pure silk, but even cheaper than worsted yarn, and it was rapidly adopted in hosiery manufacture. In weaving, its progress was slower; the first fabrics made entirely of artificial silk were not introduced until 1930. But before this the material was being increasingly used in combination with cotton and worsted yarns. Then it was found possible to mix it, in short staple form, with cotton and wool and spin it into a mixture yarn. Thus artificial silk came to be recognised on its own merits as an extremely versatile material; the early prejudice against it disappeared, assisted, no doubt, by giving it a better name: 'rayon'.[2]

It is surprising that Hollins, with all their experience in mixture yarns, played so little part in these developments. They did, for a time, offer yarns with artificial silk in various combinations with other materials for knitting and weaving, but their prices were not competitive. Then they produced a cloth of their own weaving which con-

---

[1] The guarantee was now advertised in the form: 'If it shrinks we replace.'
[2] Based on C. K. Ward-Jackson, *A History of Courtaulds*. 1941.

tained rayon, but which was eventually dropped. There is a record in the board minutes during 1936 stating that 'in view of the loss realised last year and in previous years and the intensely competitive nature of the trade in artificial silks, their sale will be discontinued unless, at any future time, we can succeed in introducing some unique feature which will enable us to make it a profitable line'.

Twenty years later, the range of manmade fibres had been greatly extended, with revolutionary effects on the textile and clothing industries. Hollins now began to realise that their basic products were vulnerable to the competition of new materials possessing qualities that found increasing favour with consumers. Nylon was especially successful, on account of its appearance and durability, and Hollins introduced certain lines containing 10 per cent nylon. These sold under the brand names of Viyellon, Clydellon and Sportellon. But British Nylon Spinners, who dominated the British market, were trying to popularise their own brand name—Bri-Nylon—and textile manufacturers were invited to use the name, and share in the benefits of BNS advertising, on certain conditions. These stipulated a nylon content of at least 15 per cent, and that BNS should be the sole supplier. Hollins, however, could not agree; they feared that the Bri-Nylon label might distract attention from their own trade-mark; moreover, they were not convinced that British nylon was so distinct from imported nylon as to justify the adoption of a brand name. Whatever the objections in this particular instance, it was clear that Hollins had to take account of the new fibres and to determine what their policy should be. The whole matter was discussed at a special board meeting in 1959, when Herbert told his colleagues that they must 'keep in the closest possible touch with research and development throughout the world, to ensure that we have the earliest possible information about anything likely to be of interest to us—we must lead the world and not follow others'.

But it was not only the competition of new materials that Hollins had to face. In the garments trade knitted fabrics were gaining at the expense of woven. The most striking development was in warp knitting, a process which combined the characteristics of weaving and knitting and produced a fabric with more elasticity than woven cloth and more stability than knitted fabric. It was especially suitable for cut-out garments. Warp knitting frames had been in use since the early nineteenth century, but lately they had been vastly improved. The great advantage of the modern warp knitting machine is speed; it is also particularly suited to synthetic yarns, from which remarkably fine fabrics can be made. At the meeting just referred to, the director of merchandise and sales emphasised the growing importance of warp knitting and suggested that it should not be overlooked in the discussion of Hollins's future policy.

The poor financial results of 1960 increased the sense of urgency in such discussion. The position had improved in 1959, largely as a result of a recovery in raw material prices, but at the end of the following year net trading profits were down to £191,927. Hollins seemed to have reached the limits of expansion along existing lines. Except in garment making, where the Marks and Spencer connection helped, its productive capacity tended to exceed requirements, yet in its sales organisation, and the prestige won for the brand name Viyella, Hollins had a great asset which could not be fully exploited. It had to seek entry into a new field and the directors became convinced that manmade fibres offered the best opportunity. It would be far better, however, to acquire an existing business in this line rather than undertake the slow and costly task of developing it themselves.

The opportunity soon occurred. Towards the end of 1960 Herbert was introduced to Joe Hyman of Gainsborough Cornard. This was effected through his fellow director, Sir Charles Hughes Hallett, who was also a member of Tyzack and Partners, the consultants. Gainsborough Cornard was a medium-sized firm, located in the Stour Valley area of Suffolk, manufacturing synthetic yarns and warp knitted fabrics. It also owned Cooper Brothers, a Nottingham firm of hosiery manufacturers. Gainsborough Cornard's policy, as explained by the chairman in his 1960 report, was 'to move with the tide of a new synthetic expansion'; so far it had been remarkably successful, and it looked forward to sharing the benefits expected to result from the massive investments of the chemical industry in the development of synthetic fibres, the merits of which were only just coming to be appreciated. Much of the firm's success was due to Joe Hyman himself, still under forty and a man of conspicuous business ability and vision.

Here, it seemed, was the answer to Hollins's problem. Herbert lost no time in starting negotiations for a take-over, after consulting his fellow directors and getting a report from the firm's accountants. The lowest price that Hyman was prepared to consider was 25s for each 5s ordinary share in Gainsborough Cornard. This was on the high side; the estimated value of the shares on an assets basis was 12s, and 25s could only be justified on the expectation of profits over the next three years. Then there was the question of how the purchase was to be effected, whether wholly in cash, or partly in cash and partly in Hollins' shares, and, if the latter, what value was to be placed on Hollins' shares. The current market price was about 30s per £1 share; on an assets basis they were said to be worth 50s, but the price was, of course, more a reflection of earnings than of assets. It was possible too, that Hollins's shares might fall in price as a result of the offer for Gainsborough Cornard. This point was stressed by Hyman and his colleagues, and a representative of the Charterhouse Finance Corporation advised Hollins that if a rights issue were made to raise funds for a cash offer the price could not be put higher than 25s in the most favourable circumstances.

It took only a few weeks to reach agreement. On 13 January 1961 Hollins announced its offer of 25s in cash for each of the 5s ordinary shares of Gainsborough Cornard, and shareholders accepting the offer were given the right to apply three-fifths of the cash to which they became entitled in subscribing for new £1 ordinary shares in Hollins at a price of 30s a share. Hyman was the major shareholder in Gainsborough Cornard and the limitation just mentioned was designed to prevent his acquiring an unduly large holding in

Hollins. In the event, over 98 per cent of holders, with 1,007,746 Gainsborough Cornard shares, accepted the terms of the offer but they subscribed for only 281,919 of Hollins shares, so that cash payments of some £840,000 had to be made. It was thought that a debenture issue might be necessary, but it subsequently appeared that this could be avoided by a reduction in merchandise stocks over the next two years by some £750,000. In the meantime a sufficient bank overdraft was arranged.

Under the terms of the agreement, Hyman retained his office as chairman and managing director of Gainsborough Cornard, and also joined Hollins' board. Shortly afterwards he was appointeds executive vice-chairman of the company, but his primary responsibility, as stated by Herbert, was to ensure that Gainsborough Cornard achieved the increases in turnover and profits that Hollins had been led to expect when making their take-over bid. It was clearly unsound, however, to regard the subsidiary as a means of subsidising the parent company. The aim must be to integrate the two firms for their mutual benefit, and when this was considered it was evident that Gainsborough Cornard represented the growth sector of the enterprise. The market for Hollins's traditional lines seemed to have reached the limit of expansion; in any event it was unlikely that all the present capacity could ever be employed so as to make satisfactory profits, which, according to one estimate, would require a sales increase of 50 per cent.

The point about excess capacity was reiterated by Hyman at successive meetings of the Hollins board and most of his fellow directors appear to have agreed, though there were differences of opinion as to the amount of redundant capacity and where it should be eliminated. Hyman argued for the concentration of spinning and weaving into two units, and for obtaining supplementary supplies from commission weavers when required. Eventually it was decided that Newhouse should go. The plant was technically efficient, but the enterprise had been built up at the expense of Pleasley and Boden Street, which had been starved of capital in the last few years. Accordingly, much of the equipment was transferred, and some of the workers were found employment at Boden Street. The withdrawal from Newhouse, which was re-leased to another firm, thus left Hollins with ample capacity, concentrated, as before, in two units, and with reduced overheads.

Although Herbert acquiesced in the decision, it must have been profoundly disappointing to see the project he had sponsored, and fostered with such enthusiasm, end in this way. But the Newhouse decision was only a tactical move in a strategy that was soon revealed. The take-over of Gainsborough Cornard had been regarded by Hollins as the acquisition of a new subsidiary, much as Seedhill had been acquired in the past. It gave Hollins a stake in a new and growing field and it brought to their own board a valuable recruit in the person of Mr Joe Hyman. But Hyman had a very different idea of the relationship. He was already thinking in terms of a group, of which William Hollins, Gainsborough Cornard and their subsidiaries would form the nucleus. The general policy of the group would be determined by a holding company.

Within six months of Hyman's joining the board this scheme had been formulated and at a meeting on 31 July 1961 it was accepted by most of the directors. Herbert had already indicated his support and had decided upon his own action. For some time he had been far from well, and he now announced his intention, on medical advice, to relinquish the chairmanship and his seat on the board. His resignation was accepted 'with understanding and regret'.[1] Hume, as deputy-chairman, took over and was duly appointed chairman of the company, with Hyman as deputy-chairman and managing director. This, however, was merely a temporary arrangement. As the plan for the group's reorganisation and future development was

---

[1] Herbert died in 1963 at the age of seventy-one. After serving with distinction in the First World War he continued his career as an engineer for a time, but before joining Hollins his interests had turned to management and sales organisation. In the Second World War he was in the Ministry of Aircraft Production and afterwards he became chairman of Short Bros and Harland Ltd. While chairman of Hollins he held a number of other directorships and public appointments, including membership of the Dollar Exports Council. He was knighted in 1951.

Hyman's, he was clearly the man to lead it—a fact which was formally recognised by his election as chairman at the end of 1961.

The first step in the reorganisation of the group's structure was to change the name of William Hollins to Viyella International Ltd. The idea of using the famous name in the style of the firm had been contemplated long before, and in 1947 a dormant company was registered as Viyella Ltd. The new style was entirely appropriate and the addition of 'international' signified the world-wide reputation of Viyella.[1] On the other hand, Viyella International embraced more than William Hollins; it stood for a group in which Hollins was merely one subsidiary, like Gainsborough Cornard. Accordingly, when Hyman assumed the chairmanship, Viyella International divested itself of all its manufacturing and trading assets. Those attributed to the Hollins organisation were transferred to a new William Hollins & Co Ltd, a wholly owned subsidiary of Viyella International.

The present William Hollins, together with the Seedhill Finishing Company, carries on much the same range of manufacturing and trading activities as before, but as a member of a group or federation as it has come to be called. Like the other subsidiaries, it enjoys considerable autonomy and has found wider opportunities within the federation. But it is ultimately subservient to a London headquarters. Nothing was more symbolic of the change than the sale of Viyella House in Nottingham. Yet something of the old William Hollins lives on in the federation. Firstly, there is the name Viyella, which made Hollins famous throughout the world, and in which it had created an asset of immense value. Secondly, there is the principle of vertical organisation. Hollins had demonstrated its possibilities in an industry where the characteristic form was horizontal, with each stage in production undertaken by separate, specialised firms; but Hollins was too small to realise its full advan-

---

[1] A Royal Warrant of Appointment for Viyella and Clydella was granted to William Hollins & Co Ltd in August 1961.

tages, and in Viyella International vertical organisation has been given full scope. Then there is the physical embodiment of past enterprise which still makes its contributions to the prosperity of the whole, including Pleasley Mills, where the first Hollins and his partners set up their business nearly two centuries ago.

Postscript

SINCE its formation in 1961 Viyella International has set the pace in a movement that has transformed the organisation of a large part of the British textile industry. Hitherto, reorganisation had usually involved the combination of firms in particular sections, thus emphasising the characteristic horizontal structure; the modern emphasis has been on vertical integration.

For many years William Hollins had been an outstanding example of this form, not so much on account of its size, but because of its comprehensive scale, ranging from spinning, through weaving, finishing and garment-making to direct selling to retailers. For reasons that have been shown, it could never be completely self-contained, and the question of how far to go in this direction was a matter of recurrent controversy for forty years. The decision to go into garment-making in a big way was especially critical; it is arguable that Hollins might have done better to sell cloth to garment manufacturers in the home market under franchise agreements, as it was virtually forced to do abroad because of tariff discrimination against made-up goods. But within a larger grouping of firms vertical organisation, as pioneered by Hollins, could yield many advantages.

By 1960 these advantages had been greatly increased by technological developments. The variety of manmade fibres now available, the progress of warp knitting, the extending range of finishing processes, and the combination of the new resources with traditional materials and methods, were all transforming the textile industries. A new multi-fibre, multi-process industry was emerging and the old classification was becoming irrelevant.

This tendency is reflected in the appearance of four large groups in the textile trades: Courtaulds, Viyella International, English Sewing Cotton, and Carrington and Dewhurst. All are vertically integrated concerns, and, except for the last, their activities range from spinning to garment-making. This is not to imply that each is self-contained. For instance, Courtaulds can use within its own organisation only a fraction of the cotton yarn it spins, and Viyella International does a great deal of dyeing and finishing on commission for other firms. Some imbalance is almost inevitable, if only because the optimum scale of production varies from one process to another. But in so far as successive stages of production are linked together within the same enterprise, these groups have substituted integration through administration for integration through the market.

In two cases—Courtaulds and Viyella—the synthetic fibre manufacturers have exerted a powerful influence, though in different ways. Synthetic fibre manufacture is a capital—intensive industry, responsive to economies of scale and the prospect of a steady demand for its products. It is dominated in Britain by Courtaulds and Imperial Chemical Industries and each has had the same problem of creating and maintaining an adequate market for a product which must pass through many stages before reaching the final consumer. Courtaulds, besides absorbing other firms operating in the basic processes, adopted the policy of taking over existing or potential users of its products and so secured a captive market for its fibres and fabrics. This was appropriate for a firm which had always been in textiles. ICI, on the other hand, is based on chemicals. In 1962 it tried to secure a controlling interest in Courtaulds, but it got only 38 per cent of the equity and two years later this was exchanged for Courtaulds' share in British Nylon Spinners. By this time ICI had decided against further penetration into textiles by take-over methods, but it still had to secure the market for its fibres in the face of intense competition, especially from Courtaulds. Its plan now was to encourage the growth of strong points in textile manufacture by the judicious distribution of capital among progressive firms.

It was this situation which gave Hyman his opportunity. Viyella International was now firmly established and its creator had ambitious plans for its growth as a multi-fibre, multi-process textile group. But more capital was needed. So Hyman took his plans to ICI, and the result was an agreement to lend Viyella £10 million and take 20 per cent of the equity.[1]

This was the beginning of a spectacular expansion. Viyella's first acquisition was the British Van Heusen Co Ltd, itself a large diversified concern with substantial interests in spinning and weaving, as well as being one of the best-known makers of branded shirts and household textiles. Other acquisitions quickly followed, in spinning, weaving, knitting, finishing, garment making and merchanting. From a group employing less than £6 million of capital and about 4,500 people, Viyella International had grown by 1966 into a major industrial organisation, with a capital of over £45 million and 25,000 employees.

Although ICI funds provided the initial impetus, the process of expansion was sustained by internally-generated resources. Some £5 million was realised by the sale of surplus properties and other assets incompatible with the plans of the federation. Only the best machinery was retained and this was redistributed, if necessary, so as to form compact, highly productive units. Capital, much in the form of bank credit, was released by reducing stocks. Then, as profits benefited from the rationalisation of resources within the federation, still more capital became available through retained earnings.

To give a full account of this still developing organisation would require another book, and a brief indication must suffice here of Hollins's position within the federation, which comprises ninety companies in twelve trading groups. Hollins, with its spinning,

---

[1] Several other firms, including Carrington and Dewhurst, attracted ICI investment about this time, and some excess capacity resulted.

weaving and garment-making units, forms one group, employing
net assets of £4,489,000 and 2,990 people, representing about 10
per cent of the federation's productive capacity. Seedhill is one of
seven firms forming the dyeing and finishing group, but it has close
links with Hollins, which supplies about one-third of its business.
It is also the main warehouse for Hollins' cloth, and the Viyella
Design Centre adjoins its premises. The federation itself, for all its
size and diversified resources, is by no means self-contained. Seedhill still does commission finishing and Hollins' traditional trade
with outside hosiery manufacturers is still carried on, providing a
check on its competitive ability. The bulk of Hollins' yarn—60 per
cent in 1965—is woven into Viyella, Clydella and other branded
cloths; but there is an increasing demand for Hollins' yarn from
outside firms, including other members of the federation. Pleasley's
strong position in this trade derives from its unique experience in
spinning short-staple wool on the cotton spinning system, which
lends itself particularly well to the production of acrylic-wool
blends. Of the cloth output, 40 per cent was exported in 1965,
mainly to enfranchised makers-up. A slightly bigger proportion was
made up in Hollins's own garment factories and the rest was sold
retail, in the piece. Federation had thus left the character of Hollins's
trade substantially unchanged, but with an increased emphasis on
cloth exports—of Viyella itself, over half the output was exported in
1965.

In developing its export trade the federation has been selective;
for it was realised that some of the constituent companies which had
been exporting at a loss, were exporting the wrong things. As the
chairman said, 'to exhort people to export who are concerned with
the ordinary run of mass produced merchandise which is not capital
intensive and which is not of a craft nature, is . . . largely a waste of
time'. Hollins is not a capital-intensive concern; its net assets per
employee were £1,500 in 1965, in contrast with warp and circular
knitting with a figure of £6,060. But it makes quality products
which, backed by appropriate selling effort, can be sold very profit-

ably in the more affluent sections of overseas markets, and, of course, in the home market too.

It would be unfair to suggest that William Hollins, in their latter years as an independent firm, failed to understand the true nature of their trade and where their prosperity lay. Their fault was rather in overestimating its capacity for expansion. They built up an industrial and commercial organisation too large for the traditional trade and then had to try to support it by branching out into other lines in which they had no special competence or in which they could not achieve an optimum scale of production. Within the federation Hollins has been restricted to a size appropriate to the prospects of its tradi-tional trade, and capital and expertise were applied where they could be most effectively employed. The Pleasley spinning mills and the Glasgow weaving plant benefited particularly from the installa-tion of modern machines, many of them transferred from New-house when that establishment was closed down. On the commer-cial side too, there was considerable redeployment of resources. Effort was concentrated on the more profitable lines and there was more emphasis on exporting, which, in contrast with the home trade, means supplying a limited number of large customers at relatively low selling cost. The initial effect was to reduce sales; but they were much more profitable: in 1964 profits, before tax, in-creased by some 50 per cent. Afterwards both sales and profits in-creased.

By virtue of its distinctive trade Hollins retained its identity within the federation. But in the meantime the federation itself was being reshaped on a divisional basis and this eventually involved changes in the Hollins unit. The first step, was the disposal of Viyella House and the dispersal of its commercial activities: yarn sales to Pleasley, garment sales to Hucknall, where most of the gar-ments are made, the cloth warehouse to Seedhill, which does the finishing process. A small headquarters staff was retained in Not-tingham, but only as a temporary arrangement. Finally, in 1967 William Hollins split into three companies. The senior company, which holds the Royal Warrant, is at Somercotes in Derbyshire, being accommodated with Aertex Ltd, another member of the federation. In addition to its functions as the senior company, Somercotes is responsible for the sale of hosiery made from Hollins' yarn. The other companies are William Hollins (Spinners) Ltd, Pleasley, and William Hollins (Fabrics) Ltd, based on Paisley.

Yet through all these changes the Viyella image, created and fostered by Hollins, has been consistently maintained. Its character emerges in the early advertisements, the appeal of which is well described by Pigott.[1] 'The pipe-smoking young men who chat so casually in their Viyella shirt sleeves or pyjamas are obviously men-about-town when fully dressed. The children who 'snuggle in bed' between Viyella sheets inhabit a Peter Pan world stretching from their enormous nurseries to Kensington Gardens, a world ruled jointly by leisured mothers and indulgent nannies. For such families Viyella occupied a place as one of the unchanging things they never did without. They bought it because it was the best.' Sixty years later the best techniques of modern advertising are used to make the same appeal. Discussing a recent advertising campaign for children's Viyella, a specialist journal examines the reasons for its success. 'The copy and the shots, each in their own way, enter the fantasy world of children, but since they are Viyella children naturally their world is one of almost Edwardian security, where all afternoons are golden walks in the park, and where red-coated guardsmen play nursery rhymes on golden trumpets, and golden hearted nannies pirouette among the rhododendrons.'[2] In the advertisements for women's clothes new styles, patterns and colours are naturally emphasised, but so are the traditional qualities of the fabric, its softness and warmth without weight. In the more conservative men's trade the traditional qualities are a main selling point. After the war they had to be spelt out again, especially in American advertising.[3] But in 1967

[1] Op cit, p 122. The reference is to the advertisement reproduced on p 107.
[2] 'Analysis and Planning', *Journal of Advertising Media*. October 1966.
[3] See example, p. 218.

it was thought sufficient to explain that 'Viyella shirts look and feel and behave like no other shirts because they're made of Viyella'. Not many products could be advertised in this way. The appeal is to tradition rather than novelty and the appeal is reinforced by the current slogan: 'the most natural fabric in the world'.

Viyella International Limited

A FEDERATION OF TEXTILE BUSINESSES

R

Appendix

CHAIRMEN OF WILLIAM HOLLINS & CO LTD, FROM ITS ESTABLISHMENT IN 1882, TO THE FORMATION OF VIYELLA INTERNATIONAL LTD, IN 1961

William Hollins	1882–90
W. B. Paget	1890–1908
Henry Ernest Hollins	1908–19
Arthur Remington Hollins	1919–23
C. H. Hill	1923–4
Sir Ernest Jardine	1924–34
Sir Frederick Aykroyd	1934–8
P. C. Cooper-Parry	1938–9
F. J. Dickens	1939–43
Douglas Hamilton	1943–55
Joseph Wild	1955–8
Sir Edward Herbert	1958–61

BOOKS

Baines, E. *History of the Cotton Manufacture*. 1835.

Blackner, J. *History of Nottingham*. 1815.

Church, R. A. *Economic and Social Change in a Midland Town*. 1966.

Cunningham, W. *The Growth of English Industry and Commerce in Modern Times*. 1925.

Daniels, G. W. *The Early English Cotton Industry*. 1920.

Erickson, C. *British Industrialists: Steel & Hosiery*. 1959.

Felkin, W. *A History of the Machine-Wrought Hosiery and Lace Manufactures*. 1867.

Fitton, R. S. and Wadsworth, A. P. *The Strutts and the Arkwrights*. 1958.

Henson, G. *The Civil, Political and Mechanical History of the Framework Knitters*. 1831.

Macpherson, D. *Annals of Commerce*. 1785.

Owen, R. *Life of Robert Owen*. 1857.

Pigott, S. *Hollins: A Study of Industry*. 1949.

Singer, C. J. (ed). *A History of Technology*. 1958.

Unwin, G. *Samuel Oldknow and the Arkwrights*. 1924.

Ward-Jackson, C. K. *A History of Courtaulds*. 1941.

Wells, F. A. *The British Hosiery Trade*. 1935.

NEWSPAPERS AND PERIODICALS

The Nottingham Journal. 1785–1890.
The Nottingham Review. 1829–44.
The Economist. 1908–66.
The Statist. 1908–65.
The Viyella Standard. 1946–61.
Viyella International. 1961–7.

PARLIAMENTARY PAPERS, ETC

Report of Select Committee on the State of Children Employed in Manufactories	1816
Report of the Commissioners on the Employment of Children in Factories	1833
Report of the Commissioners appointed to inquire into the Condition of the Framework Knitters	1845
Official Catalogue of the Great Exhibition of the Works of Industry of all Nations	1851
Report of the Royal Commission on the Depression of Trade and Industry. XXI	1886
Report of the Committee on the Position of the Textile Trades after the War. XIII	1918
Reports of the Committee on Industry and Trade: Survey of the Textile Industries	1928

COMPANY MINUTE BOOKS, REPORTS AND PAPERS

Minute Books of the Directors, W. H. & Co	1890–1961
Minute Books of the Executive Committee, W. H. & Co	1935–61
Annual Reports and Accounts, W. H. & Co	1908–60
Reports of Chairman's Address at Annual General Meetings of Shareholders, W. H. & Co	1919–60
Reports of Extraordinary General Meetings of Shareholders, W. H. & Co	1923, 1938, 1939
Report of Sir William Plender to Directors of W. H. & Co	1923
Accountants' Reports to Directors of W. H. & Co on valuation of capital and costing	1934
Reports of Shareholders' Consultative Committee to Directors of W. H. & Co	1935, 1939
Paper by A. Huskisson on proposals for reorganisation W. H. & Co	1938
Paper by James Ross on the Seedhill Finishing Co	Undated

Annual Reports and Accounts of Viyella International   1961–66
Reports of Chairman's Address at Annual General   1961–6
    Meetings of Shareholders, Viyella International

INDENTURES, DEEDS AND ARTICLES OF CO-PARTNER-SHIP

Copy of Indenture of Co-partnership with Indenture   1 March 1785
    Lease of Land and buildings at Pleasley, signed
    20 September 1784
Indentures of Apprenticeship   various dates 1791
Deeds of Co-partnership   9 March 1844
Indorsement to above   15 February 1847
Deed of Co-partnership   1 August 1859
Articles of Co-partnership, W. H. & Co   13 December 1865
Articles of Co-partnership, W. H. & Co   15 November 1870
Supplemental Deed to above   7 January 1874
Articles of Co-partnership, W. H. & Co   26 April 1875
Supplemental Deed to above   30 November 1880
Memoranda and Articles of Association of W. H. &   4 February 1882
    Co Ltd
Deed of Dissolution of partnership of W. H. & Co   26 November 1883
Resolution amending Articles of Association of   7 March 1898
    W. H. & Co (Nottingham) Ltd

ASSIGNMENTS OF SHARES IN PARTNERSHIP, PROPERTY, STOCK AND EFFECTS AT PLEASLEY

Siddons-Pearsce   21 January 1792
Cowpe-Paulson and others   23 March 1796
Hollins-Howitt   23 April 1815
Howitt-Hollins   4 September 1819
Hollins-Henry Hollins II   27 June 1820
Pearsce Trustees-Hollins   26 March 1827
Paget T.-Oldknow heirs (Declaration of Trust)   28 December 1829
Wragg-Paget, C.   30 September 1834
Oldknow-Paget, T.   7 October 1840
Hollins, H. (III), Hollins, H. and C.   30 December 1840
Hollins, H. (II)—Paget and others   29 April 1841
Hollins, H. & C.—Hollins, E.   16 May 1843
Paget, T. and others—Partners in W. H. & Co   31 December 1846

YEARLY ACCOUNTS AND STATEMENTS OF THE PARTNER-SHIP

Book of Yearly Account Statements and Partnership   1786–1813

Appendix

Settlements. (Probably the copy belonging to
Henry Hollins I)
Book of Yearly Account Statements and Partnership   1786–1806
Settlements. Also containing Private Ledger
Accounts for each Partner
Book of Yearly Account Statements and Partnership   1797–1806 and
Settlements. (Originally the copy belonging to   1831–47
Henry Hollins II)
Book of Yearly Accounts Statements. Also containing   1873–81
Private Ledger Account of William Hollins I.
(Originally the copy belonging to William
Hollins I)

Index